NEW SCROLL SAW
HANDBOOK

NEW SCROLL SAW HANDBOOK

Patrick Spielman

Sterling Publishing Co., Inc.
New York

Library of Congress Cataloging-in-Publication Data Available

6 8 10 9 7

Published by Sterling Publishing Co., Inc.
387 Park Avenue South, New York, NY 10016
© 2002 by Patrick Spielman
Distributed in Canada by Sterling Publishing,
% Canadian Manda Group, 165 Dufferin Street,
Toronto, Ontario, Canada M6K 3H6
Distributed in the United Kingdom by GMC Distribution Services,
Castle Place, 166 High Street, Lewes, East Sussex, England BN7 1XU
Distributed in Australia by Capricorn Link (Australia) Pty. Ltd.,
P.O. Box 704, Windsor, NSW 2756, Australia

Sterling ISBN-13: 978-0-8069-7877-2
ISBN-10: 0-8069-7877-5

For information about custom editions, special sales, premium and
corporate purchases, please contact Sterling Special Sales
Department at 800-805-5489 or specialsales@sterlingpub.com.

ACKNOWLEDGMENTS

 am very grateful to all those many talented people who helped with the first edition and to those who also have directly impacted the content of this new, revised edition.

Special thanks to Jennifer Blahnik, my personal editor and secretary, for her assistance with research and for converting my wild scribbles into a discerning form.

Thanks with love to "Mrs. Pat," my wife and personal designer, who always contributes more than she or anyone knows. And, thanks to our children, Bob, Sherri, and Sandy, who have helped in various ways.

A profound debt of gratitude to each of the many experts in the various fields of scroll-sawing, from all around the world, whom I've had the privilege to know as good friends and to count on as trusted consultants and key advisors. The combined wisdom and expertise of these individuals is absolutely awesome. Collectively, they have made this a good book and the only one of its kind. I shall forever be thankful to all for their immeasurable contribution to this work. These people are:

Henry Aldinger	Don Frechette	Julia Meader	Kerry Shirts
Robert A. Becker	Sandra Friedenfels	Ernie Mellon	Robert Spielman
James Beckerdite	Monty Gould	John Nelson	George Stefureac
Dirk Boelman	Barry Gross	John Nickalls	Gus Stefureac
Willard Bondhus	Garnet Hall	Chuck Olson	Robert Stroulger
Anthony Borgatti	Alan Hoyt	Cathy Peck	Diana Thompson
Gary Browning	Rick Hutcheson	Barbara Peters	Sherri Valitchka
Roger Buse	Julie Kiehnau	Bob Phillips	Carl Weckhorst
Bev Carmody	Dan Kihl	Bill Pickens	Joan West
Lucille Crabtree	Silas Kopf	John Polhemus	Burt Whitman
Gösta Dahlqvist	Dean Larson	Kirk Ratajesak	Robin Wirtz
Terry Davy	Ray Lawler	Jim Reidle	J.D. Woodward
Hanns Derke	Roxanne LeMoine	Carl Roehl	Don Zinngrabe
Frank Droege	Carmen Lucke	Bob Schuttleworth	
Harold Foos	Lawrence Luser	Ray Seymore	

CONTENTS

PREFACE

he primary purpose of this book is to provide new and experienced scroll-saw users with a single, comprehensive reference embracing all significant subjects related to the scroll saw. Scroll-sawing, as we know it today, has been an ongoing activity for the past 130 to 200 years. Every effort has been made to include all relevant time-tested information as well as current information concerning the recent explosion of new scroll saws and accessories and innovative ideas and techniques for using them. Scroll saws—and the level of functional and artistic works produced with them—have advanced tremendously since I wrote the first edition of this book in 1986. This new edition also includes updated information about all relevant scroll-sawing techniques, plus new facts of historical significance that have surfaced since my first book.

A close review will actually reveal that fundamentally there is not much new or revolutionary in terms of scroll-saw design or cutting techniques. You will, however, become familiar with numerous refinements—the best ideas from the past used with unique new materials in many different ways. All of this has made scroll-sawing one of the most popular craft and art activities of today for people of all ages around the world.

—Patrick Spielman, 2002

INTRODUCTION

The modern scroll saw **(I–1)** is a woodworking machine designed to carry very narrow blades **(I–2)** that saw curves, lines, and openings in flat wood **(I–3)** with a reciprocating (up-and-down) cutting action **(I–4)**.

The "reciprocating action" fundamentally cuts only on the down stroke, but some blades are designed to cut in both directions. Overall, scroll saws cut slower and are much safer than other machines such as circular saws and band saws that have continuous cutting actions. These machines also have blades with large teeth that move at lightning speed, which makes them comparatively much more dangerous. Breathing the fine dust created by the scroll saw should be more of a concern for one's long-term health than cutting one's finger, which, in the unlikely event of ever happening, would be considered a comparatively minor accident.

The band saw is sometimes compared to the scroll saw because it can make some of the same kinds of cuts. The two primary advantages of the band saw are that it cuts faster and it is capable of cutting much thicker stock (4 to 12 inches). The scroll saw is limited to stock thickness of 1½ to 2½ inches. It does, however, offer these major advantages:

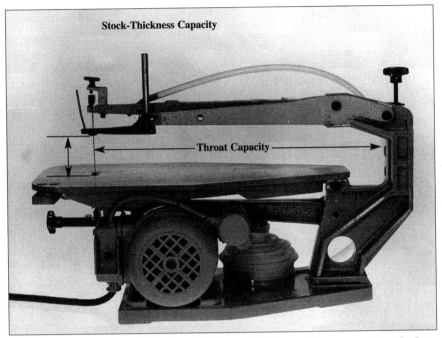

Stock-Thickness Capacity

Throat Capacity

I–1. ▶ The size of a scroll saw is usually designated by its throat capacity, which is measured in inches.

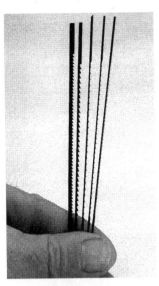

I–2. ▶ Better scroll saws carry very narrow, thin plain-end blades such as those shown that are capable of cutting highly detailed work in a variety of materials.

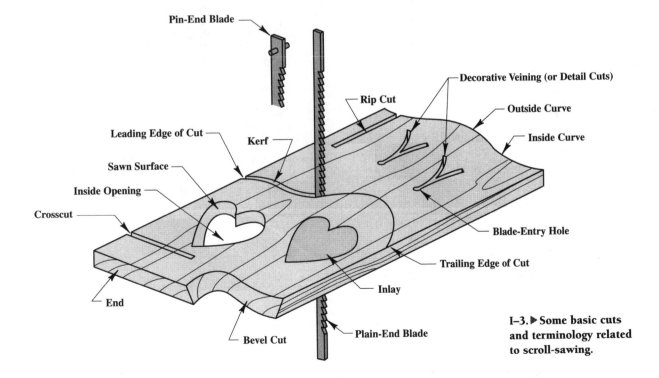

Pin-End Blade

Decorative Veining (or Detail Cuts)

Rip Cut

Outside Curve

Leading Edge of Cut

Inside Curve

Kerf

Sawn Surface

Inside Opening

Crosscut

Blade-Entry Hole

Trailing Edge of Cut

End

Inlay

Bevel Cut

Plain-End Blade

I–3. ▶ Some basic cuts and terminology related to scroll-sawing.

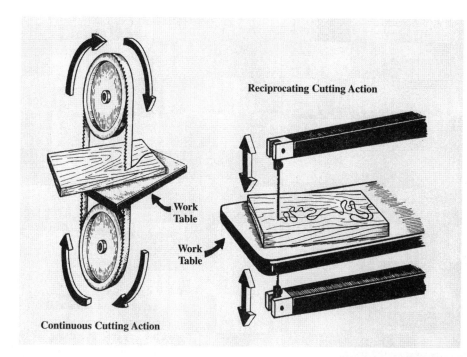

Reciprocating Cutting Action

Work Table

Work Table

Continuous Cutting Action

I–4. ▶ Comparing the continuous cutting action of a band saw on the left to the reciprocating cutting action of the scroll saw on the right.

1. It is safer to use.

2. It can cut inside openings, as shown in **I–3.**

3. Scroll-sawn surfaces are so smooth they usually do not require sanding (**I–5).**

4. It can cut more intricate designs with much finer detail.

5. It is easier to master.

6. It is easier to adjust and maintain.

SCROLL-SAW SIZE

Sizes of scroll saw are classified according to throat capacity, maximum thickness-cutting capacity, stroke length, and cutting speed in terms of strokes per minute (spm) (refer to **I–1**).

Throat capacity is the open distance from the blade to the back of the machine. Throat capacity is the most commonly used designation of scroll-saw size, which ranges from 12 to 30 inches. A saw with a 16-inch throat, for example, can cut to the center of a workpiece 32 inches in diameter.

Thickness capacity is the maximum thickness of material the saw can cut. This generally varies from 1 to almost 2¾ inches and more with large industrial saws.

Stroke length is the distance the blade moves from the top to the bottom of its reciprocation. Typically,

Band Saw

Scroll Saw

I–5. ▶ Comparing sawn surfaces of a piece of oak hardwood. The upper piece was cut with a medium-size band-saw blade. The lower smooth cut was made with a relatively coarse, No. 9 scroll-saw blade.

stroke lengths range from ⅝ to 1½ inches. Longer strokes are generally more favorable because they clear the cut from sawdust more quickly, cut thick stock more readily, distribute wear to more of the blade, and cut cooler.

Cutting speed is specified in terms of strokes per minute and is abbreviated as spm. Scroll-saw speeds range from 0 to 1,800 strokes per minute depending upon the saw's type of drive system or speed control—that is, whether the scroll saw is single-, two-, or electronic variable-speed, or whether it has belted pulleys or is foot-powered. Matching the optimum speed to the material being cut is critical.

TYPES OF SCROLL SAW

Scroll saws can be broadly categorized as either floor models or bench-top machines. They can also be categorized according to the way tension is applied to the very fine blades to keep them taut and stiff so they cut properly. One type is called a *strained* or *rigid-arm saw*. It has a spring housed in a fixed over-arm that pulls at the top end of the blade with an increasing force as it moves on the downstroke (**I–6**). This type of saw was popular between the 1920's and the 1980's until the modern reengineered parallel-arm saws appeared. The major objective of the rigid-arm saw was to provide a true, vertical stroke. Problems revolved around using very thin blades with the spring. The primary limitations of these saws are:

1. The driving mechanisms devised to convert rotary energy into a true up-and-down blade motion are complex.

2. The blade is fully tensioned only when it reaches the bottom of the stroke, and tension is substantially less at the top of the stroke when the spring compresses.

Saws of this type have, by and large, fallen out of favor with scroll-sawers and manufacturers alike. Powermatic is the only remaining United States company manufacturing a nonindustrial rigid-arm scroll saw (refer to pages 88 to 90).

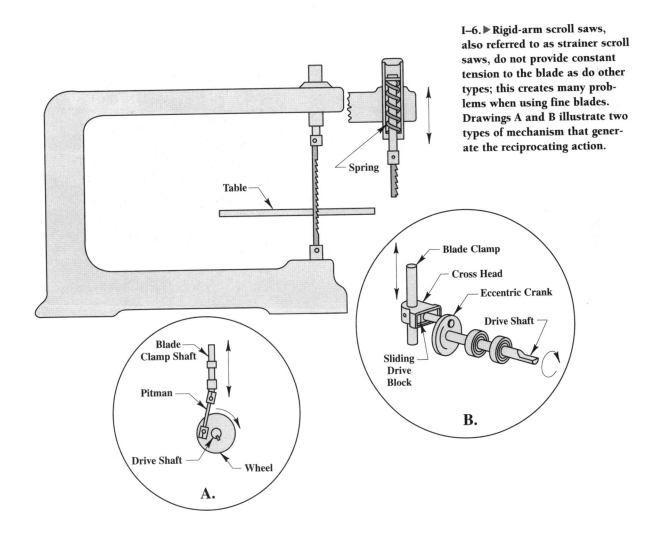

I–6. ▶ Rigid-arm scroll saws, also referred to as strainer scroll saws, do not provide constant tension to the blade as do other types; this creates many problems when using fine blades. Drawings A and B illustrate two types of mechanism that generate the reciprocating action.

Constant-Tension Saws

Constant-tension saws are of various types and designs. They all, however, have blades that are consistently kept taut at the same level throughout the entire stroke, so that unlike rigid-arm saws, the tension is the same at the bottom and the top of the stroke. Today, constant-tension saws are overwhelmingly the most popular and are available in the following styles: *parallel-arm*, *C-arm*, *double parallel-link*, and *oscillating loop*.

Parallel-Arm Saws

The parallel-arm scroll saw (**I–7**) is the oldest type of constant-tension saw. It first appeared 130 or more years ago. Many of these early parallel-arm saws are illustrated in Chapter 1. The German manufacturer Hegner introduced a version of a reengineered, upgraded parallel-arm saw in the mid-1980's, and since then many other parallel-arm saws of the same type have appeared (see Chapter 2).

Parallel-arm saws have two pivots incorporated into a general parallelogram design. This creates a blade-reciprocating action that keeps the blade in a vertical position. By and large, saws of this type are favored because of their few operating parts, and their design is such that the cuts are vertical and square to the table.

C-Arm Saws

C-arm saws (**I–8**) are definitely in the minority. They are, however, favored by some production scrollsawers because of their faster and more aggressive cutting action. The C-arm design may be of one or several connected pieces assembled in a C-shape, but the common factor is that all C-arm saws have only one major pivot point, as shown in **I–8**.

One shortcoming of a C-arm saw is that the blade is not consistently vertical throughout the stroke. Therefore, the C-arm saw is not usually the first choice for highly detailed work or curved cuts in thick material that must be square to the table. Another concern is that when a blade breaks, the upper arm does not automatically lift as do the arms on parallel-arm saws. This means that a broken blade may be reciprocating wildly and dangerously until the power is shut down.

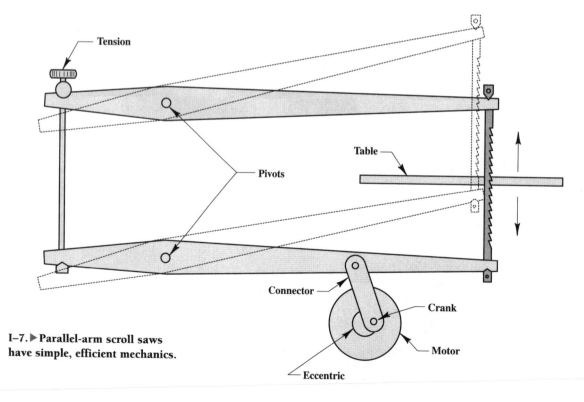

I–7. ▶ **Parallel-arm scroll saws have simple, efficient mechanics.**

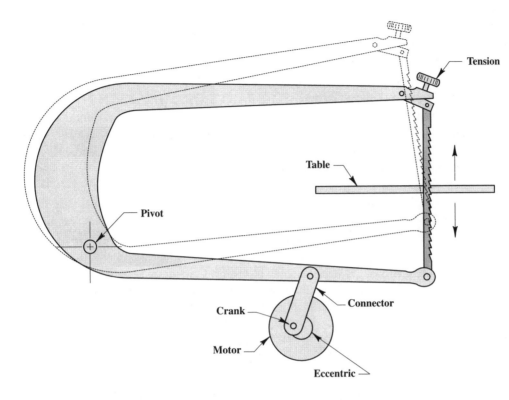

I–8. ▶ C-arm scroll saws have a cutting action that takes the blade off of a true vertical reciprocation, which is a concern of some scroll-sawers.

Double Parallel-Link Saw

The double parallel-link saw, the newest of the constant-tension scroll saws, has probably the most complex drive system of all. It is also the most difficult saw in which to understand how its reciprocating action is generated. (Refer to **I–9** and also to **2–45** and **2–66 to 2-69,** which depict the DeWalt and Excalibur saws, which exclusively incorporate this design.)

The major advantage of the "link" drive system is reduced vibration. It also provides a vertical blade action. This blade is held between the short upper

I–9. ▶ The double parallel-link saw is the most recently developed constant-tension scroll saw. It has the most complex drive system.

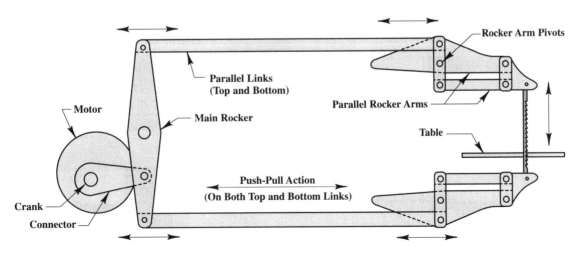

and lower rocker arms. These pivot in reaction to the push-pull motion of the linkage, thereby creating a reciprocating movement of the blade at the ends of the hollow and fixed arms enclosing most of the moving parts. Because the pivoting rocker arms are generally much shorter than the arms of parallel- or C-arm saws, the result is a blade action with more front-to-back movement during the stroke. This may create some problems of accidentally "overcutting" when making tight, highly detailed cuts. And, there also exists the ever-present danger—also likely with C-arm saws—that a broken blade will continue to reciprocate, with a stabbing action, until the power is shut down.

Oscillating-Loop Saw

An oscillating loop (**I–10**) is simply a blade connected to the two ends of a toothed flat belt that forms a loop and moves (oscillates) back and forth. This concept was applied to scroll saws over 100 years ago using leather and steel belts to generate a reciprocating action (refer to page 47 for more information about this type of saw). Today, the oscillating-loop design is found exclusively in the Eclipse scroll saws described on pages 73 to 77. The Eclipse incorporates high-tech

materials and engineering to make it a very efficient machine and the only one of the constant-tension saws that provides a "true-on-the-spot" vertical blade travel.

MAJOR PARTS OF THE SCROLL SAW

There are a number of parts that are common to most scroll saws. Since parallel-arm saws are the most popular, this style is selected as the illustrative example (**I–11 and I–12**).

Blades

The blade (**I–13**) is a disposable item that either breaks or simply wears out with use. There are only two types of blade: pin- and plain-end (also called pinless). (Refer to Chapter 5 for more information.) Some saws only take pin-end blades, some only plain-end, and some both types.

Pin-end blades are primarily used in light-duty, lower-priced saws. These blades are easily installed by simply "hooking" the pins into indents of simple holders located on the ends of the arms (**I–14**). Pin-end blades, by necessity of design, are larger in size than plain-end blades and, therefore, limit the amount of fine detail that can be sawn with them.

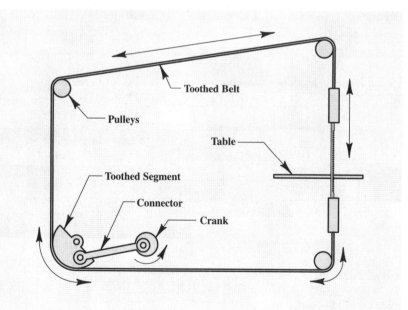

Toothed Belt

Pulleys

Table

Toothed Segment

Connector

Crank

I–10. ▶ The oscillating-loop mechanism is based on a very old concept that has been currently refined and upgraded.

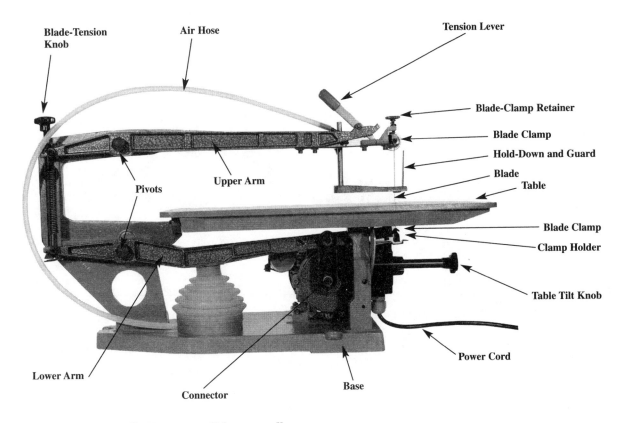

I–11. ▶ The major parts of a Hegner parallel-arm scroll saw.

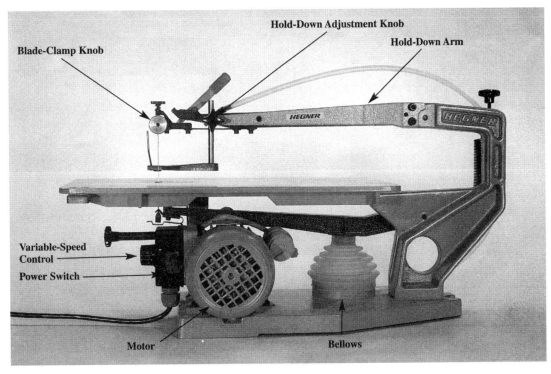

I–12. ▶ Another view of the scroll saw shown in 1–11, with the major parts identified.

I–13. ▶ Two basic blade types: Pin-end (left) and plain-end. Notice that the pin-end blade is larger and that a larger hole is required for inside sawing.

I–14. ▶ Pin-end blades are easy to install and some scroll saws have holders that allow their teeth to face in any of four directions: front, back, to the left, or to the right, as shown.

Plain-end blades are available in a much greater selection of sizes, tooth styles, and designs for cutting a wider variety of materials. Saws equipped to carry plain-end blades that can be easily and quickly installed are preferred by most scroll-sawers.

Blade Clamps

Blade clamps (sometimes called "chucks") are mounted onto the ends of the arms and designed to hold either just pin- or plain-end blades or both kinds of blades. Blade-clamp designs vary greatly from manufacturer to manufacturer and have dramatically improved in recent years (I–15 and I–16). There are two types of blade clamp: those that are permanently fixed to the ends of the arms, and detachable types that are removable from the saw. Blade clamps that are referred to as "toolless" are now more or less preferred because they speed up and simplify blade changes.

I–15. ▶ The wrench-tightened blade clamps found on older saws and shown here are frustrating and very time-consuming to use.

through the table opening. There are saws that have *replaceable table inserts* with various-size slots or custom-drilled holes that fit into machined openings in the table.

Arms

The arms are made of machined or cast aluminum, cast iron, or of a new, reinforced graphite-composite material. They are connected to a base or supporting casting with pivoting provisions consisting of bolts and bearings. Many saws have a protective shroud or cast-aluminum cover that almost totally encloses or protects the moving arms, linkage, or belts (**I–17**).

I–17. ▶ **This Tradesman scroll saw and many other saws do not have separate hold-down arms. Instead they have housings that enclose the upper moving arms, protecting the user from accidental injury. Here, the motor and lower moving parts are also well-enclosed. Notice the tension-control lever located at the upper rear and the adjustable air hose.**

I–16. ▶ **New toolless blade clamps such as this one from RBI are a great improvement over the older types.**

Tables

Tables support the workpiece during cutting. They are available in different sizes and shapes. Tables are made of aluminum or cast iron and various alloys, and are available in various finishes and/or levels of smoothness.

Most saws have tables that tilt to the left, right, or both directions in various degrees. The sizes of the openings in the table for the blade also vary. Some saws have large blade openings that provide a good view of the lower blade clamp. Other saws have relatively small table openings that provide more support close to the blade. The latter is advantageous when sawing small pieces that might otherwise drop

The *hold-down arm*—not found on all scroll saws—is a nonmoving auxiliary arm that extends horizontally, usually to the right side of the top arm. It can serve several functions:

1. It supports the workpiece hold-down foot and its vertical-adjustment mechanism.

2. It provides a mounting location to get the air hose close to the saw blade.

3. It acts as a mounting provision for an auxiliary light.

4. It incorporates a blade-changing fixture to hold detachable blade clamps while a wrench tightens or loosens the blade clamp.

Hold-Down

The hold-down (**I–18**) prevents the material being cut from flopping up and down on the table. Hold-downs are made of spring steel, flexible plastic, or cast metal; these materials make the hold-down rigid.

The hold-down is sometimes coupled with a blade guard. Both items are important safety devices and especially helpful for beginners. Experienced scroll-sawers often remove these devices to improve work-piece maneuverability and saw-line visibility and to simplify the cutting of inside openings and small parts.

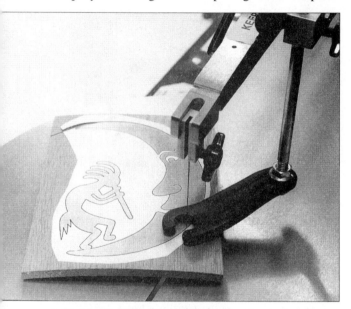

I–18. ▶ RBI's hold-down is made of a plastic that flexes with changing material thickness such as when cutting warped material as shown.

Blade-Tensioning Devices

Blade-tensioning devices essentially do two things: set the amount of tension and provide a mechanism that quickly releases or reapplies the preset tension when blades are being changed or installed.

Some saws have a cam-action flip lever that provides for a quick-release or tension application. Other saws may have a turn knob just to set the tension level and a lever tension release. Some saws are designed to have both actions controlled by a single lever that rotates, like the hands of a clock, to set the amount of tension and then also flips to activate or deactivate the full amount of tension (refer to **I–17**).

Dust-Blower System

Most saws have an adequate means of blowing the sawdust away to keep the cutting line visible. A bellows of rubber or plastic that operates automatically and is driven from the action of the arms is the most common air source. The air is directed through a straight nonadjustable or adjustable hose to a spot near the blade. Scroll saws with a blower system that directs the airflow away from the operator (refer to **I–17**) are preferred. Otherwise the fine dust, which is dangerous to one's health, is inhaled by the operator unless other safety precautions are taken. (Refer to pages 151 to 157 for further discussions about dust and operator safety.)

Switches and Speed Controls

Switches and speed controls are conveniently located up front on newer saws. On older saws, they are located below the table near the motor or are attached to the stands. Some saws have a separate power switch and another control knob for adjusting the variable speed. Some saws incorporate the switch into the speed control. Pulling the switch knob out turns the saw on, for example, while pushing it in turns it off; rotating the knob changes the speed. Better variable-speed saws have scales calibrated in actual strokes per minute, while others have meaningless division marks.

Refer to Chapter 2 for a look at typical switch-and-speed-control dials.

Motors

Motor sizes and types also vary from brand to brand. They range from 1/10 to 1/4 in horsepower, and from 1.2 to 2.8 in amps. Most saws are sufficiently powered for their cutting capacities.

Generally, motors are either the induction or the universal type. Induction motors have no brushes and require minimal maintenance. Universal motors have brushes that wear and contaminate the internal components of the motor and eventually require repair or service. Induction motors are more expensive than universal motors. Some experts claim that universal motors are better because they do not lose power at slow speeds; others insist that induction motors hold up best for continuous use in dusty environments.

Finally, it should be noted that in addition to variable-speed saws, there are single-speed, two-speed, and foot-powered saws available. There are also saws that require shifting a belt on step pulleys to change the blade speed. This old concept is still mechanically sound and is incorporated in the modern PS Wood Machine's two saws, Hegner's heavy-duty Polymax, and Delta's new 20-inch saw. (Refer to Chapter 2 for descriptions and for more information about these saws.)

Stands

Scroll-saw stands are either standard or available as optional accessories. Any bench-top saw can be made into a floor model by simply attaching it into a stand. (Turn to pages 112 and 113 for more information about floor stands.)

SCROLL-SAW CAPABILITIES

Scroll saws are used to make an endless variety of things, both decorative and functional. Scroll-sawers everywhere are exploiting the full potential of these machines to have fun and to earn extra income. Some are full-time working professionals, and others are weekend hobbyists, using the scroll saw to entertain themselves and their families.

What follows are some examples of work that can be made with a scroll saw. New ideas and techniques emerge regularly. The work samples illustrated here range from simple wooden cutouts to large, ornate pieces of freestanding fretwork. Some samples also show work made of plastic, paper, and metal.

Simple Toys and Cutouts

Almost any single- or multiple-speed scroll saw with pin- or plain-end blades can be used for this class of work (**I–19 and I–20**). Some inexpensive saws, however, may not be able to saw material thicker than ¾ inch effectively and may leave sawn edges that need sanding. (Review Chapter 8 for basic scroll-sawing techniques.)

I–19. ▶ **Simple shapes such as these kitchen tools made from relatively thin material can be cut with almost any scroll saw.**

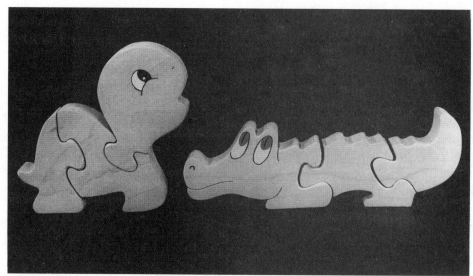

I–20. ▶ Toys and puzzles from simple profiles as shown to more complex designs can be made with the scroll saw.

Architectural Woodwork and Home-Restoration Projects

Architectural woodwork and home-restoration projects are often perfect for the scroll-sawer. Making Victorian gingerbread such as scroll-sawn brackets (**I–21**), corbels, valances, and grilles requires a saw capable of sawing thick material and providing a large throat capacity to handle big pieces.

Miniatures and Models

This category of scroll work (**I–22 and I–23**) generally requires a reasonably good variable-speed saw that can slow the cutting action down for controlled cutting of tight turns and for following precise lines in a variety of thin materials. Plain-end blades are a must when small inside openings need to be cut.

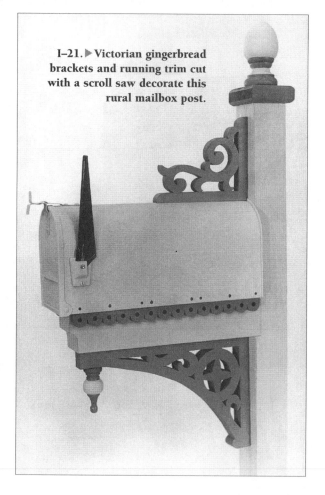

I–21. ▶ Victorian gingerbread brackets and running trim cut with a scroll saw decorate this rural mailbox post.

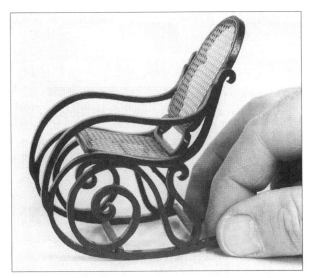

I–22. ▶ This ornately sawn chair was made from thin plywood and painted.

I–23. ▶ Architectural models such as this one can be made with the scroll saw.

Jewelry-Making

Jewelry-making (**I–24**), like miniature and model work, requires fine, plain-end blades in a scroll saw capable of smoothly cutting small parts in wood, metal, and plastic. A variable-speed precision saw is required to produce high-quality work. (Refer to Chapter 19 for more information.)

I–24. ▶ Jewelry-making involves sawing many kinds of material. In addition to wood, various plastics, Corian, brass, silver, and copper alloys are easily cut with scroll saws.

Signs

Everything from small desktop name signs (**I–25 and I–26**) to large, commercial advertising signs can involve various levels of scroll-saw work. Small interior signs requiring accurate, smooth cuts can be made in thin and thick stock in a variety of materials. Continuous sawing of tough, thick materials for making larger signs will be handled easily with medium- to low-priced saws. A larger-than-usual throat capacity may be necessary if sawing big pieces. A saw with a choice of speeds to cut a variety of materials will also be a major benefit. (To see more sign projects and some easy-to-do techniques, refer to pages 329 and 330.)

Ornaments, Silhouettes, and Paper-Cutting

Work in this broad category can range from simple to very complex shapes with fine details (**I–27 and I–28**). Cuttings are routinely made from a variety of materials, all involving specific sawing requirements. Normally, fine blades and slow speeds work best.

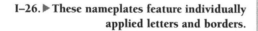

I–25. ▶ This desk nameplate features connected scroll-sawn letters cut from thick hardwood.

I–26. ▶ These nameplates feature individually applied letters and borders.

I–27. ▶ An old German-style ornament cut from waste aluminum house siding. (Design courtesy of Karl Gutbrod.)

I–28. ▶ **Hanging ornament with inlays of contrasting wood. Notice the detail cuts (also called veining) to accentuate the hair and add facial expression.**

I–29. ▶ **Thin plywood design applied to a prefinished plaque.** (Design by Bev Carmody.)

Overlays

Overlays (**I–26 and I–29**) are generally thin decorations sawn from flat materials that are glued to a solid background. Overlays are usually made of wood, but a variety of other materials can also be used. Again, a saw providing a choice of fine blades and slow cutting speeds best handles all of the variables. (Some general techniques and tips for creating this kind of scrollwork are given in Chapter 17.)

Inlays and Marquetry

Inlays (**I–28 and I–30**) and marquetry (**I–31**) involve cutting and fitting together different species of wood on or into a flat surface to create a decorative design or picture. There are a variety of techniques that can be employed, but all usually require fine blades and fairly slow cutting speeds. Usually this work involves some scroll-sawing of very small pieces in thin materials, and sometimes it requires sawing with the saw

I–30. ▶ **These simple bevel-cut inlays with ¼-inch hardwood plywood are Julie Kiehnau's first attempt at this work.**

I–31. ▶ This exquisite scroll-sawn marquetry of a typewriter-and-book design on the tambour of the roll-front desk is by professional woodworker Silas Kopf.

table tilted slightly to the blade. Inlaying thick materials requires a saw that is capable of providing greater-than-usual blade tension and accurately cutting material that is twice the thickness of the inlay. (Turn to Chapter 13 for how-to techniques.)

Segmentation and Intarsia

Segmentation (**I–32 and I–33**) and intarsia (**I–34**) involve sawing solid woods of various species and thicknesses into separate pieces, and then fitting them together after rounding the edges or otherwise

shaping the individual pieces. The result is a sculptural-looking piece that is usually mounted onto a flat backing.

Segmented work generally involves cutting pieces of a design from a single board, whereas intarsia designs call for a variety of natural-colored woods. The scroll saw used for these types of work should be capable of carrying small plain-end blades that can make true, tight radius cuts in stock of ¾ inch and less thickness. (The various techniques and project examples are given in Chapter 22.)

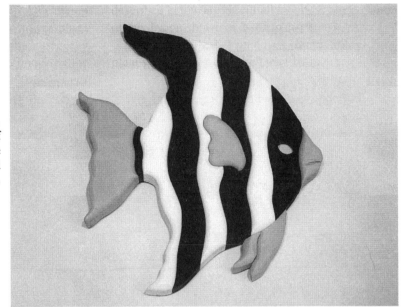

I–32. ▶ An example of segmentation. All pieces are cut from one piece of wood. The edges are rounded and the individual parts are painted and glued to a backer.

I–33. ▶ Pictorial segmentation is a new technique developed by Kerry Shirts. It utilizes only one piece of wood that's been cut into detailed segments that are individually stained before being reassembled into a dramatic work of art.

I–34. ▶ This excellent example of intarsia by Lucille Crabtree features different pieces of various-colored natural woods that have been cut, shaped, and fitted together.

Fine Fretwork

Fine fretwork (**I–35**), also known as "pierced cutting," involves making numerous inside cutouts usually in thin stock, although this work is not necessarily restricted to just thin material. A scroll saw that features fast and easy changing of small plain-end blades is essential. The saw should also be designed to make it easy and fast to get the blade threaded through the workpiece regardless of its size. Minimum vibration, a large scroll-saw table to support big pieces that are often very delicate and fragile, and sufficient throat clearance are also important considerations. (To see other examples of fretwork and learn basic techniques, turn to Chapter 16.)

I–35. ▶ **Fine fretwork by professional scroll-sawer John Polhemus.**

Bevel-Sawing Shapes in Relief

Bevel-sawing shapes in relief (**I–36**) involves sawing various inside openings with the table tilted, producing pieces with beveled edges. The pieces are made to intentionally bind at a position of relief to the surrounding background. Variations of the technique can provide stunning sculptural or carved effects with the design raised in relief or recessed below the surface. Any saw carrying fine plain-end blades with greater-than-average tension and a table that tilts a few degrees both left and right can be used. (Turn to Chapter 12 for more information on this work.)

Compound-Sawing

Compound-sawing (**I–37**) involves a simple technique of sawing an object by cutting on two or more surfaces of the workpiece. A saw with a higher-than-usual thickness-cutting capacity is less restrictive; however, it must be able to make square and accurate cuts in thick stock. Work of this type is not highly dependent on a saw with a large throat capacity, and a broad range of speed choices is usually not essential. (This easy and fun-to-do technique is discussed in Chapter 11.)

I–36. ▶ Bevel-edged scroll-sawn shapes pushed up in relief to appear as if the background were cut away. The shapes sawn to be recessed below the surface appear to be routed or carved into the surface.

I–37. ▶ A chess set in progress utilizes the compound-scrolling technique.

Incise-Carving

This technique utilizes the scroll saw to cut and remove triangular chunks of wood from the surface of a board so the resulting design appears as if it were hand-carved with a V-gouge or router bit (**I–38**). The saw used must carry plain-end blades, provide good blade tension, and have a tilting table. (The techniques for this unusual class of scrollwork are described in Chapter 15.)

Making Simulated Baskets and Vessels

Making simulated baskets and vessels (**I–39**) involves scroll-sawing and stacking rings together that have either straight or bevel-cut edges. The amount of cutting detail and stock thickness can vary from ¼ inch upward to 1½ inches or more. Any saw carrying fine plain-end blades and with a speed control for sawing thin stock can be used for this class of work. (Turn to Chapter 12 for more information.)

I–38. ▶ Some designs created with the scroll saw that resemble incise-carving.

I–39. ▶ Simulated baskets, made of scroll-sawn ring-like layers, are very authentic-looking and are actually very easy to make.

Wood Joinery

Fine woodworking joints such as through dovetails, pin-and-cove joints (**I–40**), tight miter joints, and a variety of others can be cut with the help of the scroll saw or exclusively with it. The scroll saw may or may not require the assistance of other tools such as routers and table saws. (For further details about making joints with the scroll saw, see Chapter 18.)

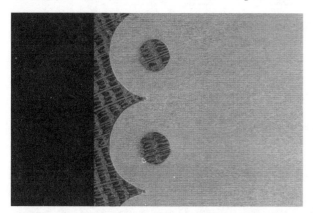

I–40. ▶ Making this elegant pin-and-cove joint involves the use of a router and the scroll saw.

Specialty Jobs

Specialty jobs include sawing a variety of materials, among which are soft-foamed plastics (**I–41**), fabrics, the hard bone of animal antlers, glass, ceramics, and steel. In short, almost anything imaginable can be cut to some extent with the scroll saw.

I–41. ▶ Acrylic plastic is just one of many great materials available for scroll-sawing special projects.

CHAPTER ONE

HISTORICAL OVERVIEW OF SCROLL-SAWING

his chapter examines significant developments of the past leading to today's modern scroll saws and the marvelous works made with them. In actuality, however, scroll-sawing and the fundamental designs of scroll saws have changed very little in the last 130 to 150 years.

EARLY PATTERNS AND PUBLICATIONS

There were at least 14 known scroll-saw project designers or publications that printed scroll work in the 1800's (1–1 and 1–2). Many mail-order houses that sprang up during that time offered everything the fret-sawer needed, including tools, blades, wood, hardware, machines, and project patterns. Of the many project designers of that era, the most illustrious include Adams and Bishop. They founded their company in 1879 and later sold it to J.R. Bowman. "Russell's Designs of 1884–85" featured patterns by Arthur Hope and H.L. and William Wild. Other names involved with the creation and/or distribution of patterns include Fleetwood, Pomeroy, and Ware.

No. 551. Swiss Clock.
12x18 in. 20c.

No. 545. Mantel Clock. 13x19 in. 20c.

No. 598. Handkerchief Box.
7x7 in. 10c.

No. 651. Corner Cabinet.
10½x28 in. 25c.

No. 594. Hanging Swiss Clock. 30x10 in. (Large enough for 8-day strike clock. Put together like 519.) 25c.

No. 689. Corner Bracket.
12½x33 in. 15c.

1–1. ▶ Sample project patterns from the 1880 A.H. Pomeroy catalog that were purchased and cut by scroll-sawers utilizing hand frames and early foot-powered scroll saws.

1–2. ▶ Various publications were available for the early scroll-sawer. The longest running was this English publication *Hobbies Weekly*, which was launched in 1895 and ran for almost 60 years.

Patterns were also imported. They were of English, Dutch, Italian, German, and French origins that were developed primarily for hand-sawn fretwork. When the total quantity of early pattern designers is considered, relatively few were American. There was also a magazine published in the 1800's entitled the *Fretsawer's Monthly and Home Decorator*, which provided tips and introduced new patterns, tools, and supplies.

In 1895, a British magazine, *Hobbies Weekly*, appeared that concentrated on fretwork (refer to **1–2**). It enjoyed an enormous worldwide readership until sometime in the 1950's or 60's. In the early 1900's, a Scandinavian publication, The *Aller's Familie Journal*, provided hundreds of patterns for "figure sawing" (fretwork). In the United States, *Home Craftsman* magazine featured many projects for scroll-sawers between the 1930's and 60's. Delta Manufacturing published numerous scroll-saw projects between 1932 and the early 1970's with its periodical *Deltagram & Flying Chips*. Thousands of designs from these old publications are now being redrawn, redesigned, and reissued by contemporary designers, authors, and publishers.

By and large, scroll saws still function much like they did in the 1800's. Early antiquated machines all had a reciprocating cutting action as do the modern ones, and scroll saws still have the same major parts: a narrow blade clamped and tensioned between two arms, a table, and a power source (hand crank, foot power, steam, water, or electricity) that drives the blade up and down. In the following pages, you will see many early saws with features and components that are currently being promoted as "new" or "revolutionary" by today's scroll-saw manufacturers. Some of these features/components were in fact developed over 100 years ago. They include up-front lever tensioning, toolless blade clamps, sawdust blowers, oscillating belt drives, speed control, true vertical strokes, hinged upper arms, hold-downs, and more.

HAND FRAMES
In scroll-saw work, as in all other forms of woodcutting, power tools essentially evolved from hand tools (**1–3 to 1–7**). It is difficult to determine exactly where and when hand-cut scrollwork originated. We know that Egyptian furniture removed from sealed tombs provides proof that ornamental fretlike veneer overlays were used some 3,000 years ago. Veneers were somehow delicately cut and applied to early Greek and Roman furniture as well. Ornamental overlays on furniture were also found in European and Scandinavian countries in the 16th and 17th centuries.

Elaborate fretwork furniture parts were clearly evident in works by the famous 18th-century European craftsmen including Duncan Phyfe, Thomas Chippendale, and others. Some of Chippendale's fret designs were inspired by the repetitious geometrical patterns found in early Chinese temples. It is believed that the first fine scroll- or fret-sawing blades were invented by a German clock-maker in the late 1500's.

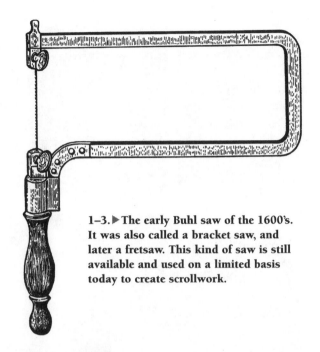

1–3. ▶ **The early Buhl saw of the 1600's. It was also called a bracket saw, and later a fretsaw. This kind of saw is still available and used on a limited basis today to create scrollwork.**

1–4. ▶ **Buhl sawing circa 1775. The work is held vertically with the foot-operated clamp of this "Buhl Horse." Sawing was done with a push stroke.**

Basic fretwork techniques and special tools can clearly be traced back to a famous French craftsman, André Charles Boulle (1642–1732). His works involved the decoration of furniture with brass, tortoiseshells, and exotic wood inlays. Boulle is regarded by some historians as the father of inlay and marquetry techniques. His ornamental work became so specialized and well known that eventually it was simply described as Buhl work ("Buhl" was the German corruption of Boulle). (Refer to **1–3 and 1–4**.)

The U-shaped saw frame Boulle used was called the Buhl saw and various other names over the ensuing years (refer to **1–3 and 1–4**). This hand tool was the forerunner of the scroll-saw machine. It was once called a bracket saw because shelf brackets were a popular project cut with it. Eventually, it became known as the fretsaw, a name that has survived up to today.

The early metal fretsaw frames were available only from Germany or the United States until the 1890's, when *Hobbies Limited* of England produced high-quality frames made of British steel. The hand fretsaw remains virtually unchanged in its basic design.

Fretwork became very popular in Italy during the mid-1700's, where it was actually called Sorrento carving because most of the famous fretworkers practiced their art in the city of Sorrento. The term spread throughout the world and became used for fretwork, even in the United States (refer to **1–6**).

The Sorrento Wood-Carving Company of Boston and Chicago was founded in 1865, and claimed to be the only mail-order house in the world devoted solely to fretwork. It provided all the necessary tools and featured patterns and expensive, high-quality German saw blades made from clock-spring steel. It also is quoted as claiming to be "the first to introduce knowledge of this pleasing work into this country."

In an old catalog, *Schroeter's Scroll Saw Designs, Revised Edition No. 1*, dated 1915, the following is written on the inside cover: "Fretsawing of fancy articles originated in Switzerland using in all case the old style hand frame..." There were no changes to the hand frame until a motorized version produced by Dremel appeared in 1939 (refer to **1–7**). The basic design of the metal frame was incorporated into some clever bench-top devices that ensured true vertical cuts (**1–8 and 1–9**).

1–5. ▶ **Other styles of early saw frame made of wood.**

1–6. ▶ Fretwork, also called Sorrento wood carving, was a popular hobby for everyone—including women and children—from the 1800's through the 1940's and 50's. When long frames such as this were used, they were supported on the upper arm to reduce fatigue.

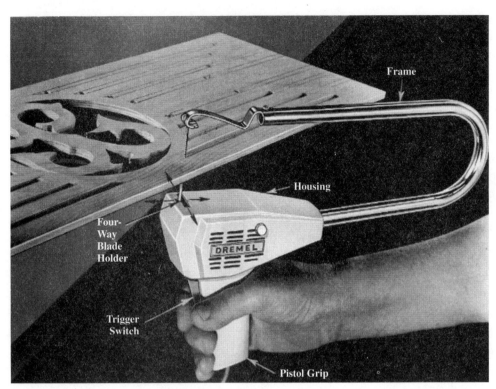

Frame

Housing

Four-
Way
Blade
Holder

Trigger
Switch

Pistol Grip

1–7. ▶ Hand frames essentially did not change until Dremel's electric version came along in 1939. It was, however, discontinued in 1972.

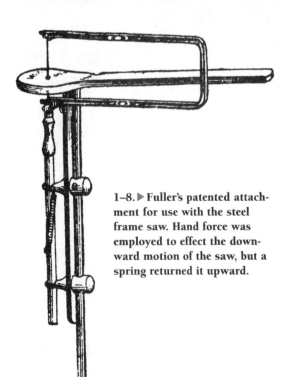

1–8. ▶ Fuller's patented attachment for use with the steel frame saw. Hand force was employed to effect the downward motion of the saw, but a spring returned it upward.

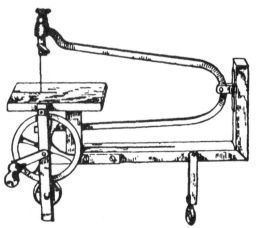

1–9. ▶ This English-made device known as the Original Eclipse No. 1333 was operated by a hand crank.

(Reprinted by permission of Terry Davy.)

FOOT-POWERED SAWS

Reciprocating foot-powered saws with spring-pole tensioning have been documented in Europe and the United States prior to the 1800's. Around 1867, crude foot-powered scroll saws for home use began to appear (**1–10**). In fact, during the last half of the 1800's, 60 or more different models or variations of foot-powered scroll saws arrived on the market.

Prior to the foot-powered scroll saws that were made for home use, crude factory saws were already developed. Some could stack-cut 25 to 30 pieces of veneer at a time. Most operated according to the movable-sash (wooden-frame) principle (**1–11**). These saws incorporated some fundamental design principles that were retained in some of the saws made early in the 20th century and even in today's modern saws.

Historian Harold Barker has documented over 300 home and industrial jig or scroll-saw machines that appeared in the United States between 1800 and 1960. When you add the early saws imported from England and other countries and the scroll saws introduced since the 1960's, the total number of saws is staggering. Space constraints limit the following discussion to descriptions of only some of the most popular early saws—and only those with significantly important features.

The actual development of foot-powered scroll saws intended for the amateur or home craftsman began in the 1870's. Once it began, many saws appeared in rapid succession. In 1876, A.H. Shipman of Rochester, New York, claimed to be the first to manufacture a cheap, practical foot-powered scroll saw for home use (**1–12**). Appropriately named the

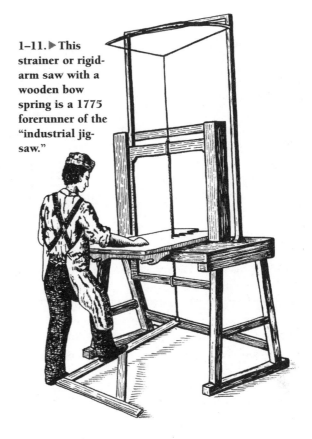

1–11. ▶ This strainer or rigid-arm saw with a wooden bow spring is a 1775 forerunner of the "industrial jig-saw."

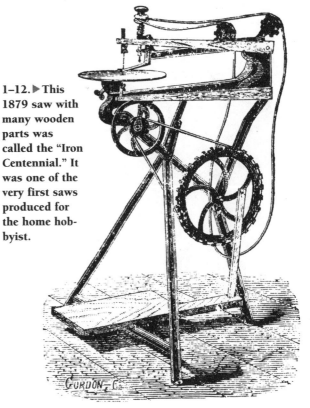

1–12. ▶ This 1879 saw with many wooden parts was called the "Iron Centennial." It was one of the very first saws produced for the home hobbyist.

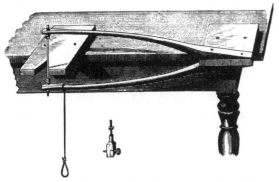

1–10. ▶ One of the earliest foot-powered scroll saws dates back to the 1800's.

Iron Centennial because of the year, Shipman's saw, though crude, was sold in the United States and abroad with great success.

The treadle on Shipman's foot-powered saw produced a rotary motion that was converted to a vertical reciprocating sawing action. Other saws produced by Shipman's company were given names such as the Demas for 1880, Demas Nos. 4 and 5, the Prize Demas, the Holly, and the Prize Holly.

The Millers Falls Company of New York also produced some saws in the 1870's and 1880's that became very well known, and were used throughout the United States and presumably in Europe. The most popular were its Cricket and Rogers saws, which were very inexpensive and could be afforded by almost all home craftspeople (**1–13**). Other saws produced by Millers Falls Company include the Millers Falls Saw, the Star, the Lester, and the New Lester. It is interesting to note that the New Rogers saw featured a toolless blade-clamp system and an up-front, toggle-type lever tensioning device that operated two pivots on a linkage (**1–14 and 1–15**). The Millers Falls Saw, the Star, and the Cricket were all very similar.

Hobbies Limited of England copied the popular American-made Rogers saw, calling it the Briton (**1–16**). In the 1800's, Hobbies Limited imported

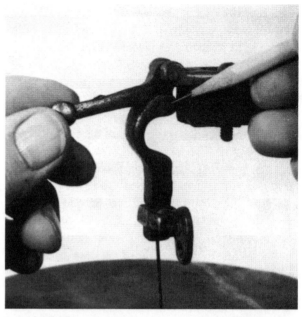

1–14. ▶ The lever position on an untensioned blade in the New Rogers Saw.

1–13. ▶ The New Rogers Saw (1880–1915) was perhaps the most popular of all treadle saws.

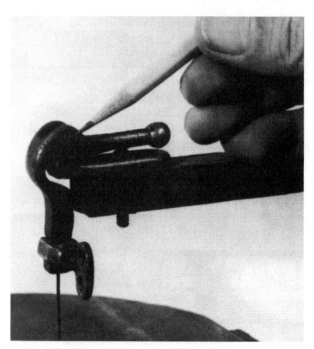

1–15. ▶ The lever in the tensioned position.

1–16. ▶ The Briton saw made by Hobbies Limited of England was a copy of the Rogers saw. (Drawing courtesy of Terry Davy.)

1–17. ▶ The Brittania, made by Hobbies Limited, circa late 1800's, was one of the first to have a true vertical blade stroke with a spiral spring tension. (Drawing courtesy of Terry Davy.)

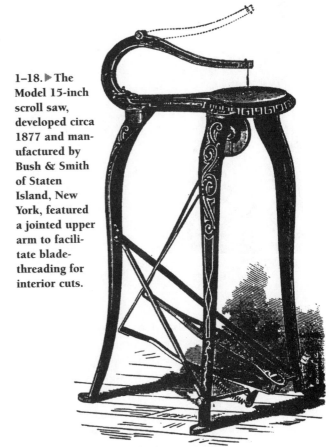

1–18. ▶ The Model 15-inch scroll saw, developed circa 1877 and manufactured by Bush & Smith of Staten Island, New York, featured a jointed upper arm to facilitate blade-threading for interior cuts.

many other American saws, copied them, and made improvements where practical. Hobbies was one of the first companies to produce a spiral, spring-tensioned blade and a true vertical stroke (1–17). This was actually the forerunner of the rigid-arm machines popular from the 1930's to 60's.

Another interesting early development is the concept of a hinged upper arm. This feature, found on today's DeWalt scroll saws, was first developed around 1877 on the 15-inch Model saw manufactured in New York (1–18).

The Trump Brothers of Wilmington, Delaware, introduced a number of saws in the 1870's. One of the company's earliest introductions was the Fleetwood, which had a friction drive (1–19 and 1–20). Later models (1879) were redesigned from friction to the more conventional belt drives. In addition to three different models of the Fleetwood saws, the Trump Bros. also made the Dexter saws—models A, B, and C.

The Seneca Mfg. Co. of Seneca Falls, New York, made at least six high-quality saws. They were given names such as the Challenge or Boss, the Rival, the Victor (1–21), and the Empire.

1–19. ▶ The bench-mounted, foot-powered Fleetwood scroll saw, patented in 1872, was claimed to be the best for delicate and accurate fret-sawing. It had unique, guided blade clamps, a 14½-inch throat, and could cut stock ¾ inch and under rapidly.

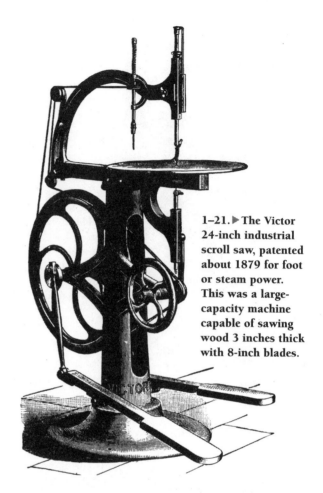

1–21. ▶ The Victor 24-inch industrial scroll saw, patented about 1879 for foot or steam power. This was a large-capacity machine capable of sawing wood 3 inches thick with 8-inch blades.

1–20. ▶ Another friction-driven Fleetwood saw with a "first-class ornamental stand."

shapers, table saws, and other tools. It had 14 patents on various foot-powered mechanisms. The Barnes catalog of 1872 carries this statement: "The only true economy is to secure a strong and durable machine." The catalog also made this claim: "With the effort of an ordinary walk, 800 to 1,200 strokes per minute can be generated." The Barnes machines became extremely popular, and the scroll saws are now highly sought by tool collectors.

Some Barnes machines were made for light industrial use, and others were developed primarily for home use. Illus. **1–22 to 1–28** show some of the first foot-powered Barnes saws. The Velocipede saw had a bicycle-like operation that was incorporated in both the lighter and heavier saws. The Barnes No. 6 Amateur Saw (1883–1901), shown in **1–27 and 1–28**, was one of the forerunners of the "oscillating loop drive" now found on the modern Eclipse scroll saw shown on pages 73 to 77.

The W.F. and John Barnes Co. of Rockford, Illinois, was the major foot-powered scroll-saw manufacturer in the Midwest. Two brothers, one a model-maker and the other an inventor, organized their company in 1868. The company made a number of innovative and efficient foot-powered scroll saws and eventually branched into all kinds of woodworking machinery, including foot-powered lathes,

1–22. ▶ This model No. 7 scroll saw was one of the first foot-powered scroll saws manufactured by Barnes, making an appearance in 1872. It was a 24-inch machine that carried a 7-inch blade. Ordinary operation produced 800 to 1,200 cutting strokes per minute. It was capable of cutting at the following rates: 1-inch pine at 4 feet per minute; 2-inch pine at 1 foot per minute; 1-inch walnut at 2 feet per minute; and 3-inch walnut at ½ foot per minute.

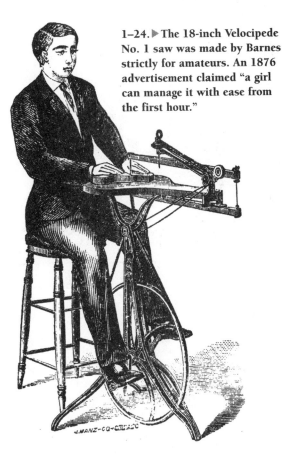

1–24. ▶ The 18-inch Velocipede No. 1 saw was made by Barnes strictly for amateurs. An 1876 advertisement claimed "a girl can manage it with ease from the first hour."

1–23. ▶ The No. 7 Barnes saw shown with a vertical hickory stick attached to the rear leg, which served as a spring return.

Velocipede Scroll Saw No. 2.

Price, with Boring Attachment, $20.00
Without Boring Attachment, $18.00

1–25. ▶ The 24-inch Barnes No. 2 scroll saw. With a 7-inch blade, it could cut stock 3 inches thick at the rate of 1 foot per minute. This improved version, made after 1880, had a perforated belt drive.

1–26. ▶ Reprint from an early Barnes catalog. Other ads stated: "All muscles of the limbs are brought into healthful exercise which should be a good consideration when selecting a machine"; and "many a boy has been saved from vice by his growing interest in working with tools."

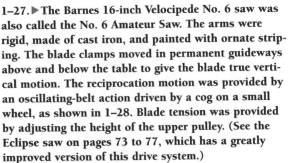

1–27. ▶ The Barnes 16-inch Velocipede No. 6 saw was also called the No. 6 Amateur Saw. The arms were rigid, made of cast iron, and painted with ornate striping. The blade clamps moved in permanent guideways above and below the table to give the blade true vertical motion. The reciprocation motion was provided by an oscillating-belt action driven by a cog on a small wheel, as shown in 1–28. Blade tension was provided by adjusting the height of the upper pulley. (See the Eclipse saw on pages 73 to 77, which has a greatly improved version of this drive system.)

(Photo courtesy of George Stefureac.)

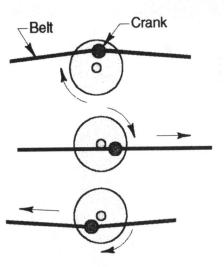

1–28. ▶ How the oscillating-belt action was generated on the Barnes No. 6 Velocipede saw with a crank on the small pulley. (Photo courtesy of George Stefureac.)

Some foot-powered saws from England that appeared in the 1870's and later include the Excelsior and the Goodell Scroll Saw and Lathe Combination (**1–29**). The Imperial (**1–30**), the Norfolk (**1–31**), the Triumph, the Victory, the Gem (**1–32**), and the Anchor (**1–33**) are among many scroll saws manufactured by Hobbies Limited of England that had some noteworthy features. Hobbies Limited sold a series of over 20 foot-powered saws, many in the United States, within a span of 60 years that extended well into the 20th century. Some historians contend that Hobbies Limited of England was, at one time, the largest manufacturer of scroll-sawing tools and supplies in the world.

A few other names either associated with a manufacturer or that identify certain models of foot-powered scroll saw include: Beach, Bentel, Bush, Clinton, E.O. Chase, Gardner's (a saw featuring two

1–29. ▶ **The British-made Goodell Scroll Saw and Lathe Combination shown here appeared in 1887 and remained in production for more than 60 years. Notice the grinding wheel and horizontal drill on the left.**

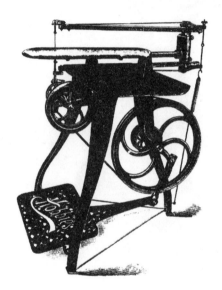

1–31. ▶ **The British Norfolk, introduced in 1904, featured a speed control using a system of small and large pulleys. This machine could also be power-driven from line shafts.**
(Drawing courtesy of Terry Davy.)

1–30. ▶ **The Imperial, introduced in 1889 by Hobbies Limited of England, was one of many machines developed to improve upon the flaws in American machines.**
(Drawing courtesy of Terry Davy.)

1–32. ▶ **The Gem machine, introduced in the 1920's, was the first with all-metal arms. It was very popular. See the Hobbies Limited treadle scroll saw on page 85, which is a foot-powered saw that is still available today.**
(Drawing courtesy of Terry Davy.)

1–33. ▶ The Anchor saw, produced by Hobbies Limited in 1934, utilized a revolutionary flexible steel band running over pulleys to operate the blade in a true vertical stroke. An oscillating cam shaped like an anchor provided the movement to the steel band much like that of the modern Eclipse saw shown on pages 73 to 77. (Drawing courtesy of Terry Davy.)

1–34. ▶ An early electric saw, brand name unknown. (Photo courtesy of Henry Aldinger.)

heavy flywheels that perpetuate inertial energy into the driving system), Griffin, Lewis, New American, New Giant, Plummer, Pomeroy's House Saw, Sears, Stafford, Wilds, and Walker, Wright & Smith.

In the 1850's, bellows and air piston-type sawdust blowers were already in common use. In the early 1860's and 1870's, machines were produced in the United States and England that employed spiral-spring tensioning and blade guides that moved inside fixed housings, ensuring true vertical strokes. Apparently this was a feature desired and in demand by earlier scroll-sawers for cutting very fine details.

An interesting patent was incorporated into an 1871 machine called "Moors Revolving Blade Scroll Saw." With this machine, the blade rotated (on a vertical axis) while sawing so you didn't have to turn the piece being cut. The operator turned the blade "to conform to the curvature of the pattern, instead of making the outline (of the work) conform to the direction of the saw."

Illus. **1–34 to 1–39** show some early electrified large-capacity saws and how they were used in industry. In the early 1920's, small electric motors for individual machines were becoming more widely accepted, even though the induction motor had been in existence since 1888. Electric motor-powered machines were not quickly purchased because rural

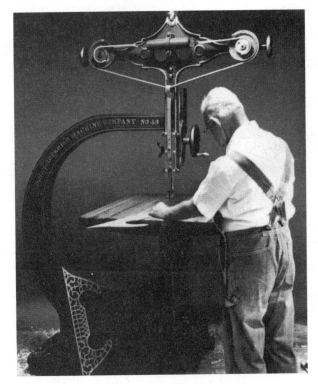

1–35. ▶ This Superior No. 46 industrial-quality scroll saw was designed to provide large pieces of Victorian fretwork on a production basis. It was manufactured circa 1882, and an electric motor was added in 1906. Blade tension consisted of leather belts connected to a large spring.

1–36. ▶ This 1927 Barnes electrified scroll saw had a 24-inch throat, a 7-inch blade, and a ¼-horsepower motor. It suffered in competition with other brand saws such as Delta, which featured cast-iron, rather than wood, tables.

1–37. ▶ Fay's early-industrial scroll saw was driven by line shafts from water or steam power. The overhead straining mechanism provided unlimited throat capacity. Reciprocation was provided by the wheel-and-pitman (page 15) action, which moved the blade in vertical guides.

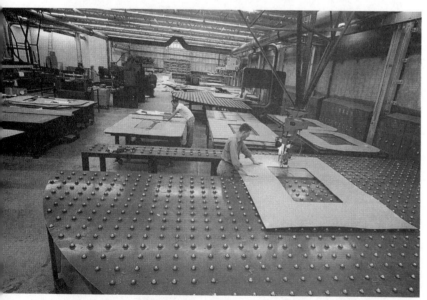

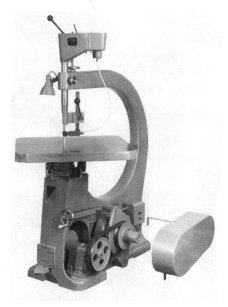

1–38. ▶ A scroll-sawing operation in a wood-product factory. Notice the large, ceiling-supported scroll saw. The casters on the worktable facilitate the movement of heavy workpieces.

1–39. ▶ An Oliver 36-inch industrial, variable-speed scroll saw. This machine weighs 1,600 pounds, stands 6 feet high, carries blades up to 18 inches in length, and cuts stock up to 10 inches thick with a 2½-inch stroke.

America did not get electricity for quite a while. In fact, some rural areas didn't receive electricity until the late 1930's.

In 1921, Carl Moberg of Chicago invented a crank-operated scroll saw for boys. Around 1925, Herbert Tautz, a manufacturer of sewing machines in Milwaukee, Wisconsin, started to produce it (**1–40 and 1–41**). In the years following the Great Depression, this production effort expanded into the Delta Manufacturing Company, and the famous heavy, rigid-arm jigsaws eventually came into existence. These saws were a standard school-shop item from the 1930's through the 1970's. Illus. **1–42 to 1–45**

1–41. ▶ A close-up look at the grooved crosshead, in which the inner end of a crank (extending from the shaft) rides. When the hand crank revolves, the crosshead carrying the saw frame is driven up and down on the two vertical guide posts. This basic system for converting rotary motion to a reciprocating action was employed in the rigid-arm, 24-inch Delta jigsaws manufactured until 1995.

1–40. ▶ Shown here is the first scroll saw manufactured by Herbert Tautz in Milwaukee, Wisconsin, who eventually expanded the company to create the Delta Power Tool Company. The frame carrying the blade moves up and down with the operation of the hand crank. The lower frame is a hold-down that is adjustable to stock thickness.

1–42. ▶ A 1930 version of Delta's popular 24-inch rigid-arm jigsaw. Manufacturer's claim: "5 years in development...opens new era in scroll sawing."

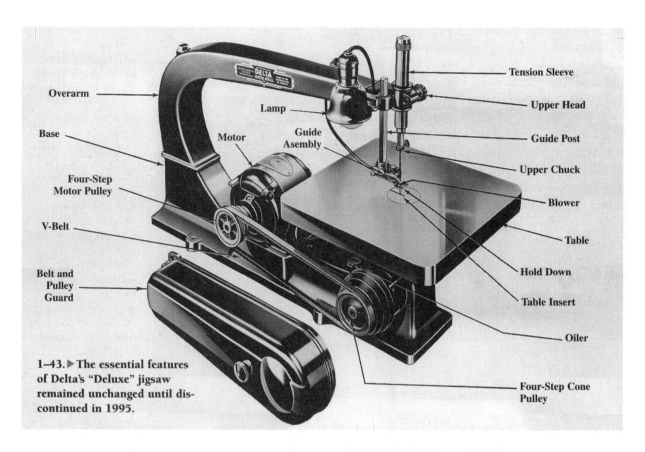

Overarm

Lamp

Base

Motor

Guide
Asembly

Four-Step
Motor Pulley

V-Belt

Belt and
Pulley
Guard

Tension Sleeve

Upper Head

Guide Post

Upper Chuck

Blower

Table

Hold Down

Table Insert

Oiler

Four-Step Cone
Pulley

1–43. ▶ The essential features
of Delta's "Deluxe" jigsaw
remained unchanged until discontinued in 1995.

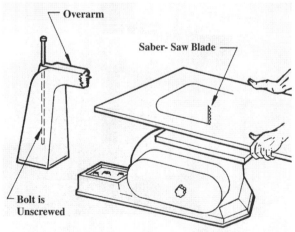

Overarm

Saber- Saw Blade

Bolt is
Unscrewed

1–44. ▶ The Delta jigsaw could be converted to a saber
saw by removing the upper arm.

1–45. ▶ View
with a "cut-
away" table
showing the
saber-saw blade
clamped only in
the lower
chuck. Saber-
saw blades were
coarse-cutting
and $3/16$ to $1/4$
inch in width to
provide suitable
stiffness.

show the development and features of Delta's popular 24-inch rigid-arm saw. Scroll saws of this type were actually called jigsaws because of their spring-type blade-tensioning mechanisms. Some other names of 24-inch rigid-arm jigsaws that followed Delta's lead were: American, Atlas, Boice-Crane, Craftsman, Crescent, Dunlap, Duro (which was a 26-inch saw), Powermatic, Yates, and Walker-Turner.

Scroll saws did not undergo a major change in design and manufacture until 1974 when Helmut Abel of Germany patented the Hegner constant-tension scroll saw (1–46 and 1–47). This scroll saw, an electric, high-tech, well-engineered product of modern metal alloys, quickly proved to be a vastly popular version of the constant-tensioned, foot-powered saws of the 1800's. Many other manufacturers have since rushed to claim a piece of this huge and ever-expanding market. In 1982, R.B. Industries of Missouri became the first United States company to enter the revived scroll-saw market (1–48).

In the 1980's, Canadian inventor Tom Sommerville designed the "double parallel-link" drive system and introduced it in two saws: a 24-inch floor model (1–49) and a 19-inch bench-top saw bearing the brand name Excalibur. The 24-inch model has been discontinued. The bench-top model and the new 30-inch Excalibur and DeWalt saws shown in Chapter 2 are made by the Sommerville Group in Canada.

1–47. ▶ Hegner's first scroll saw was called the Multi-Max 2.

1–48. ▶ The RBI Eagle—a C-arm scroll saw with a 16-inch throat, 1⅛-inch stroke, two-speed belt drive, 2-inch maximum-cutting thickness, and tilting table—was discontinued in 1986 due to the success of the company's other parallel-arm machines.

1–49. ▶ The discontinued Excalibur 24-inch variable-speed scroll saw.

1–46. ▶ Helmut Abel of Germany is the 1974 patent holder for the Hegner line of scroll saws.

In the late 1980's and 90's, a rush of inexpensive bench-top scroll saws entered the market. Many of these saws have since been either discontinued or improved as new models (**1–50 to 1–54**).

A large number of essentially identical saws were made in the Far East for various United States companies by the Rexon Group. These included machines for many major companies, including Delta, American Machine & Tool, Jet, and Craftsman. Although modern materials and manufacturing techniques were used to make these saws, in many ways they were not as "user friendly" as some of the older, foot-powered saws. These single-speed saws had blade clamps, for example, that were crude and difficult to use, requiring wrenches and special holders (refer to **1–53**). Some experts contend that saws of this type did more to discourage the craft of scroll-sawing than popularize it because of the difficulty of changing or threading the blade for making inside cutouts.

Within the last few years, we have seen great improvements that make even many of the less-expensive saws more user friendly. Most of the new saws available today are discussed in the next chapter.

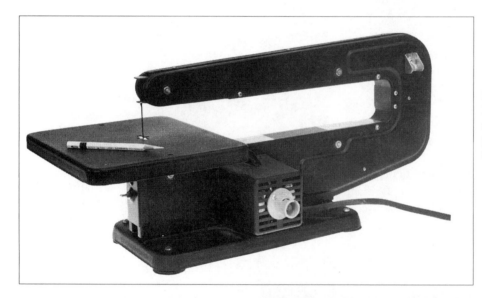

1–50. ▶ This light-duty, 15-inch Dremel scroll saw, which carried 3-inch pin-end blades, was recently discontinued.

1–51. ▶ The 18-inch Hobby Hawk, manufactured by RB Industries, was discontinued early in the 1990's.

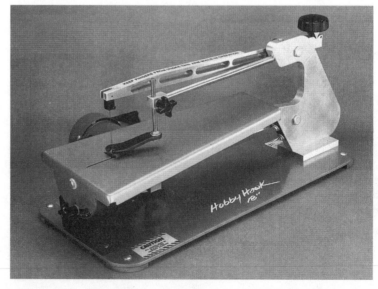

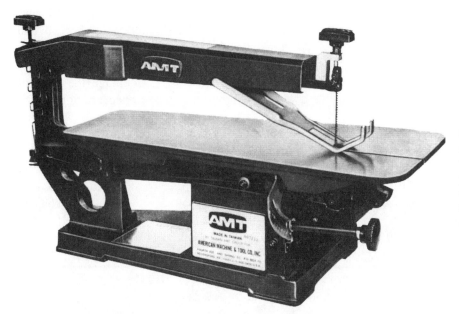

1–52. ▶ A typical design of many imports from Taiwan and China manufactured for various United States companies imitated the look and some features of the Hegner saws. Some are still available today.

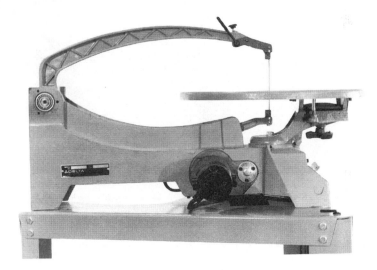

1–54. ▶ This 18-inch, heavy-cast, C-arm, variable-speed Delta scroll saw was popular for a few years before giving way to a high-tech, Q-3 version that is 40 pounds lighter (shown on pages 65 to 67).

1–53. ▶ Poorly designed blade clamps that require a wrench, such as the clamp shown here, were typical of the inexpensive saws imported from the Far East.

CHAPTER TWO

CURRENT
SCROLL SAWS

*his chapter provides a brief overview of approximately 50 scroll saws currently available in North America and Europe. The scroll saws are presented alphabetically, and the major features of most of them are described and illustrated. Complete specifications for each saw are given in **Table 2–1** on pages 100 to 109.*

In this chapter, you will see a variety of designs and find that a number of saws are similar. Similarity exists because certain saws are produced by the same manufacturer and just given different colors and names.

Within the past few years, we've seen major improvements from nearly every manufacturer. Today's scroll saws perform better and are easier to use than previous ones. Even most of the inexpensive Asian imports now come loaded with "user-friendly" features. These include toolless blade clamps, easy tensioning, variable speeds, adjustable-direction sawdust blowers and dust extraction, positive locking tables, and a variety of special features and options. You will, however, also learn that some saws still have features that are not desirable for the serious scroll-sawer, and others are designed to better perform certain kinds of work. Most manufacturers do have ongoing programs to upgrade and improve their products.

The information presented here is as current as possible. Some saws may have been discontinued entirely as dictated by sales and market conditions. In fact, a number of saws sold during the last decade are now discontinued. Although some may still be in use, they are not included in this chapter due to space limitations.

This information is intended to assist the first-time buyer so he or she may acquire the best saw available within size, performance, and price limitations. Experienced scroll-sawers and professionals planning to upgrade to a special-purpose, larger, or more durable saw will also find the comparisons helpful.

AXMINSTER SCROLL SAWS

Two English saws bearing the Axminster name are sold by the Axminster Tool and Machinery Co., located in Axminster, England.

The Axminster FS410 bench-top scroll saw (2–1) is sold as a beginner's saw and is designed to carry pin-end blades. Plain-end blades may also be used; however, a special conversion kit must be purchased. This is a parallel-arm machine with a thickness-cut-ting capacity limited to one inch. It is a well-guarded, single-speed machine operating at 1,400 spm (strokes per minute). The polished aluminum saw table tilts for bevel-sawing and has a zero-degree-setting bolt.

The Axminster FS18 scroll saw (2–2) is an 18-inch C-arm single-speed (1,720-spm) machine. The table is cast iron and tilts 45 degrees. Although the saw is designed essentially to carry pin-end blades, a conversion kit comes with it to hold plain-end blades. Its stock-thickness capacity is 1⅜ inches.

Refer to **Table 2–1** on pages 100 to 109 for complete specifications for the Axminster scroll saws.

BLACK & DECKER SCROLL SAW

Black & Decker's first and only entry into the scroll-saw market is the 16-inch bench-top machine shown in 2–3. This new saw has a 2-inch thickness-cutting capacity and a thumbscrew on the top and bottom of the toolless blade-clamping system (2–4). A rear tension lever sets the amount of tension by rotation and releases or applies tension to the blade with a simple flip of its cam-action design.

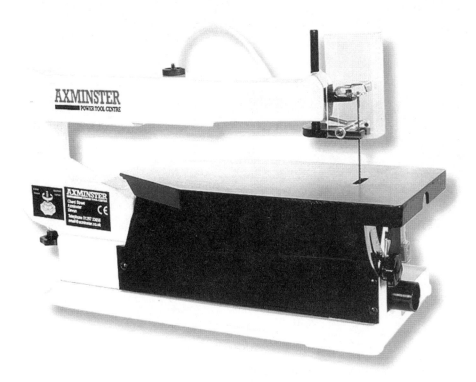

2–1. ▶ **This Axminster FS410 beginner's scroll saw is available in England.**

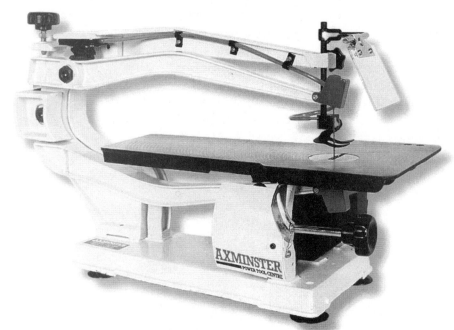

2–2. ▶ Axminster's FS18 C-arm scroll saw, also available in England.

2–3. ▶ Black & Decker's 16-inch variable-speed scroll saw.

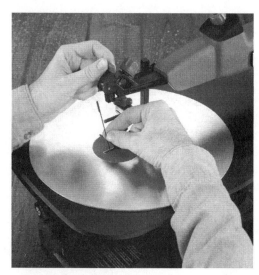

2–4. ▶ Blade installation on the Black & Decker scroll saw.

An up-front variable-speed control (**2–5**) provides a choice of 400 to 1,700 spm. The table tilts more than 45 degrees and has a zero-degree stop that can also be adjusted to tilt up to two degrees to the right. The adjustable air hose is standard. The combination blade guard and hold-down is removable. A special light accessory that mounts onto the saw is available.

Refer to **Table 2–1** on pages 100 to 109 for complete specifications for the Black & Decker scroll saw.

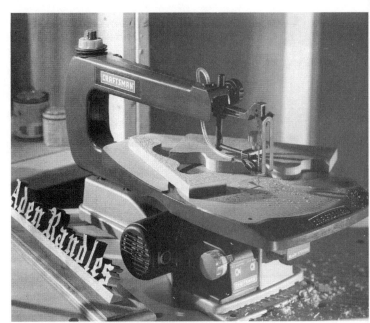

2–6. ▶ **The Craftsman 16-inch variable-speed machine— Sears's newest saw—has toolless blade clamps and other quality features.**

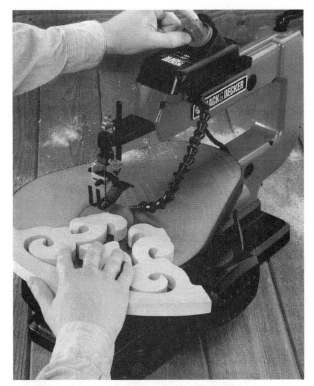

2–5. ▶ **The variable-speed control on the Black & Decker scroll saw is conveniently located.**

CRAFTSMAN SCROLL SAWS

The current line of Craftsman scroll saws offered by Sears, Roebuck and Company is improved over previous models. Today's Sears saws, for example, are considerably easier to use with plain-end blades. Earlier Sears saws were essentially designed for use with the more limited pin-end blades unless the machines were fitted with a blade-holder conversion-kit accessory.

The new line of Sears saws consists of three models: a 16-inch variable-speed, bench-top saw (**2–6**); a 24½-inch, two-speed, bench-top machine (**2–7**), and

2–7. ▶ **The Craftsman "deep throat" bench saw is a two-speed unit with a 24½-inch throat and a 2-inch thickness-cutting capacity.**

a 20-inch variable-speed Professional floor-model saw (**2–8**). All accept pin- or plain-end blades and offer some other favorable features.

The Craftsman 16-inch variable-speed saw has an innovative design and user-friendly features, although it also has some questionable functions that could be annoying to serious scroll-sawers. This machine does have very adequate safety features. The upper arms move inside a protective housing, reducing the chance of pinched fingers between the arm and the workpiece. The blade on the bench models is so well protected, the guard is a visual obstruction for some jobs.

The dual blade clamps are unique in that the operator can quickly switch from pin- to plain-end blades without modifying or adjusting anything (**2–9**). The blade clamps provide for the pin-end blades to be "hooked" on at the left side, while plain-end blades

2–9. ▶ The blade clamps on the Sears saws feature toolless, side-by-side pin- and plain-end blade-mounting provisions.

are inserted to the right into the pivoting jaws and clamped with thumbscrews. The guard/hold-down is actually a visual obstruction when the blade is attached into the upper clamp, as shown in the operator's view of **2–10**. Making inside cuts also requires pivoting the hold-down to the side to make room to thread the blade through the workpiece (**2–11**). The blade must also be threaded through the guard/hold-down regardless of what kind of cut you intend to make. The blade-tension-and-release control is located to the rear, but works very well (**2–12**).

2–8. ▶ The Craftsman Professional 20-inch floor model with its variable-speed control located up front.

2–10. ▶ It can be difficult to install a plain-end blade on the 16-inch Sears saw when making an inside cut. First, the blade must also be threaded through the combination guard and hold-down foot. Second, the guard—especially the upper end of it—obstructs visibility to the blade clamp.

2–11. ▶ Making room for threading the blade through the workpiece requires raising the hold-down/guard and swinging it to the side.

2–13. ▶ View showing the combination push-pull power switch and variable-speed control knobs. Notice the shallow blade-storage drawer located under the table.

2–12. ▶ Craftsman's unique dual-control system for blade-tensioning. The outside is rotated to quickly engage or release the tension as shown. The smaller, inside knob is rotated to adjust the tension level. Notice the cast boss on the side provided for mounting an accessory light.

2–14. ▶ Making a bevel cut requires adjusting the hold-down and guard.

Illus. **2–13 and 2–14** show some more features of the 16-inch bench-top saw and its setup for bevel-sawing.

Only the Craftsman Professional model has an independent, adjustable dust-blower hose. The fixed air hoses of the bench-top saws are attached to the hold-down mechanism, with the inside end of the hose fitted over a metal "finger" that will obviously obstruct the amount of airflow (**2–15**).

Most experienced scroll-sawers eventually elect to remove the hold-down so they can maneuver the workpiece more easily, make quick turns, and control the cutting of small parts. If the hold-downs are removed from the Sears bench saws, the air hoses would also need to be disconnected.

By and large, the Sears bench-top saws have good features, but they also have some limitations that need to be considered for certain kinds of scrollwork. The more-expensive Professional saw has features that, in the long run, will allow the operator more flexibility and allow a broader range of scroll-saw work to be performed without difficulty.

2–15. ▶ **View showing how the airflow is obstructed with the open end of the hose fitted onto a "finger" of the hold-down.**

Refer to **Table 2–1** on pages 100 to 109 for complete specifications for all three models of Sears scroll saw.

DELTA SCROLL SAWS

Delta Woodworking Machinery, based in Jackson, Tennessee, produces six models of scroll saw: four 16-inch parallel-arm saws, a 20-inch parallel-arm saw, and an 18-inch C-arm saw. Over a span of some 75 years of manufacturing scroll saws, Delta has developed a long-standing reputation for innovation. Its current 18- and 20-inch saws are no exception. The arms are made of a strong, reinforced graphite composite—an exclusive in the industry.

Below I describe each of the scroll saws.

16-Inch Scroll Saws

Delta offers a group of three machines that look very similar to each other and which have the same work capacities: a 2-inch-maximum cutting thickness with a ⅞-inch stroke. The single-speed unit, operating at 1,725 strokes per minute, has blade clamps that require the use of wrenches to install blades. The two-speed machine offers a choice of 850 or 1,725 strokes per minute, with a separate "high–low" speed-selector switch. This saw features Delta's Quickset II blade clamp and quick-tension release, which are lever-operated. Delta's 16-inch variable-speed saw (**2–16**) is the same as the two-speed unit, but offers a wider range of speed selection—anywhere from 400 to 1,800 strokes per minute.

2–16. ▶ **Delta's 16-inch variable-speed scroll saw has essentially the same design elements as the 16-inch two- and single-speed saws.**

Illus. **2–17 to 2–22** show the types of blade clamp found on the various Delta saws. The lower blade clamps of the 16-inch saws require the use of a wrench (**2-20 to 2-22**). Otherwise, all clamps on the newest 16-inch saw and the 18- and 20-inch saws

described below are essentially toolless blade clamps of the design shown in **2–17 to 2–19**.

Refer to **Table 2–1** on pages 100 to 109 for complete specifications for the Delta 16-inch scroll saws.

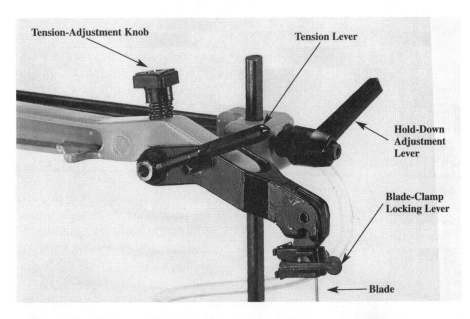

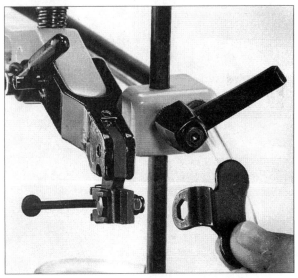

2–17. ▶ The upper blade clamp and tension lever on the Delta 16-inch variable-speed saw.

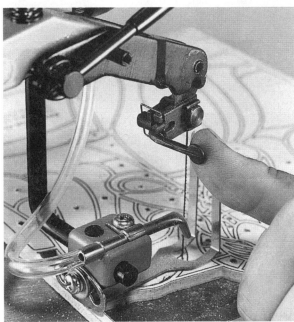

2–18. ▶ Releasing the upper blade clamp. Notice the tension lever above in release position. Also shown here is a close-up of the hold-down and the nonadjustable sawdust blower.

2–19. ▶ Blades of different thicknesses require an adjustment to the opening size and clamping action of the blade clamp. This special wrench turns a locknut on the right of the blade clamp that tightens or loosens the clamping action.

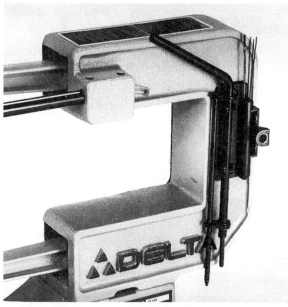

2–20. ▶ **All early Delta 16-inch saws require an Allen wrench to work the lower blade clamp. Wrenches are stored on the saw as shown.**

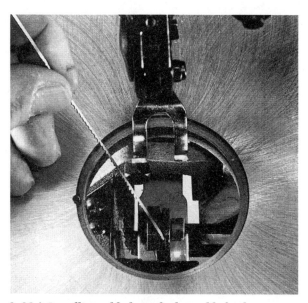

2–21. ▶ **Installing a blade in the lower blade clamp.**

2–22. ▶ **The blade-changing wrench engaged in the lower blade clamp.**

Model 40-570 16-Inch Saw

Delta's model 40-570 (**2–23**) saw—its latest one—has some very innovative features. One that makes good sense is the carrying handle built into the housing (shroud) that encloses and protects the upper arm. Another unique and helpful feature is the table-tilt-degree scale, which is located at the top rear of the table (**2–24 and 2–25**). This saw also addresses the problem of handling fine dust. It has one of the new-style adjustable dust blowers and a built-in provision for dust pick-up under the table.

The under-the-table area is enclosed to contain the dust and/or to provide extraction through a sawdust port to your shop vacuum (**2–26**). The dust enclosure covers and protects the end of the lower arm and the table-lock knob. This device only needs to be removed when changing to a new blade or making table-tilt adjustments.

The saw has an all-toolless blade-changing system featuring Delta's popular Quickset II devices and up-front tensioning (**2–27 to 2–29**).

The variable-speed control (**2–30**) provides 600 to 1,650 spm and is located next to the power switch.

Refer to **Table 2–1** on pages 100 to 109 for complete specifications for the Delta model 40-570 16-inch saw.

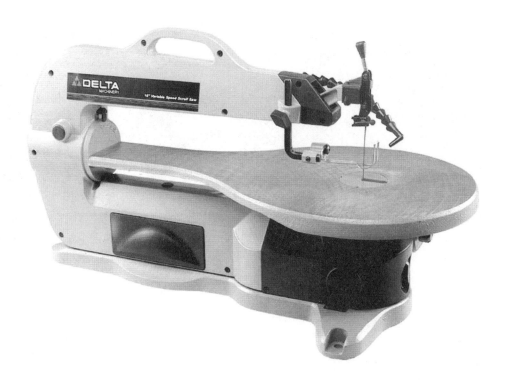

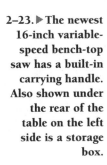

2–23. ▶ The newest 16-inch variable-speed bench-top saw has a built-in carrying handle. Also shown under the rear of the table on the left side is a storage box.

2–24. ▶ The table-tilt-degree scale located at the above rear of the table is just one of Delta's new design innovations.

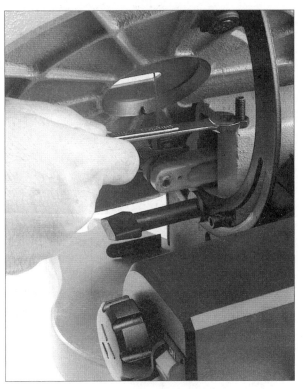

2–25. ▶ A stop screw can be set to simplify repositioning the table 90 degrees to the blade.

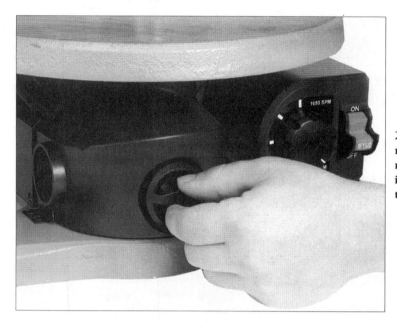

2–26. ▶ This knob must be released to remove the "dust cup" (box), which is necessary when installing a new blade into the lower clamp or accessing the table-tilt lock handle.

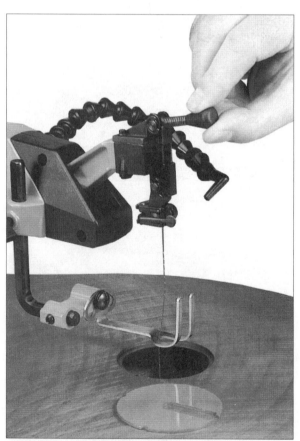

2–27. ▶ Delta's new blade-tension lever is pivoted toward the rear to apply tension or toward the operator to release the tension.

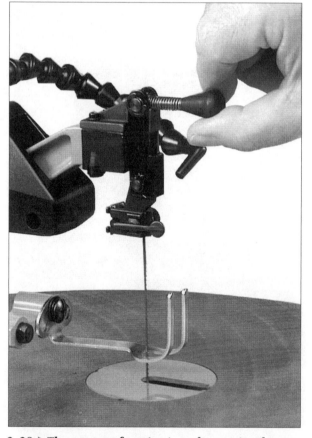

2–28. ▶ The amount of tension is set by rotating the tension-lever knob clockwise to increase the amount of tension or counterclockwise to decrease blade tension.

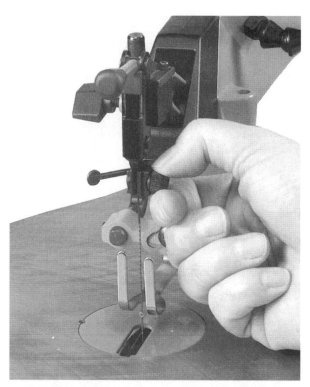

2–29. ▶ Adjusting the clamping action of the blade clamps to accommodate different widths of blade is accomplished by turning the chuck clamping knob slightly as shown.

2–30. ▶ View showing the on-off switch at the right and the variable-speed dial at the left.

Q-3 18-Inch Variable-Speed Saw

Delta's Q-3 18-inch, variable-speed saw (2–31) is promoted as its most innovative scroll saw. This machine features a graphite-composite C-arm construction and the Quickset II blade-changing system. The Q3 has all its controls located up front, including a dial-controlled electronic variable-speed control that ranges between 300 and 2,000 strokes per minute. An

2–31. ▶ Delta's 18-inch, C-arm, variable-speed scroll saw has a more aggressive cutting action than Delta's other parallel-arm saws.

adjustable-direction dust blower and floor stand are standard. This machine has a 2-inch thickness-cutting capacity, a ⅞-inch stroke, and a table that tilts right 45 degrees and 9 degrees left (**2–32 to 2–34**).

One shortcoming that is characteristic of all C-arm saws is the danger involved when a blade breaks. There is no automatic shut-off and the arm does not lift, so there is the ever-present possibility of a broken blade piercing the operator's hand or fingers.

Refer to **Table 2–1** on pages 100 to 109 for complete specifications for the Delta Q-3 18-inch variable-speed saw.

2–32. ▶ Making inside cuts on Delta's Q-3 saw. Notice the up-front controls.

2–33. ▶ A close-up view of the Q-3's upper blade clamp.

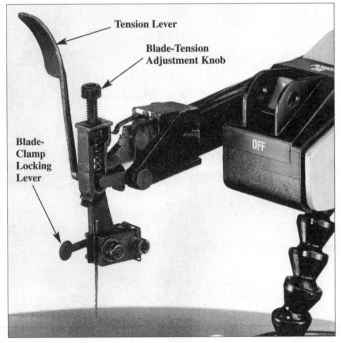

2–34. ▶ View showing table-tilt mechanism and access to the lower Quickset II blade clamp on the Q-3.

20-Inch Scroll Saw

Delta's 20-inch scroll saw (**2–35**) has parallel arms made of a graphite material. This is a belt-driven machine that provides a choice of six speeds (400, 700, 1,200, 1,400, 1,600, and 2,000 spm) by shifting the belt to different pulley-size combinations (**2–36**). The toolless Quickset II blade-chuck system ensures fast blade threading and changing. An adjustable blower and floor stand are standard. Other noteworthy features include up-front switches that can be padlocked, a convenient tension lever, and a port for a 2¼-inch dust-extraction vacuum.

An interesting feature is that when a blade breaks or you wish to thread the blade when cutting an inside opening, the upper arm can be locked in the "up" position (**2–39**). Illus. **2–37 to 2–40** show additional features of Delta's parallel-arm saw.

The Delta 20-inch scroll saw, like the 18-inch machine, has a rear leg adjustment (**2–40**) that permits tilting the entire saw toward the operator for easier operation and improved visibility.

Refer to **Table 2–1** on pages 100 to 109 for more information on the Delta's 20-inch scroll saw.

2–35. ▶ Delta's 20-inch, six-speed, belt-driven saw has parallel arms made of a graphite-composite material and wrench-free upper and lower blade clamps.

2–36. ▶ Blade-speed changes require shifting the belt on step pulleys according to a chart located on top of the belt guard; the belt guard for the scroll saw in this photo has been removed and is not shown.

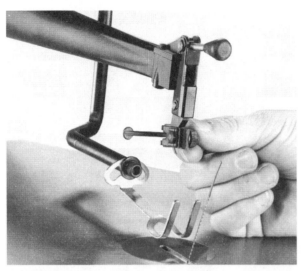

2–37. ▶ The finger-operated locknut changes the blade-clamp opening to accommodate blades of various thicknesses.

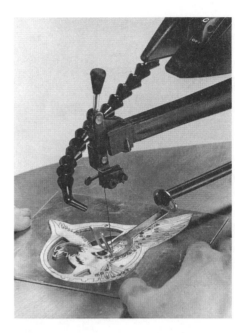

2–38. ▶ This excellent dust blower directs fine dust away from the operator.

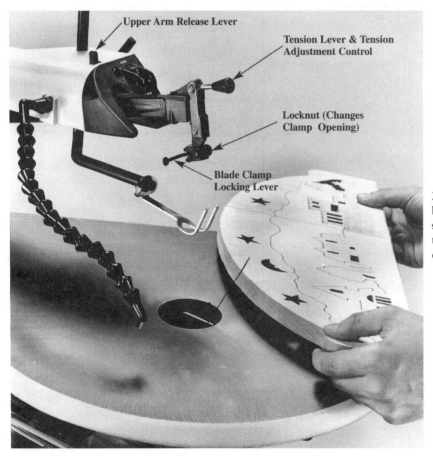

Upper Arm Release Lever

Tension Lever & Tension Adjustment Control

Locknut (Changes Clamp Opening)

Blade Clamp Locking Lever

2–39. ▶ This view shows the upper blade clamp on the Delta 20-inch scroll saw. The tension lever is also the tension control. Rotating it clockwise increases the tension.

2–40. ▶ On the 18- and 20-inch Delta scroll saws, an adjustment screw shifts the blade clamp (right or left) if necessary to align the lower blade clamp to the upper blade clamp, ensuring a perfectly vertical blade travel.

DEWALT 20-INCH SAW

The DeWalt 20-inch bench-top variable-speed saw (**2–41**) arrived in the market in 1996 with much fanfare. This saw, with its double parallel-link drive system, is made by Canadian manufacturer Sommerville Design, in Pickering, Ontario, which is also the manufacturer of the Excalibur saws. Turn to pages 77 to 79 for a discussion of Excalibur saws and to see a diagram of their drive system, which is essentially the same as DeWalt's.

The mid-priced DeWalt saw has a number of design innovations in addition to its unusual drive system. Some of the most notable features are the up-

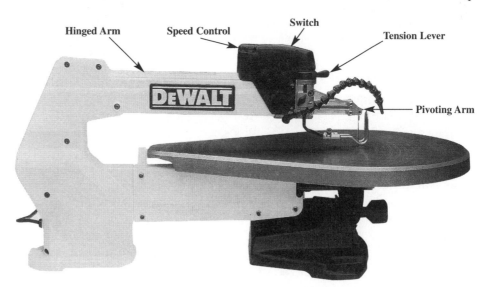

Hinged Arm   Speed Control   Switch   Tension Lever   Pivoting Arm

2–41. ▶ The DeWalt 20-inch variable-speed scroll saw is one of the first machines to offer full up-front controls and toolless blade clamps.

front controls and the upper arm. The entire upper arm assembly can be lifted (**2–42**), which permits an unclamped lower end of the blade to be threaded into the workpiece from the top. Or, with the lower end of the blade clamped, the blade can be threaded upward through the bottom of the workpiece if desired. Many experts commend the "top-down" method for inserting the blade when making inside cutouts in large fretwork pieces. The DeWalt also has very simple toolless blade clamps, as shown in **2–43**. The guard and holddown do not interfere with line visibility (**2–44**).

2–43. ▶ **Blade installation is quick and easy with DeWalt's simple, toolless blade clamps.**

2–42. ▶ **The upper arm lifts, which makes blade threading easy. It can be done by inserting the blade through the workpiece either from the bottom up or top down as desired.**

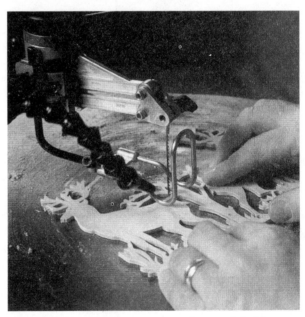

2–44. ▶ **The DeWalt in use. Notice the guard, holddown, and adjustable sawdust blower.**

Critics of the DeWalt, however, do not favor the many wear points of the parallel-link drive mechanism shown in **2–45 to 2–47**. There is also a safety concern when a blade breaks. On many saws, the upper arm rises instantaneously when a blade breaks. Not so with the DeWalt scroll saw. There exists the possibility of a broken blade stabbing the workpiece or your hand before the saw can be turned off. Finally, the short arms of the DeWalt pivot or move through much shorter radii than other saw types (parallel & C-arms, etc.). This gives the blade a measurable front-to-back motion, which some scroll-sawers dislike for

doing extremely fine and highly detailed cutting.

A floor stand (**2–48**) and work light are available accessories. Various "arm-lift" devices are also available as accessories to keep the arm in an "up" position or move it to any down position with fingertip control. These accessories are helpful when changing or threading blades for cutting inside openings. (See pages 113 and 114.)

Refer to **Table 2–1** on pages 100 to 109 for complete specifications on the DeWalt 20-inch saw.

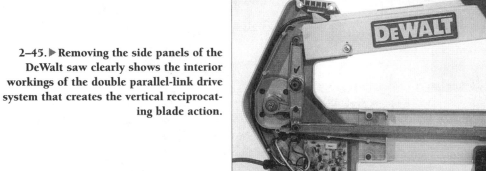

2–45. ▶ Removing the side panels of the DeWalt saw clearly shows the interior workings of the double parallel-link drive system that creates the vertical reciprocating blade action.

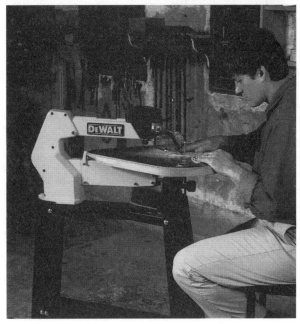

2–46. ▶ This close-up of the drive system shows the main rocker and connector, which create the back-and-forth movement of the upper and lower drive links.

2–48. ▶ The DeWalt in use on a floor stand.

2–47. ▶ A look at the stamped metal lower drive link and the rocker arm pivots.

DIAMOND HEAVY-DUTY FRETSAW

The Diamond (**2–49**) is an extraordinary English-made saw that has been available for nearly two decades. The machine was developed and is manufactured by Douglas Woodward of Hinckley, England.

Diamond machines have a number of innovations other saws do not have. A wide variety of different types and sizes of blade can be used, from the finest 5-inch fret blade for sawing veneer up to a 12-inch length of a band-saw blade, and even a hacksaw blade for metal-cutting. It has a 4-inch thickness-cutting capacity, with a 1⅛-inch stroke. The toolless blade clamps can be swiveled 360 degrees, so material can be cut in any direction, such as from the side in band-saw fashion.

Woodward offers the Diamond in three sizes: 16, 19, and 24 inches. The latter two sizes are the most popular. They are driven by a ½-hp motor. A ¼-hp motor drives the smaller machine. The 16-inch, bench-top hobbyist saw shown in **2–50** has a 3-inch thickness-cutting capacity. The 19- and 24-inch models have electronic variable speed that provides 0 to 1,400 strokes per minute.

The Diamond can be fitted with some unusual accessories, including a long fence, a circle-cutting jig, a magnifier, and a "bridge." The latter device ensures perfect blade travel for deep scrolling, stack-cutting, and metal work. Illus. **2–49** shows the 24-inch saw with a stand-mounted seat, fences (on the floor), and a flexible shaft with a ¼-inch chuck.

Refer to **Table 2–1** on pages 100 to 109 for complete specifications for all Diamond saws.

DREMEL SCROLL SAW

Dremel Tools of Racine, Wisconsin, offers a model-1680 variable-speed 16-inch scroll saw, made by Rexon in Taiwan (**2–51 and 2–52**). This saw is a major upgrade from Dremel's earlier two machines of the same size (models 1672 and 1695). This saw is almost identical to the Tradesman saw shown on page 98. It is recommended that the reader also review the descriptions of the Tradesman saw.

The Dremel is loaded with many desirable features. Some of the noteworthy improvements are as follows: toolless blade clamps (**2–53**), an adjustable-direction dust blower, up-front controls (**2–54**), and

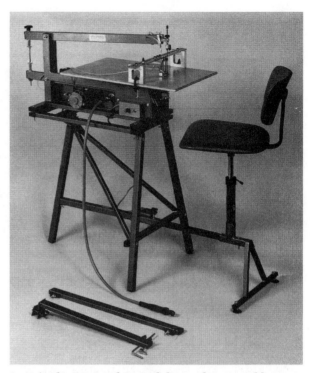

2–49. ▶ The Diamond 24-inch heavy-duty, variable-speed scroll saw, made in England, has a 3-inch cutting capacity and many unusual features and uncommon accessories such as the "tool bridge" shown attached to the table. This "bridge" acts as a hold-down and also ensures perfect blade alignment.

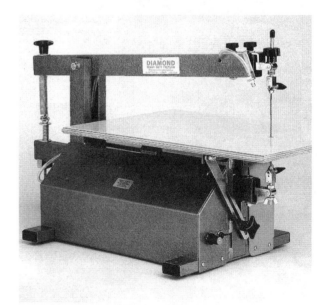

2–50. ▶ The Diamond 16-inch bench-top saw has a thickness-cutting capacity of 3 inches.

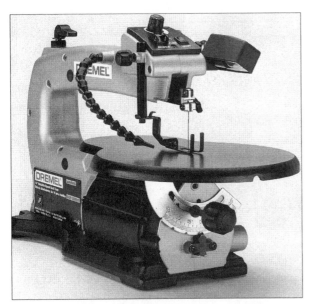

2–51. ▶ The Dremel model 1680 16-inch, variable-speed, bench-top machine features convenient up-front controls and toolless clamps that require no wrenches for blade changes.

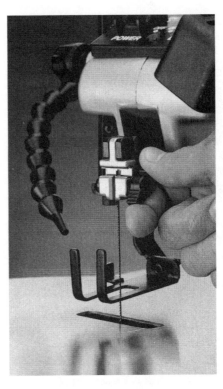

2–53. ▶ A good view of the improved upper blade-clamp design shows the reflective, zinc-oxide-coated surfaces that visually make blade installation much easier.

2–52. ▶ The Dremel model 1680 scroll saw has features such as improved blade clamps that allow it to cut the many inside openings required of fretwork projects easier and faster than previous Dremel scroll saws.

45-degree left-and-right table tilt with positive stops at 90, 15, 30, and 45 degrees (2–55).

Another enormously helpful feature is the reflective coating on both blade clamps that makes blade installation visually much easier—especially with the lower clamp, which normally on all scroll saws is hidden in a dark shadow cast from the table.

A quick, lever-tension release speeds blade changes and threading for sawing inside openings. A light improves cutting-line visibility, and a lower port is provided for dust extraction with a shop vacuum.

Refer to **Table 2–1** on pages 100 to 109 for additional machine specifications and features.

ECLIPSE SCROLL SAW

The Eclipse 20-inch variable-speed saw (**2–56 to 2–58**) is one the newest and most revolutionary saws to come on the market. It is the only current machine known to be driven by the "oscillating-loop" mechanism (**2–59 and 2–60**).

This high-end, well-engineered saw was invented

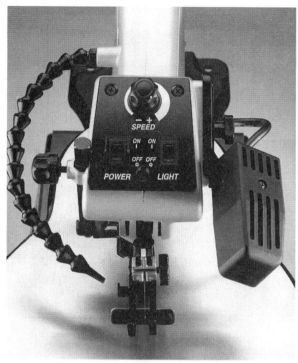

2–54. ▶ **The operator's view of the convenient up-front controls.**

2–55. ▶ **The table tilts both ways with positive stops at 90, 15, 30, and 45 degrees to the blade.**

by scroll-sawer Ernie Mellon and is manufactured by his company, which is based in Quinton, Virginia. The Eclipse has many advantageous features, but two of the most significant are a true, on-the-spot, vertical-blade travel without any front-to-back blade action, and a full 1½-inch stroke that is almost twice that of most other major-brand saws.

Because the blade is always vertical (in one spot) throughout the stroke, extremely delicate and accurate work is more easily performed with less chance of miscuts. The long stroke quickly carries sawdust out of the kerf. It cuts cooler and wear is distributed to more of the blade, which ensures a longer blade life and less breakage.

The oscillating-loop drive consists of a flat belt attached to one end of each of the two blade clamps. With a blade inserted, a continuous loop is formed. The loop is tensioned and moves back and forth over a series of pulleys that are driven by a toothed segment, which is shown in **2–59**. The variable speed provides between 200 and 1,350 strokes per minute.

Even though the top speed is just 1,350 strokes per minute, the long stroke produces 2,025 inches of blade travel per minute compared to the 1,531 inches of blade travel per minute of a typical saw operating at 1,750 strokes per minute with a ⅞-inch stroke.

2–56. ▶ **The Eclipse 20-inch saw is one of the most revolutionary saws to arrive on the market. It has many features other machines do not have.**

2–57. ▶ At first glance the Eclipse looks like a rigid-arm saw, but inside the hollow C-shaped aluminum housing is a belted oscillating-loop drive mechanism.

2–58. ▶ The up-front control panel includes a timer that starts and stops as the saw is turned on and off. Also included on the control panel are a light switch (left), the variable-speed control (center), and the power switches (right).

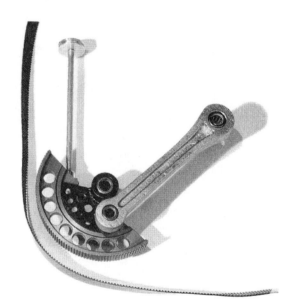

2–59. ▶ The internal toothed drive segment that converts the rotary motion of the motor into the oscillating action of the drive belt.

2–60. ▶ The toothed belt is connected to the upper blade clamp.

Two significant safety features of the Eclipse are an automatic shut-off that is instantly activated if a blade breaks and the fact that there are no exposed moving parts whatsoever other than the blade. Everything is contained within the hollow aluminum housing.

Here is a quick rundown of some other exclusive features of the Eclipse:

1. Large clamping and tensioning levers **(2–61 to 2–63)** that provide for quick and easy blade changes.

2. A complete, up-front control panel (refer to **2–58**) that includes the power switch, the variable-speed control, and a timer that starts and stops when the machine is turned on and off. This way, you can record the time spent cutting a project.

3. A 45-degree (right or left) table-tilt scale **(2–64 and 2–65)** that is readable from above through the table-insert openings.

4. A built-in light that provides a field of light to the cutting area.

5. A repositionable, three-slot table insert has a wide-to-narrow opening that supports small, delicate cuts **(2–65).**

The Eclipse saw has a long stroke which uses more of the blade; thus its thickness-cutting capacity is limited to approximately 1½ inches. Because there is limited space under the table for a blade clamp hand knob, a special tool is necessary for the lower blade clamp. The positive features of this machine far outnumber these minor limitations.

Refer to Table **2–1** on pages 100 to 109 for complete specifications for the Eclipse saw.

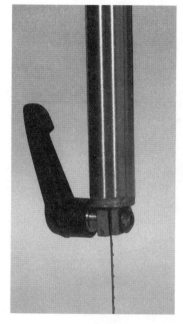

2–61. ▶ A close-up look at the upper blade clamp. Notice the large, multipositionable clamp lever and that the blade is inserted from the rear rather than the front, as done with other saws.

2–62. ▶ Another unique feature is that the upper blade clamp can be raised far beyond the top end of the blade, as shown, to facilitate threading for sawing inside openings.

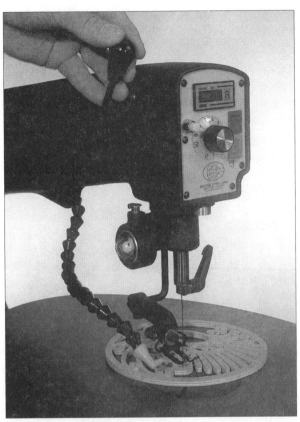

2–63. ▶ The up-front blade-tension lever is easy to reach and of a large size that is easy to use.

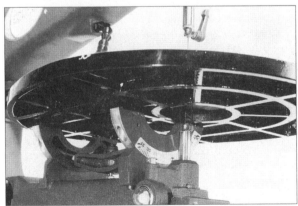

2–64. View showing the substructure of the Eclipse saw table that tilts 45 degrees both ways.

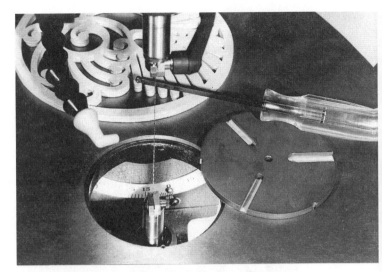

2–65. ▶ The table-tilt scale is readable from above through the insert opening. Notice the three-slot insert with a choice of wide-to-narrow openings to support small cuttings. Also shown is the hex tool used for installing blades into the lower clamp; this can be done while viewing the clamp through the table.

EXCALIBUR SCROLL SAWS

There are essentially two models of Excalibur saw (**2–66 and 2–67**), including one with a 30-inch throat—the largest capacity of nonindustrial saws. Excalibur saws are manufactured by Sommerville Designs in Ontario, Canada. Sommerville also makes the DeWalt scroll saw discussed on pages 69 to 71. The Excalibur 19-inch saw (**2–68**), like the DeWalt, can be used as a bench-top machine or with a floor stand.

The two Excalibur models and the DeWalt saw are the only machines available featuring the "double parallel-link drive" system. (Illus. **I–9, 2–69,** and **2–45 to 2–47** show how the drive mechanisms of these saws work.)

Critics of the double parallel-link drive system claim that there are too many "wear points" with this type of mechanism. Sommerville designers and dealers, however, insist that there have been no problems and that their saws have recently been upgraded from plain bearings to needle bearings to further ensure high performance. They claim the Excalibur saw is one of the smoothest-operating saws because its parallel-link design minimizes vibration.

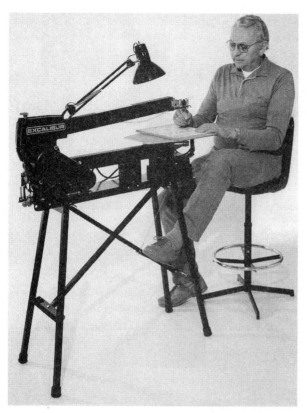

2–66. ▶ The setup for the Excalibur 30-inch saw, operated here by master scroll-sawer Carl Weckhorst, utilizes a stool, lamp, and Seyco's "top arm-lift pedal." (Photo courtesy of Seyco Sales.)

2–67. ▶ The Excalibur 19-inch variable-speed saw on a standard floor stand.

2–68. ▶ The Excalibur 19-inch saw on an optional stand. (Photo courtesy of Seyco Sales.)

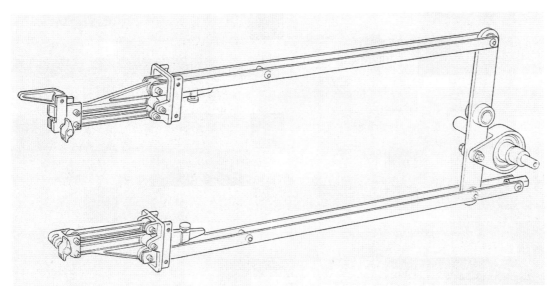

2–69. ▶ Inside view of Excalibur's mechanism that converts rotary motion into a push-pull reciprocating action known as the Double Parallel Link Drive System.

The design of the Excalibur saws keeps the blade vertical throughout the stroke. The short pivoting action of the front rocker arms, however, causes the blade to oscillate (front to back) somewhat more than other saw designs. This may present some problems for extremely fine and highly detailed cutting.

In addition to Excalibur's exclusive drive system, another distinctive feature is that the upper arm lifts, as shown in **2–70**. Even with a standard five-inch blade fastened in the upper blade clamp, the operator can have sufficient clearance under the lower end of the elevated blade. This unique feature is especially desirable when sawing large and/or thick pieces of fretwork with numerous inside openings. In fact, a "top-down" blade-threading procedure is recommended as follows:

1. With the tension and the lower blade clamp released, raise or lift the arm.

2. Lower the blade (while it is still fastened in the upper blade clamp) through the workpiece and the table opening.

3. Clamp the lower end of the blade into the bottom blade clamp and retension the blade.

The Excalibur saws have toolless blade changes that come with a flip tension lever (to release the tension) and thumbscrew-activated blade clamps of the type that are always attached to the machine. The large worktables tilt 45 degrees left and right. The air hose is the nonadjustable type.

2–70. ▶ Excalibur's upper arm lifting capability facilitates an easy "top-down" blade-threading technique that is desirable when making inside cuts in very thick and large stock.

Some special accessories made for Excalibur saws, such as a foot-controlled "top arm lift," magnifying work light, and dust-collector kit, are available. (See Chapter 3.)

Refer to **Table 2–1** on pages 100 to 109 for complete specifications of the Excalibur saws.

GRIZZLY SCROLL SAWS

Grizzly Industrial, Inc., of Bellingham, Washington, offers four scroll saws: three 16-inch parallel-arm models and a 22-inch C-arm saw.

The Grizzly model G7949 saw (2–71) is one of the least-expensive 16-inch saws available. It is a very basic machine that carries only pin-end blades. Its stroke length is ¾ inch, and its thickness-cutting capacity is 1³⁄₁₆ inches.

Grizzly sells two 16-inch variable-speed saws. Model G5776 (2–72) carries only pin-end blades, has a ⅝-inch stroke, and has a maximum thickness-cut-

ting capacity of 1⅝ inches. The model G1257 scroll saw (2–73) has an adapter to permit the use of plain-end blades, a ¾-inch stroke, and a 2-inch-maximum thickness-cutting capacity.

Grizzly's model G1060 saw (2–74) is a 22-inch, heavy-duty, C-arm, single-speed unit. This machine has a 2-inch thickness-cutting capacity, a ¾-inch stroke, and will accept plain- and pin-end blades. It has a maximum table tilt of 30 degrees.

Refer to Table 2–1 on pages 100 to 109 for complete specifications for the Grizzly saws.

2–71. ▶ The Grizzly model G7949 saw carries only pin-end blades and is one of the lowest-priced 16-inch saws available.

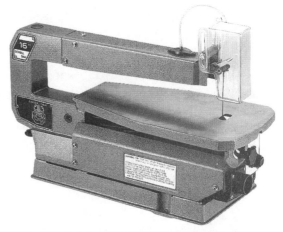

2–72. ▶ Grizzly's model G5776 16-inch, light-duty, variable-speed saw accepts only pin-end blades.

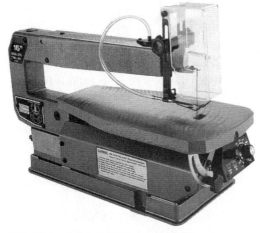

2–73. ▶ This model G1257 scroll saw has more capacity than Grizzly's other 16-inch saws. With an adapter, it will carry plain-end blades.

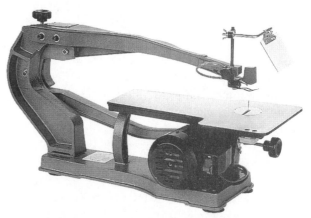

2–74. ▶ The Grizzly model G1060 scroll saw is a 22-inch, C-arm saw and has a table that tilts only up to 30 degrees.

HEGNER SCROLL SAWS

The world-famous Hegner scroll saws are made in Germany. Hegner was the first contemporary manufacturer to use innovative engineering and modern materials and technology on the basic design elements of the foot-powered parallel-arm saws of the mid-1800's.

Advanced Machinery Imports, Inc., of New Castle, Delaware, is the exclusive United States and Canadian distributor for Hegner. Hegner U.K., Ltd., of Halisham, East Sussex, is the distributor in England.

Today, Hegner manufactures several saws. There are two 14-inch saws—a single-speed (**2–75**) and a variable-speed. Both have a 1⅞-inch thickness-cut-

ting capacity. The variable-speed unit comes with a slightly larger table.

The most popular Hegner scroll saw is the model 18V 18-inch, variable-speed machine (**2–76 and 2–77**). It has a 2⅝-inch thickness-cutting capacity and an up-front quick-lock-lever tension release (refer to **2–87**). The same machine is available in a single-speed model. The Hegner 22V is essentially the same as the 18V, but with 4 inches of additional throat capacity and 17 pounds of added weight (**2–78**).

Hegner offers a heavy-duty, industrial machine designed for production or continuous use. This machine—the 20-inch Polymax (**2–79 and 2–80**)—has a four-speed, belted step-pulley drive. It has all

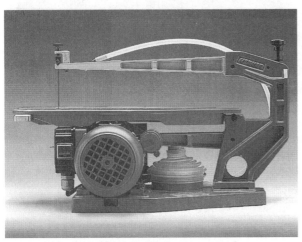

2–75. ▶ The Hegner 14E scroll saw is a single-speed machine.

2–76. ▶ Hegner's model 18V scroll saw—an 18-inch, variable-speed machine—is its most popular one.

2–77. ▶ View showing the Hegner table tilted left and the combination switch and variable-speed control at the right.

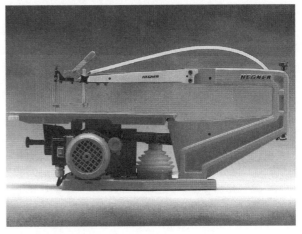

2–78. ▶ The Hegner 22V has a larger throat capacity and is slightly heavier than the 18V.

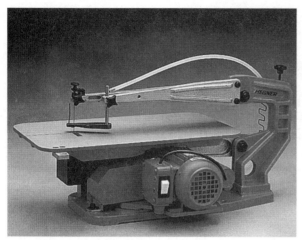

2–79. ▶ Hegner's 20-inch Polymax is a four-speed industrial saw.

2–81. ▶ Hegner UniMax with upper arm installed for maximum blade support.

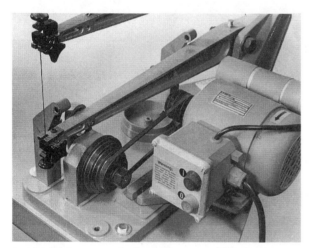

2–80. ▶ This view with the table removed shows the belted drive system of the Polymax.

cast-iron construction, a 1⅞-inch thickness-cutting capacity, and offers a choice of stroke lengths (⁹⁄₁₆ or ³¹⁄₃₂ inch). The shorter stroke length coupled with a slow speed, for example, is advantageous when sawing veneers and doing marquetry work.

Hegner's latest saw—the UniMax (2–81)—is advertised as ideal for a fretworker or miniaturist, and for general scroll-sawing in thin materials. It has three unique advantages. The overarm can be easily removed when sawing thin materials; this creates unlimited throat depth (2–82). The upper end of the saw blade is free, so no setup is ever needed for an inside cut. Finally, the ceramic guide (2–83) and direct-drive system (2–84) limit moving parts and friction; this makes the machine smooth and quiet on any surface.

Hegner officials strongly recommend that the company's three-leg floor stand be used with each machine (2–85). All Hegner saws have the same rear tensioning (2–86). The 18- and 22-inch saws also have up-front tension release (2–87).

Although Hegner has continually upgraded its saws since they were introduced to the United States in 1978, it has remained steadfast in its patented blade-clamp design for all saws. The clamps pivot on their knifelike edge at the ends of each arm. Advocates of this design claim extended blade life because the design eliminates "arm-induced flexing." The blade clamps are slotted to receive the blade, which is held in place with a screw.

The lower blade clamps on the Hegner saws require the key-type wrench shown in 2–88. The upper clamp may be fitted with a round thumbscrew accessory. The clamps are not permanently fixed to the saw arms, as they are on many machines. Users might consider this a disadvantage for some work; however, because of

2–82. ▶ Hegner UniMax with upper arm removed for unlimited throat depth.

2–83. ▶ The UniMax ceramic blade guide for wear-free control and convenience.

2–84. ▶ The UniMax motor and ingenious direct-drive system provide reliable, vibration-free operation on any surface. Also note the integrated sawdust blower.

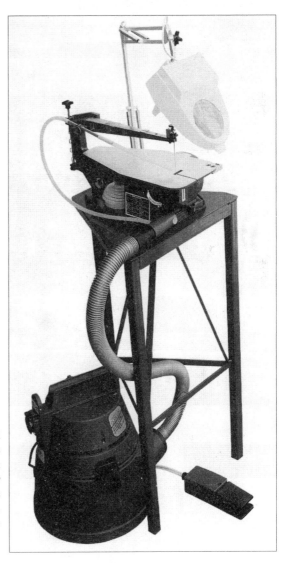

2–85. ▶ A Hegner saw on the company's typical floor stand. This saw is shown with Hegner's dust-extraction accessory, which pulls sawdust from the top of the workpiece and from under the table. A single-action foot switch controls the vacuum and machine.

(Photo courtesy of Roger Buse, Hegner U.K., Ltd.)

Hegner's slotted table (fully inward from the front), a blade can be installed or removed without threading the blade through the table opening.

One of Hegner's major design weaknesses is the nonadjustable dust blower. The design is such that the dust blower directs the dust right at the operator.

However, Hegner does offer a very effective dust-extraction accessory that connects to a shop vacuum and pulls the dust from top surfaces of the workpiece and from under the table (refer to **2–85**).

Refer to **Table 2–1** on pages 100 to 109 for complete specifications for all Hegner saws.

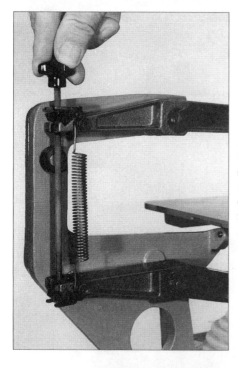

2–86. ▶ Blade tension is set at the rear on all Hegner saws.

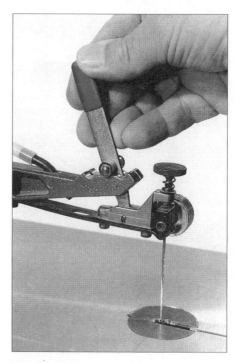

2–87. ▶ The Hegner 18- and 22-inch saws come with this up-front tension-release lever. Notice the knife-edge blade clamps and the finger-controlled knob visible on the right of the upper blade clamp (an optional accessory for all saws).

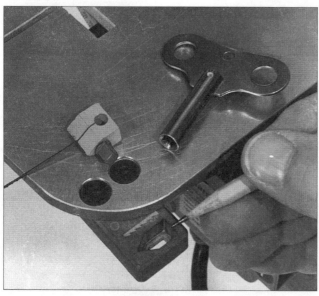

2–88. ▶ Installing a blade in the lower blade clamp is done in the fixture attached to the saw table.

HOBBIES SCROLL SAWS

Hobbies Limited, located in Dereham, Norfolk, England, has been involved in the manufacture of foot-powered scroll saws for over 110 years. Hobbies is one of the few companies in the world to still offer a foot-powered fretsaw.

The Hobbies treadle fretsaw (**2–89**) is one saw based on earlier design elements that has survived the test of time. This 18-inch, all-steel-frame saw with a blue hammered finish is still available. It has a 1-inch thickness-cutting capacity and toolless blade clamps that accept 5-inch plain-end blades. The worktable is 27 inches from the floor. The machine features a Vee-shaped belt drive and is ideal for light crafts such as making the coronation coach shown in **2–90**.

Refer to **Table 2–1** on pages 100 to 109 for complete specifications for the Hobbies saw.

2–90. ▶ **The Coronation Coach is just one of many model and toy projects designed by Hobbies for treadle saws.**

MAKITA SCROLL SAW

Makita's only scroll saw (**2–91**) is a variable-speed, bench-top unit similar in design to other Taiwanese-made scroll saws in this price category. This saw is advertised as having toolless blade change, which is true only when using pin-end blades.

An L-shaped wrench must be used to tighten the setscrews of combination pin- or plain-end blade clamps. Another tool, a "blade-change rod," must also be used to steady the blade clamp while tightening the setscrews with the L-shaped wrench (**2–92**).

2–89. ▶ **This treadle fretsaw, which has all-steel frame construction, is made by Hobbies Limited, in England, and is still available today.**

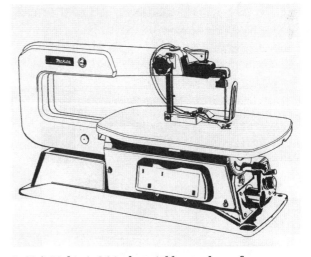

2–91. ▶ **Makita's 16-inch variable-speed saw features a combination tension adjustment and release with a single lever located up front. The saw also features an enclosed upper arm.**

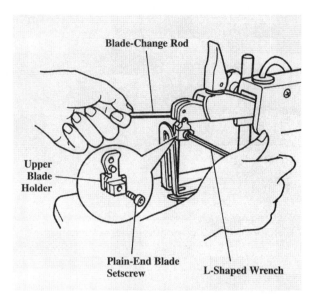

Blade-Change Rod

Upper Blade Holder

Plain-End Blade Setscrew

L-Shaped Wrench

2–92. ▶ Changing or installing plain-end blades on the Makita saw requires two special tools.

2–94. ▶ Setting the tension. Notice that the hold-down and guard are attached to the adjustable bracket that holds the dust-blower line.

2–95. ▶ Cutting a wood sign on the Makita scroll saw.

Makita's scroll saw has an easy-to-operate speed control and a vacuum port for extracting sawdust from under the table (**2–93**). The saw also features a handy lever-type blade-tension release located in the front. It allows you to loosen or tighten the blade tension by rotating the lever (**2–94**). Makita's combination hold-down-and-guard system provides good protection from the blade, but tends to impair visibility of the cutting action around the blade (**2–95**). The nonadjustable sawdust-blower hose is connected to the hold-down. This presents a problem should the operator want to remove the guard and hold-down for

2–93. ▶ A look at the Makita saw's dust-collection port and combination switch-and-variable-speed control.

whatever reason, such as when sawing small pieces. If you remove the hold-down, you also remove the mounting for the sawdust-blower hose.

Refer to **Table 2–1** on pages 100 to 109 for complete specifications for the Makita scroll saw.

PS WOOD MACHINES SCROLL SAWS

PS Wood Machines, of South Park, Pennsylvania, is owned by Barbara Peters. Her company markets mid-priced 14- and 21-inch, floor-model, parallel-arm, belted-drive scroll saws (**2–96 and 2–97**) through a dealer network, trade shows, and direct mail order.

The current PS Wood Machines scroll saws evolved from the original Lil Nugget and Scroll Mate saws that were designed and manufactured in the mid-1980's by Donald Strong. The Strong saws were acquired by Sakura Taiwan (where they were manufactured) and sold briefly in America under the Sakura U.S.A. label. When Sakura ceased production, Ms. Peters (and then-partner Alex Snodgrass) acquired the manufacturing rights in 1994, naming

2–96. ▶ PS Wood Machines 14- and 21-inch scroll saws have the same general design. They feature a belted-drive speed-change system and a 2½-inch thickness-cutting capacity.

2–98. ▶ Speed change is made by shifting the flexible round belt to a new combination of pulley sizes.

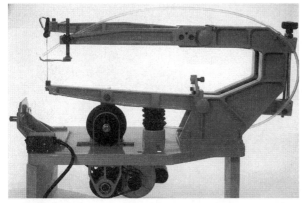

2–97. ▶ View with the saw table removed, showing the motor and step-pulley system located under the base.

upper blade clamp and a quick-acting up-front tensioning lever that speeds blade-threading for cutting inside openings. The lower clamp, however, requires an Allen wrench when changing to a new blade.

A large table opening permits the lower clamp (with attached blade) to easily pass through it (**2–99**). The removable lower blade clamp is designed to be held in the blade-changing fixture (hole) located on the right side of the hold-down arm when blades are being changed (**2–100**). The blade-suspension-and-

their company and saw brand PS Wood Machines.

The two PS Wood Machines scroll saws are of the same general design. The smaller 14-inch saw is made in the United States, and the larger one in Taiwan. In addition to their throat capacities, there are also differences in their tables, stands, motor sizes, total weights, and speed choices. The 14-inch saw is a three-speed unit, and the 21-inch machine provides five speeds.

Making speed changes (in terms of strokes per minute) is actually fairly easy. The operator must shift a round elastic belt to a new combination of pulley sizes, as shown in **2–98**.

The blade-suspension system features a toolless

2–99. ▶ The large opening permits the passing of the lower clamp (attached to the blade) through the table.

clamping system has been upgraded several times to its present design (**2–101 and 2–102**). The owner's manual, however, has not been updated to include these changes.

Changing and threading blades quickly and effectively to make inside cuts may require some practice. The recommended procedure is quite different than the common practice of feeding the blade upward through the hole in the workpiece. With the PS Wood Machines scroll saws, the procedure for threading the blade to cut an inside opening is as follows:

1. With the blade attached to the lower clamp, flip the workpiece over, thread the blade through the entry hole, and then flip the workpiece back over.

2. Install the blade into the upper clamp with the tension released.

3. Drop the lower clamp through the table opening and "hook" it into the lower arm. Apply the tension with the flip lever. With a little practice, this step can be accomplished without looking.

Some design improvements currently being contemplated for PS Wood Machines saws include a new table insert, belt guard, and adjustable blower hose.

Refer to **Table 2–1** on pages 100 to 109 for complete specifications for the two PS Wood Machines saws.

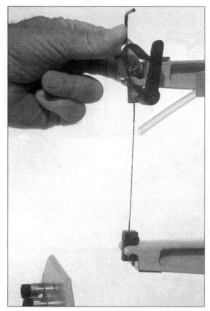

2–101. ▶ The blade-suspension system shown with the table removed for visual clarity. The blade-tension lever, which looks like an Allen wrench, is partially visible above the upper blade clamp.

2–102. ▶ Operator's view of the scroll saw. Notice the parallel-jaw blade clamp, the hold-down adjustment, and the non-adjustable air hose located to the right.

2–100. ▶ The cross pin on the lower blade clamp engages into a hole located on the hold-down arm for blade changes. This holds it stationary while the blade is locked or released from the screw-activated jaws with the Allen wrench shown.

POWERMATIC SCROLL SAW

The Powermatic Company of McMinnville, Tennessee, is the only company in the United States still making heavy-duty, rigid-arm scroll saws (**2–103**). Saws of this type have their tensioning system provided by a coil spring located inside an upper quill assembly (**2–104 and 2–105**). This system does not provide consistently uniform blade tension throughout the stroke as do other scroll saws. The greatest amount of tension is when the blade reaches the bottom of the stroke, and the tension lessens as the blade approaches

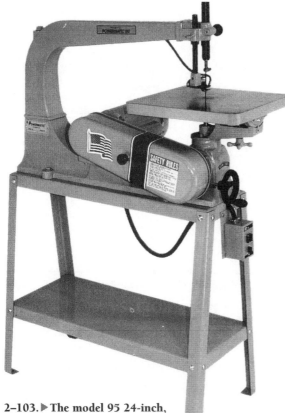

2–103. ▶ The model 95 24-inch, heavy-duty, rigid-arm scroll saw made by Powermatic weighs 220 pounds and is available in a choice of variable-speed and belted four-speed, step-pulley models.

2–104. ▶ Close-up look at Powermatic's upper blade clamp, hold-down, roller-type blade support, guide, and fixed dust blower.

2–105. ▶ The lower blade clamp requires an Allen wrench. Notice the heavy, wide blade.

the top of the stroke. This design requires extra support for the blade and by and large restricts the use of very small, fine blades for intricate fretsawing.

The overall range of scroll-saw work produced on this saw is best limited to jobs that do not require smoothly cut surfaces and work that can be cut with larger, stiff, and coarse-cutting blades.

Although this machine has a very rugged, heavy, and durable construction and all cast-iron and steel components, it does not have the capability to cut extremely fine details in stock as do other types of saw. A 1/3-horsepower motor drives both the variable-speed (**2–106**) and four-speed models.

2–106. ▶ A front handwheel changes the diameters of the pulleys and rear motor-mounted sheaves to provide a variable-speed range between 800 and 1,653 strokes per minute.

One distinct advantage of this machine is that the upper arm can be removed. Then, with the proper blade, it can be converted to a saber saw, as shown on page 50. Small files can also be clamped in the lower chuck to convert it to a reciprocating filing and sanding machine.

Refer to **Table 2–1** on pages 100 to 109 for complete specifications for the Powermatic scroll saw.

PRO-TECH 16-INCH SCROLL SAW

Pro-Tech, based in Gardena, California, entered the power-tool business in 1985. Today, Pro-Tech offers a variable-speed, bench-top, light-duty saw that is sold throughout the United States and Canada (**2–107**). The machine is similar to the Makita and other brands of the same general design. (Refer to pages 85 and 86 for a detailed description of the Makita saw.)

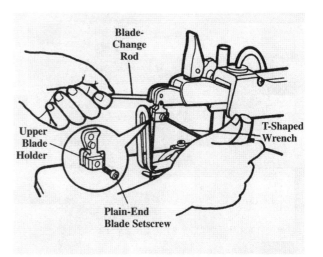

2–108. ▶ **Two tools are required to install plain-end blades into the blade clamp of the Pro-Tech scroll saw.**

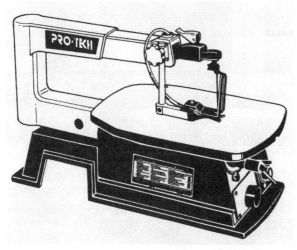

2–107. ▶ **Pro-Tech's 16-inch variable-speed scroll saw is sold in the United States and Canada.**

The Pro-Tech scroll saw carries pin- and plain-end blades. This saw requires tools to install or change plain-end blades (**2–108**), and you must tilt the table to get at the lower blade clamp. Company specifications list the saw as having a 2-inch thickness-cutting capacity with a tilting table of cast aluminum.

Pro-Tech's scroll saw has a combination tension-adjustment-and-release control lever located up front. The parallel arms are protected inside a cast-aluminum housing.

Refer to **Table 2–1** on pages 100 to 109 for complete specifications for the Pro-Tech's scroll saw.

RBI AND RECORD SCROLL SAWS

The United States-made RBI Hawk scroll saws and the English Record scroll saws, located in Shepfield, United Kingdom, are all manufactured by R.B. Industries in Harrisonville, Missouri. The "R" and "B" in the name RBI are the initials of R.B. Rice, the father of the company's owner, Verle Rice. RBI entered the scroll-saw market in 1980 and has since continually upgraded its products. It presently offers three saws: a 16-, 20-, and 26-inch saw (**2–109 to 2–111**). The latter saw is the largest United States-made saw currently available. The same saws are made with the Record label. Record's 26-inch saw is shown in **2–112**.

RBI holds seven patents on scroll-saw designs, and has been a leader in the industry. It claims to be the first manufacturer to utilize several design innovations.

All RBI and Record scroll saws have similar features (**2–113 to 2–117**), with the only essential differences being their throat capacities and table sizes. Otherwise, they all have a 2⅝-inch thickness-cutting capacity with a ⅞-inch stroke, toolless blade clamps, and a 300-to-1,725-strokes-per-minute electronic variable-speed range.

The primary components of RBI-manufactured saws are machined of extruded aluminum. The saw

2–109. ▶ RBI's Hawk Ultra 26-inch scroll saw has the largest throat capacity of any United States-made saw.

2–110. ▶ RBI's Hawk Ultra 20-inch scroll saw.

2–111. ▶ RBI's Hawk Ultra 16-inch scroll saw.

2–112. ▶ Record's 26-inch scroll saw, one of three models available in England manufactured by RBI. (Record also sells a 16- and a 20-inch saw.)

tables are cast aluminum, and the stands are made of 10-gauge sheet steel. Bright red paint identifies the RBI saws, and unpainted aluminum on a dark green steel stand identifies Record saws.

Some of the many noteworthy features of these saws include the following:

1. Toolless blade clamps (refer to **2–113, 2–114, and 2–118**).

2. A choice of cutting actions. Aggressive or normal cutting can be accommodated by positioning the lower blade clamp in either of two notches on the lower arm (refer to **2–114**).

3. A "clock-tensioning system" that indicates how to set the tension for all different-sized blades (refer to **2–115 and 2–116**).

4. An up-front tension-release lever that makes blade-threading for inside work fast (refer **2–117**).

5. A plastic hold-down foot that flexes over uneven surfaces. This flexibility is ideal when sawing warped stock (refer to **2–118**). It has a sufficiently large bearing surface that provides more-than-average support when cutting fretwork with numerous openings.

6. A removable plastic plug under the table for a shop vacuum connection.

7. A stop rod under the table that when preset guarantees a table position that is perfectly square to the blade (**2–119**).

8. A stand that can be adjusted to chair height for sit-down operations and/or for use by the wheelchair-bound.

Refer to **Table 2–1** on pages 100 to 109 for complete specifications for RBI and Record saws.

REXON SCROLL SAWS

The Rexon Group, manufacturer of low-priced Taiwanese scroll saws (**2–120**), exports a variety of woodworking machines to more than 70 countries around the world. It is the world's largest manufacturer of scroll saws. Although the Rexon name has not been highly visible on scroll saws in the United States, Rexon has indeed played a leading role in scroll-sawing over the years. It has produced and/or currently makes machines for a number of well-known North American scroll-saw companies,

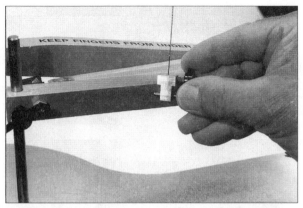

2–113. ▶ When installing a new blade into the lower clamp, the clamp is best removed and fit into a hole on the hold-down arm, as shown here, to speed and simplify the operation.

2–114. ▶ Close-up of the lower arm showing the two-position "notch" for the blade holder that offers a choice of cutting actions. Positioning the blade clamp into the rear "notch" is recommended for more aggressive sawing and square-cutting in thick stock. The front notch is recommended for normal cutting.

2–115. ▶ The blade tension on RBI and Record saws is adjusted at the rear of the saws with a cam-type lever.

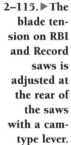
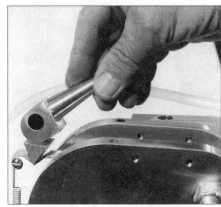

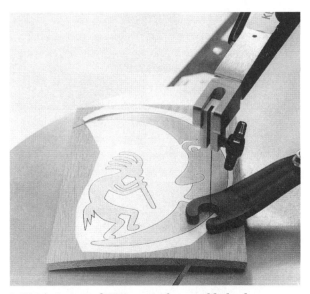

RBI HAWK™ PRECISION SCROLL SAW
Exclusive, No-Fault Blade Tensioning Chart

BLADE SIZE	CLOCK POSITION		
	216	220	226
#12	11:30	11:00	10:30
#9	11:30	11:00	10:30
#7	12:00	11:30	11:00
#5	12:30	12:00	11:00
#2	1:00	12:30	12:00
#2/0	1:00	1:00	12:30

2–116. ▶ All RBI Hawk saws have a "clock-tensioning" chart attached to them. The lever is positioned as if it is an hour hand of a clock, providing recommended "times" (positions) for various blade sizes ranging from 2/0 up to No. 12.

2–118. ▶ A view of RBI's typical upper blade clamp. Also shown is its excellent workpiece hold-down, which provides good support, yet flexes when sawing varying thicknesses of material such as this cupped stock.

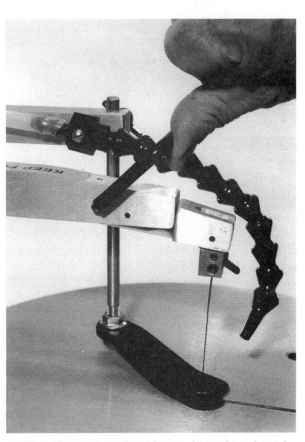

2–117. ▶ The tension-release lever is located on the end of the upper arm. A rearward push returns the tension.

2–119. ▶ RBI's table-tilt mechanism and Posi Stop rod at the left. When preset, this returns the table square to the blade after it has been used in a tilted position, without the need to check for squareness.

including: Ace, AMT, Delta, Dremel, Grizzly, Master Craft, Master Mechanic, Ryobi, Sears, Tradesman, and numerous others.

Rexon scroll saws sold under its own label are more evident in England. Rexon has specialized in smaller, inexpensive bench-top saws. It currently sells four machines with the Rexon label: one 13-inch C-arm saw and three 16-inch parallel-arm saws.

The Rexon 13-inch saw is one of the smallest and least-expensive saws made today. It handles pin-end blades more effectively than plain-end ones, which require an Allen wrench to tighten both the upper and lower blade clamps. The aggressive cutting action created by the short length of the single-pivot C-arm design creates difficulty in cutting small-radius curves in thicker stock.

The Rexon 16-inch parallel-arm saws are much better performers for all-around scroll-sawing. The model SS-16A (**2–120**) is a single-speed saw, the model SS-16SA is a two-speed, and the DTS-16A is a variable-speed. Except for the color, the DTS-16A is virtually identical to the Dremel and Tradesman saws (pages 72 and 73 and 98 and 99) sold in the United States. All Rexon 16-inch saws have a 2-inch thickness-cutting capacity.

Rexon has made major strides in recent years to improve not only its own brand of saws, but also those made for other manufacturers. The saws of a decade ago had much more troublesome blade clamps that discouraged many from attempting highly detailed fretwork requiring the sawing of numerous inside openings. Many of Rexon's early saws accepted only pin-end blades. Today, most Rexon-made saws have blade holders or clamps that will take both pin- and plain-end blades. The latter type, however, are generally still more troublesome to install.

Refer to **Table 2–1** on pages 100 to 109 for complete specifications for the Rexon scroll saws.

RIDGID SCROLL SAW

The Ridgid model 1650 scroll saw (**2–121**) is a 16-inch variable-speed, light-duty, parallel-arm, bench-top machine and one of the few saws of its size made in the United States. The Ridgid saw has a 2-inch thickness-cutting capacity, a ⅞-inch stroke, and a speed range of 500 to 1,700 spm. A combination speed control and push-pull power switch is located next to the motor housing.

A well-designed, under-the-table sawdust port exists over the motor toward the rear of the machine on the right side for connection to your shop vacuum (**2–122**). A blade-tension knob is located at the rear. Both blade clamps are thumbscrew-controlled for toolless blade changes. A nonadjustable air hose is "tied" to the hold-down and blade-guard assembly

2–120. ▶ Rexon's single-speed 16-inch scroll saw cuts at 1,450 strokes per minute, has a 2-inch thickness-cutting capacity, and will accept both pin- and plain-end blades.

2–121. ▶ This variable-speed Ridgid machine is one of the few 16-inch bench-top scroll saws made in the United States.

(**2–123**). This arrangement complicates removal of the hold-down and guard when sawing very small parts and other specialty jobs.

Refer to **Table 2–1** on pages 100 to 109 for complete specifications for the Ridgid scroll saw.

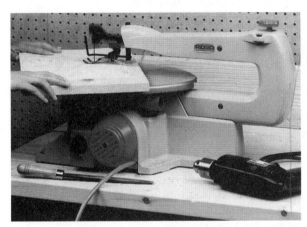

Sawdust Collection Port

2–122. ▶ An under-the-table view of the sawdust connection port that fits a 1¼-inch vacuum hose.

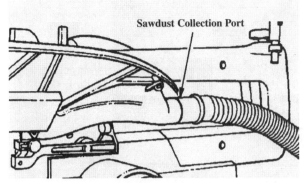

2–123. ▶ The Ridgid scroll saw in use. Notice the vacuum port visible under the rear right of the table and the non-adjustable blower hose connected to the hold-down.

RYOBI SCROLL SAWS

Ryobi Technologies, Inc., of Anderson, South Carolina, produces and distributes bench-top power tools throughout the United States and Canada. This includes two scroll saws—models SC162VS and SC163VS (**2–124** and **2–125**). Both are 16-inch saws with variable-speed drives. Model 162VS has an up-front lever-type tensioning system, and model 163VS has a tensioning knob located at the rear of the saw. The table on both scroll saws, featuring a new design,

2–124. ▶ Ryobi's model SC162VS 16-inch, variable-speed saw.

2–125. ▶ The Ryobi SC163VS model is also a 16-inch, variable-speed saw.

tilts left (**2–126**) and has a positive stop at zero degrees.

The air hoses are the nonadjustable type that is "tied" to the hold-down-and-guard mechanism. Both blade clamps of the model 162VS scroll saw require a T-shaped Allen wrench, which makes blade changing somewhat cumbersome. Pin-end blades, however, can be changed without the wrench. The newer model 163VS scroll saw features tool-less blade clamps. Both models have a ¾-inch stroke, a 2-inch thickness-cutting capacity, a blade storage facility, and rubber feet.

Refer to **Table 2–1** on pages 100 to 109 for complete specifications for the Ryobi scroll saws.

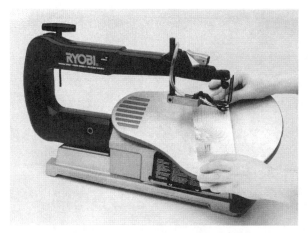

2–126. ▶ Bevel-cutting on a Ryobi saw. Adjusting the hold-down and guard for this type of work can be troublesome.

2–127. ▶ The Shopsmith 20-inch variable-speed scroll saw features new blade clamps and a speed range between 500 and 1,450 strokes per minute. Notice the switch-and-speed-control box mounted on the right front leg.

SHOPSMITH SCROLL SAW

Shopsmith, Inc., based in Dayton, Ohio, has been selling its United States-made, multiple-function machines for nearly three decades. More recently, however, Shopsmith has entered the individual free-standing stationary-machine market with a 20-inch, variable-speed scroll saw (**2–127**). A similar version that mounts to the Shopsmith Mark V (which performs the functions of several power tools) is also available (**2–128**).

Shopsmith's earlier scroll-saw machines had a complicated blade-tension system, and blade-changing was tedious and time-consuming. Recently, however, Shopsmith has upgraded its blade clamps to a quick-change, toolless design (**2–129**). An upgrade kit is available from Shopsmith to replace the entire tensioning system, blade clamps, hold-down, and guard parts of certain older saws. Some of the more recent Shopsmith saws only require replacing the two blade clamps, which are available from Shopsmith. Otherwise, the Shopsmith retains the same general design it has had for more than a decade or so.

Refer to **Table 2–1** on pages 100 to 109 for complete specifications for the Shopsmith scroll saw.

2–128. ▶ Side view of the Shopsmith scroll saw mounted to the Mark V.

2–129. ▶ A close-up look at the Shopsmith's new toolless blade-clamping system.

THE TOOL COMPANY SCROLL SAWS

The Tool Company, in Raymore, Missouri, offers two unusual scroll-saw products—a two-speed kit saw and a beautiful cast reproduction of the 1970's foot-powered Barnes Velocipede No. 2.

The kit scroll saw provides all of the essential, hard-to-find parts that allow the do-it-yourselfer to make an excellent scroll saw in a weekend (**2–130 and 2–131**). The kit is almost complete except for the wood material to build the stand and the electrical parts, including the motor. The parts are essentially the same used on the Velocipede Pedal Saw.

Plans and instructions are included to make the stand, and the required material for the stand is available at your local lumberyard. A ¼-hp, 1,725-rpm motor is required and is also available from The Tool Company.

The completed saw takes 5-inch blades and has a 1¼-inch stroke, a 24-inch throat, an oversized table, two speeds (900 and 1,200 spm), and toolless blade clamps (**2–132**). An optional 8-inch-diameter sanding disc is available that fits onto the pulley shaft on the left side of the saw.

The Velocipede Reproduction Saw (**2–133**) is not only an accurate machine with a time-proven design, it also offers the scroll-sawer beneficial exercise. The saw uses 5-inch blades, has toolless blade clamps, cuts 1½-inch stock, and has a 1¼-inch stroke, a 24-inch throat capacity, and a shipping weight of 50 pounds. A cast-bronze reproduction of the original Barnes boring attachment is also available from The Tool Company. The drill turns only when it is in the down position. (See Illus. **1–25** on page 44 for an illustration of the drilling attachment.)

Refer to **Table 2–1** on pages 100 to 109 for complete specifications for The Tool Company scroll saws.

2–130. ▶ A do-it-yourself saw made from a kit provided by The Tool Company. Notice how some of the components are the same as those of the Velocipede Pedal Saw shown in 2–132 and 2–133. The 8-inch disc sander shown is an optional accessory.

2–131. ▶ Components of The Tool Company's saw kit. The motor, motor pulley, belt, electrical switches, and wood for the stand must be obtained by the builder.

2–132. ▶ The time tested, toolless blade clamp is standard on The Tool Company's motorized scroll kit and its Velocipede Reproduction saw, shown in 2–133.

2–133. ▶ Cast-aluminum reproduction of the Barnes No. 2 Velocipede scroll saw manufactured by The Tool Company.

TRADESMAN SCROLL SAWS

The Tradesman scroll saws are made in Taiwan by Rexon and distributed in the United States by Power Tool Specialists, Inc., a division of The Rexon Group located in East Windsor, Connecticut.

There are currently four saws available: a 15-inch model and three 16-inch models (2–134). All take pin- and plain-end blades and have a 2-inch thickness-cutting capacity and a rear blade-tensioning lever (2–135). Two of the 16-inch saws are variable-speed, and the other two single-speed.

The most popular Tradesman saw is the model 8368 saw (refer to 2–134). This machine is essentially identical to the Dremel saw. (To get a more complete overview of both saws, review Dremel Scroll Saw on pages 72 and 73.)

The Tradesman model 8368 scroll saw has a combination tension-adjustment-and-release lever located to the rear of the machine. All other controls are located up front (2–136). The scroll saw has a slightly longer stroke than the other Tradesman 16-inch saws.

The model 8368 scroll saw and the Dremel saw have many user-friendly features such as a work light and vacuum port (2–137). However, at the time I tested it, the blade clamps still required a T-handle Allen wrench to make blade changes (2–138). The manufacturer intends to upgrade the upper clamp to a wrenchless type in the near future. The lower clamp

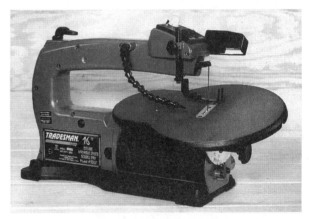

2–134. ▶ The Tradesman 16-inch variable-speed saw has many "user-friendly" features for a low-priced saw.

may remain the same, requiring a wrench. The lower clamp screw is accessible only from the left side, which is great for left-handed scroll-sawers but somewhat awkward for right-handed people.

A plastic door on the model 8368 scroll saw safely covers nearly all of the moving parts under the saw table (2–139), which would be dangerous to use without the door. The door, however, must be opened to get at the lower blade clamp. The manual recommends lubricating the arm bearings after every 50 hours of use.

Refer to **Table 2–1** on pages 100 to 109 for complete specifications for all four Tradesman scroll saws.

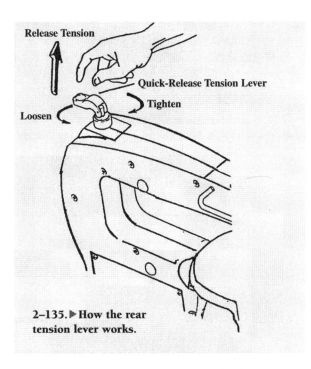

2–135. ▶ How the rear tension lever works.

2–136. ▶ Up-front controls include the power and light switches and the speed-adjustment dial. Notice the adjustable blower and the upper blade clamp that will be converted to a toolless design in the near future.

2–137. ▶ View showing the enclosed understructure, the 45-degree left-and-right table-tilt capability, and the shop vacuum connected to the port at the right.

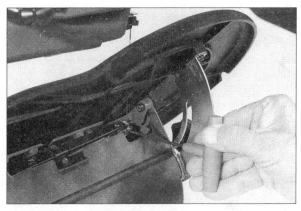

2–138. ▶ The lower blade clamp is only accessible from the left side and requires a T-handle Allen wrench.

2–139. ▶ View of the understructure with the door/cover removed. Notice the unusual motor position in which the shaft is parallel to the saw arms.

Scroll Saw Comparison Chart

KEY

Reciprocating Drive Type:

PA=Parallel-Arm

PL=Parallel-Link

OL=Oscillating-Loop

CA=C-Arm

RA=Rigid-Arm

Speed Control:

EVS=Electronic Variable-Speed

BP=Belted Pulleys

TS=Two-Speed

SS=Single-Speed

FP=Foot-Powered

*The letters L, M, and H refer to lower-priced (under $400), medium-priced ($400 to $800), and higher-priced (over $800).

**Some manufacturers claim to have toolless blade changes; this may be true, but only for pin-end blades. Toolless in this chart, however, refers to the installation of plain-end blades only.

***NA means information not available

Brand and Model	*Approx. Cost	Floor (F) or Bench (B)	Throat Capacity	Reciprocating Drive Type	Stroke Length	Thickness Capacity
Axminster FS410 (Sold in England)	***NA	B	16"	PA	NA	1"
Axminster FS18 (Sold in England)	NA	B	18"	CA	NA	1⅜"
Black & Decker BT4000 (Made in Taiwan)	L	B	16"	PA	¾"	2"
Sears Craftsman 16-21636 (Made in Taiwan)	L	B	16"	PA	⅞"	2"
Sears Craftsman 24-21623N (Made in Taiwan)	L	B	24.5"	PA	¾"	2"
Sears Craftsman 20-22620N (Made in Taiwan)	L	F	20"	PA	⅞"	2"
Delta 40-570 (Made in China)	L	B	16"	PA	¾"	2"
Delta 40-530 (Made in China)	L	B	16.5"	PA	⅞"	2"
Delta 40-560 (Made in China)	L	B	16"	PA	⅞"	2"
Delta 40-540 (Made in China)	L	B	16"	PA	⅞"	2"
Delta 40-680 (Made in Taiwan)	M	F	20"	PA	⅞"	2"
Delta Q3 40-650 (Made in Taiwan)	L	F	18"	CA	⅞"	2"
DeWalt 788 (Made in Canada)	L	F	20"	PL	¾"	2"
Diamond AF24 (Made in England)	H	F	25"	PA	1⅛"	4"

Tension Release Knob (K) or Lever (L)	Blade Clamps Wrench (W) or Toolless (TL)**	Speed (Strokes per Minute)	Speed Control	Table Tilt (Degrees)	Adj. Direction Dust Blower	Blade Types	Built-In Light	Wt. (Lbs.)	Additional Comments
K	W	1,720	SS	45	No	Pin Only	No	NA	Conversion kit available for pin-end blades
K	W	1,720	SS	45	No	Pin and Plain	No	NA	
L	TL	400–1,700	EVS	L, 47 R, 2	Yes	Pin and Plain	No	45	Up-front controls; light accessory available
K	TL	0–1,700	EVS	L, 45	No	Pin and plain	No	32	
K	TL	825 or 1,725	TS	L & R 45	No	Pin and plain	No	98	
K	TL	400–1,800	EVS	45	Yes	Pin and plain	No	68	Up-front controls
L	TL	600–1,650	EVS	L, 45	Yes	Plain	No	62	
L	W	1,750	SS	L, 45	No	Pin and plain	No	40	Quick-release tension
L	TL	850 or 1,725	TS	L, 45	No	Plain	No	46	Quick-release tension
L	TL	600–1,800	EVS	L, 45	No	Plain	No	46	Quick-release tension
L	TL	400, 700, 1,200, 1,400, 1,600, 2,000	BP	R, 45	Yes	Plain	No	115	Quick-release tension wrench-free blade changes above and below
L	TL	300–2,000	EVS	R, 45 L, 9	Yes	Plain	Yes	90	Up-front controls
L	TL	400–1,750	EVS	L & R 45	Yes	Plain	No	56	Up-front controls; arm lifts; optional floor stand
K	TL	0–1,400	EVS	R, 20 L, 45	Yes	All, Up to 12" Length	No	44	Blade holders can be rotated to cut in any direction; arm lifts

Scroll Saw Comparison Chart
(continued)

KEY

Reciprocating Drive Type:

PA=Parallel-Arm

PL=Parallel-Link

OL=Oscillating-Loop

CA=C-Arm

RA=Rigid-Arm

Speed Control:

EVS=Electronic Variable-Speed

BP=Belted Pulleys

TS=Two-Speed

SS=Single-Speed

FP=Foot-Powered

*The letters L, M, and H refer to lower-priced (under $400), medium-priced ($400 to $800), and higher-priced (over $800).

**Some manufacturers claim to have toolless blade changes; this may be true, but only for pin-end blades. Toolless in this chart, however, refers to the installation of plain-end blades only.

Brand and Model	*Approx. Cost	Floor (F) or Bench (B)	Throat Capacity	Reciprocating Drive Type	Stroke Length	Thickness Capacity
Diamond AF19 (Made in England)	H	B & F	20"	PA	1⅛"	4"
Diamond 16 (Made in England)	NA	B	16.5"	PA	1"	3"
Dremel 1680 (Made in Taiwan)	L	B	16"	PA	¾"	2"
Eclipse (Made in U.S.A.)	H	F	20"	OL	1½"	1½"
Excalibur EX19 (Made in Canada)	H	F	19"	PL	¾"	2"
Excalibur EX30 (Made in Canada)	H	F	30"	PL	¾"	2"
Grizzly 16 G7949 (Made in Taiwan)	L	B	15⅞"	PA	⅞"	2¼"
Grizzly 16 G5776 (Made in Taiwan)	L	B	15⅞"	PA	⅝"	2¼"
Grizzly 16 G1257 (Made in Taiwan)	L	B	16"	PA	¾"	2"
Grizzly G1060 (Made in Taiwan)	L	B	21½"	CA	¾"	1⅞"
Hegner 14E (Made in Germany)	M	F	14"	PA	¾"	1¹⁵⁄₁₆"
Hegner 14V (Made in Germany)	H	F	14"	PA	¾"	1⅞"
Hegner 18V (Made in Germany)	H	F	18"	PA	¾"	2⅜"
Hegner 22V (Made in Germany)	H	F	22"	PA	¾"	2⅜"

Tension Release Knob (K) or Lever (L)	Blade Clamps Wrench (W) or Toolless (TL)**	Speed (Strokes per Minute)	Speed Control	Table Tilt (Degrees)	Adj. Direction Dust Blower	Blade Types	Built-In Light	Wt. (Lbs.)	Additional Comments
K	TL	0–1,400	EVS	R, 20 L, 4	Yes	All, Up to 12" Length	No	37.5	Blade holders can be rotated to cut in any direction; arm lifts
K	TL	0–1,600	EVS	L. 45 R, 25	No	Pin and Plain	No	NA	Blade holders can be rotated to cut in any direction; arm lifts
L	TL	500–1,600	EVS	L, 45 R, 45	Yes	Pin and Plain	Yes	40	Up-front controls
L	Upper=TL Lower=W	200–1,350	EVS	L, 45 R, 45	Yes	Plain	Yes	90	Up-front controls; vertical stroke
L	TL	0–1,650	EVS	L, 45 R, 30	No	Plain	No	55	5-year warranty; floor stand optional
L	TL	0–1,650	EVS	L, 45 R, 30	No	Plain	No	65	Top arm lifts; optional foot accessory to lift up top arm available
K	W	1,720	SS	L, 45	Yes	Pin Only	No	40	
K	W	400–1,500	EVS	L, 45	Yes	Pin Only	No	40	Has dust port
K	W	400–1,800	EVS	L, 45	Yes	Pin Only	No	49	Adapter available for plain blades
K	W	1,725	SS	L, 30	Yes	Pin and plain	No	61	
K	W	1,700	SS	L, 45	No	Plain	No	40	6-year warranty
K	W	400–1,700	EVS	L, 45	No	Plain	No	45	6-year warranty
L	W	400–1,700	EVS	L, 45 R, 12	No	Plain	No	56	Optional ⅝" stroke adjustment; 6-year warranty
L	W	400–1,700	EVS	L, 45 R, 12	No	Plain	No	73	Optional ⅝" stroke adjustment; 6-year warranty

Scroll Saw Comparison Chart
(continued)

KEY

Reciprocating Drive Type:

PA=Parallel-Arm

PL=Parallel-Link

OL=Oscillating-Loop

CA=C-Arm

RA=Rigid-Arm

Speed Control:

EVS=Electronic Variable-Speed

BP=Belted Pulleys

TS=Two-Speed

SS=Single-Speed

FP=Foot-Powered

*The letters L, M, and H refer to lower-priced (under $400), medium-priced ($400 to $800), and higher-priced (over $800).

**Some manufacturers claim to have toolless blade changes; this may be true, but only for pin-end blades. Toolless in this chart, however, refers to the installation of plain-end blades only.

Brand and Model	Approx. Cost*	Floor (F) or Bench (B)	Throat Capacity	Reciprocating Drive Type	Stroke Length	Thickness Capacity
Hegner 20P3 (Made in Germany)	H	F	20"	PA	15/16"	1⅞"
Hegner UniMax (Made in Germany)	M	B	With arm, 13⅜", Without arm, unlimited		.28"	½" with arm, ¼" without arm
Hobbies Treadle Saw (Made in England)	NA	F	18"	PA		1"
Makita SJ401 (Made in Taiwan)	L	B	16"	PA	⅞"	2"
Powermatic 95-Variable-Speed Model (Made in U.S.A.)	H	F	24"	RA	1"	1¾"
Powermatic 95-4-Speed Belted-Drive Model (Made in U.S.A.)	H	F	24"	RA	1"	1¾"
Pro-Tech 3303 (Made in Taiwan)	L	B	16"	PA	⅞"	2"
PS Wood 14 (Made in U.S.A.)	M	F	14"	PA	1"	2½"
PS Wood 21 (Made in Taiwan)	M	F	21"	PA	1"	2½"
RBI 216 Hawk Ultra (Made in U.S.A.)	H	F	16"	PA	⅞"	2⅛"

Tension Release Knob (K) or Lever (L)	Blade Clamps Wrench (W) or Toolless (TL)**	Speed (Strokes per Minute)	Speed Control	Table Tilt (Degrees)	Adj. Direction Dust Blower	Blade Types	Built-In Light	Wt. (Lbs.)	Additional Comments
K	W	700, 1,100, 1,270, 1,600	BP	L, 45	No	Plain	No	96	Optional ⅝" stroke adjustment industrial, 4-speed saw
None	W	400–1,800	EVS	No	No	Special plain, 1 to 1¼", above table	No	35	Throat capacity is unlimited with arm removed . With arm attached, it is 13⅜". Uses special blades and has no specific hold-down or blade-tensioning system.
K	TL		FP		No	Plain	No		
L	W	400–1,600	EVS	L, 45 R, 15	No	Pin and plain	No	32	Has vacuum port
K	W	800–1,653	Variable-pitch pulleys	L, 15 R, 45 Front 45	No	Plain and saber	No	225	Removable upper arm for saber work
K	W	610, 910, 1,255, and 1,725	4-speed BP	L, 15 R, 45 Front 45	No	Plain and saber	No	225	Removable upper arm for saber work
L	W	400–1,600	EVS	L, 45 R, 15	No	Pin and plain	No	32	Has vacuum port
L	Upper=TL Lower=W	1,060, 1,350 and 1,575	3-speed BP	L, 45 R, 35	No	Plain	No	65	5-year unconditional warranty quick blade change; with video
L	Upper=TL Lower=W	170, 450, 790, 1,140, 1,370	5-speed BP	L, 45 R, 35	No	Plain	No	90	5-year unconditional warranty quick blade change; with video
L	TL	300–1,725	EVS	L, 45 R, 45	Yes	Plain	No	79	6-year warranty; visual tensioning; video

Scroll Saw Comparison Chart
(continued)

KEY

Reciprocating Drive Type:

PA=Parallel-Arm

PL=Parallel-Link

OL=Oscillating-Loop

CA=C-Arm

RA=Rigid-Arm

Speed Control:

EVS=Electronic Variable-Speed

BP=Belted Pulleys

TS=Two-Speed

SS=Single-Speed

FP=Foot-Powered

*The letters L, M, and H refer to lower-priced (under $400), medium-priced ($400 to $800), and higher-priced (over $800).

**Some manufacturers claim to have toolless blade changes; this may be true, but only for pin-end blades. Toolless in this chart, however, refers to the installation of plain-end blades only.

Brand and Model	*Approx. Cost	Floor (F) or Bench (B)	Throat Capacity	Reciprocating Drive Type	Stroke Length	Thickness Capacity
RBI 2220 Hawk Ultra (Made in U.S.A.)	H	F	20"	PA	7/8"	2⅝"
RBI 2226 Hawk Ultra (Made in U.S.A.)	H	F	26"	PA	7/8"	2⅝"
Record 16, 20, & 26 (Made in U.S.A.)	NA	F	16", 20", and 26"	PA	7/8"	2⅝"
Rexon 13A3 (Made in Taiwan)	NA	B	13"	CA	5/16"	1 9/16"
Rexon 16A (Made in Taiwan)	NA	B	16"	PA	3/4"	2"
Rexon 16SA (Made in Taiwan)	NA	B	16"	PA	3/4"	2"
Rexon DTS-16A (Made in Taiwan)	NA	B	16"	PA	3/4"	2"
Ridgid (Made in U.S.A.)	L	B	16"	PA	7/8"	2"
Ryobi 162VS (Made in Taiwan)	L	B	16"	PA	3/4"	2"
Ryobi 163VS (Made in Taiwan)	L	B	16"	PA		
Shopsmith (Made in U.S.A.)	H	F	20"	PA	7/8"	2"
Tool Co. Kit Saw (Made in U.S.A.)	L	F	24"	PA	1¼"	1½"

Tension Release Knob (K) or Lever (L)	Blade Clamps Wrench (W) or Toolless (TL)**	Speed (Strokes per Minute)	Speed Control	Table Tilt (Degrees)	Adj. Direction Dust Blower	Blade Types	Built-In Light	Wt. (Lbs.)	Additional Comments
L	TL	300–1,725	EVS	L, 45 L, 45	Yes	Plain	No	93	6-year warranty; visual tensioning; video
L	TL	300–1,725	EVS	L, 45 R, 45	Yes	Plain	No	97	6-year warranty; visual tensioning; video
L	TL	300–1,725	EVS	L, 45 R, 45	No	Plain	No	79, 93 and 97	All three machines identical to and made by RBI; all with 5-year warranty
L	W	1720	SS	L, 45	Yes	Pin and plain	No	26	
L	W	1,720	SS	L, 45	Yes	Pin and plain	No	46	
L	W	800–1,720	TS	L, 45	No	Pin and plain	No	44	
L	W	500–1,600	EVS	L, 45 R, 45	Yes	Pin and plain	Yes	35	Up-front controls
K	TL	500–1700	EVS	L, 5 R, 47	No	Pin and plain	No	35	Lifetime warranty; blade storage tray; dust-collection port
L	W	400–1,600	EVS	L, 45	No	Pin and plain	No	24	Rubber antivibration feet; built-in blade storage
K	TL	400–16,00	EVS	L, 45	No	Pin and plain	No		
L	TL	500–1,450	EVS	L, 45 R, 45	No	Plain	No	85	
	TL	900 and 1,200	TS	No tilt	No	Plain	No	90	Must provide own 1,725, ¼-horsepower motor and wood motor and wood table

Scroll Saw Comparison Chart
(continued)

KEY

Reciprocating Drive Type:

PA=Parallel-Arm

PL=Parallel-Link

OL=Oscillating-Loop

CA=C-Arm

RA=Rigid-Arm

Speed Control:

EVS=Electronic Variable-Speed

BP=Belted Pulleys

TS=Two-Speed

SS=Single-Speed

FP=Foot-Powered

*The letters L, M, and H refer to lower-priced (under $400), medium-priced ($400 to $800), and higher-priced (over $800).

**Some manufacturers claim to have toolless blade changes; this may be true, but only for pin-end blades. Toolless in this chart, however, refers to the installation of plain-end blades only.

Brand and Model	*Approx. Cost	Floor (F) or Bench (B)	Throat Capacity	Reciprocating Drive Type	Stroke Length	Thickness Capacity
Tool Co. Pedal Saw-Velocipede Reproduction (Made in U.S.A.)	H	F	24"	PA	1¼"	1½"
Tradesman 15-8350SL (Made in Taiwan)	L	B	15"	PA	¾"	2"
Tradesman 16-83545L (Made in Taiwan)	L	B	16"	PA	¾"	2"
Tradesman 16-8365SL (Made in Taiwan)	L	B	16"	PA	¾"	2"
Tradesman 16-8368 (Made in Taiwan)	L	B	16"	PA	⅞"	2"

Tension Release Knob (K) or Lever (L)	Blade Clamps Wrench (W) or Toolless (TL)**	Speed (Strokes per Minute)	Speed Control	Table Tilt (Degrees)	Adj. Direction Dust Blower	Blade Types	Built-In Light	Wt. (Lbs.)	Additional Comments
	TL	600–900	FP	No tilt	No	Plain	No	50	Cast aluminum; bronze drill attachment available
L	W	1,725	SS	L, 45	No	Pin and plain	No	42	5-year warranty
L	W	1,725	SS	L, 45	Yes	Pin and plain	No	46	
L	W	400–1,800	EVS	L, 45	No	Pin and plain	No	44	
L	W	400–1,800	EVS	L, 45 R, 45	Yes	Pin and plain	Yes	45	Up-front controls

CHAPTER THREE

ACCESSORIES

*T*oday, there is an ever-increasing list of accessory products that can be purchased to improve the performance of scroll saws or to broaden the range of work possible for the scroll-sawer/woodworker, making his or her craft more fun and/or profitable.

There are general accessories such as foot switches and lights that can be adapted to any saw. There are also, however, a number of aftermarket accessory products developed specifically for certain brands or models of scroll saw. This chapter examines a variety of accessories, including those used directly with the scroll saw and those used indirectly but in conjunction with various scroll-sawing activities.

FOOT SWITCH

A foot switch (**3–1 and 3–2**) is perhaps the number-one-recommended accessory because it offers added safety, speed, and convenience. A foot-controlled saw allows you to use both hands to hold and control the work, and should a problem develop during a cut, you do not have to let go of the workpiece to shut off the saw. A light-duty, 10-amp foot switch is ideal for almost all scroll saws. A 15-amp foot switch costs a few dollars more; it can be used with other power tools such as routers and sanders. No wiring is necessary; simply plug your machine into the switch and plug the switch into an outlet.

3–1. ▶ Lower left: Foot switch. Center: Hand drill with a flutter sanding wheel mounted on a stand. Lower right: Small air-inflated sanding drum that will fit the drill.

3–2. ▶ General accessories shown in use include a round, fluorescent magnifier light and foot switch; Hegner's chair-height (20-inch) floor stand and lamp bracket; and an aftermarket adjustable sawdust blower from another manufacturer.

MAGNIFIERS AND LIGHTS

Plain work lights (**3–3**) are good for improved visibility, but for highly detailed work a magnifying light (**3–2 and 3–4**) will make it easier to follow the cutting line, etc. Many saws have a lamp-mounting "boss" cast into the body or a mounting bracket that attaches to the hold-down arm. An inexpensive type of magnifier lamp that is suitable for occasional work is shown in **3–4**. The better lamps are larger and rated for continuous use. They come with a circular fluorescent lamp and have a larger viewing area (refer to **3–2**).

Head-held magnifiers are ideal for use with scroll saws that vibrate and which may cause an uncomfortable sense of movement. Two types are shown in **3–5 and 3–6**.

3–3. ▶ Special DeWalt scroll-saw accessories shown here are a work light with a flexible neck and a floor stand. The stand has a rear leg-height adjustment that, when elevated, tips the saw toward the operator for more comfortable operation.

3–4. ▶ An inexpensive magnifier light on a small saw attached with a shop-made wooden mounting block and a large hose clamp.

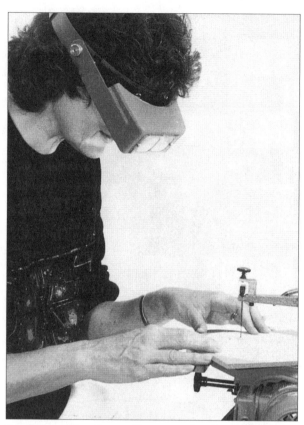

3–5. ▶ A headband magnifier is used with or without glasses and tips up when not needed.

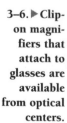

3–6. ▶ Clip-on magnifiers that attach to glasses are available from optical centers.

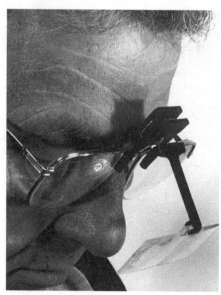

FLOOR STANDS

Floor stands (**3–2, 3–3, and 3–7**) convert bench-top saws to freestanding floor-model scroll saws. Almost any saw can be mounted to a stand. Stand options are available from various manufacturers for their own brand of saws, and some stands accept other brands of saw. Some stands are of the three-legged version that does not need leveling on uneven floors. Some saw stands also have adjustable legs to either bring the saw to a comfortable working height or tip the saw toward the operator.

Roller stand bases (**3–8**) make your floor-model scroll saw mobile. Mobile bases are useful in crowded shops and great for off-site locations such as when working craft shows.

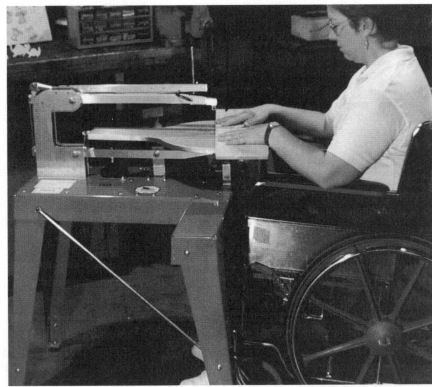

3–7. ▶ **This RB Industries chair-height floor stand allows for wheelchair accessibility.**

3–8. ▶ **A mobile base adds convenience for in-shop or off-site work.**
(Photo courtesy of HTC.)

DUST BLOWER

"Harold's" adjustable dust blower (**3–9**), invented by Harold Foos of Lakewood, Colorado, is essentially designed for Hegner saws, which otherwise have a nonadjustable airline that directs sawdust directly toward the operator. (Turn to pages 156 and 157 for a description of Hegner's dust-extraction system, which connects to a shop vacuum.)

ARM LIFTS

DeWalt arm lifts (**3–10 and 3–11**) are aftermarket accessories which can be set so the upper arm of a DeWalt saw will stay either raised or at whatever position you want it to. Currently there are two man-

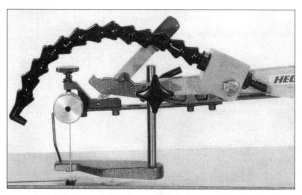

3–9. ▶ An aftermarket adjustable blower developed for Hegner saws attaches to the hold-down arm with a single bolt.

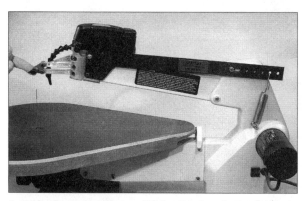

3–10. ▶ The Easy Lift arm lift by Jim Dandy Products works with a spring (shown at the rear).

3–11. ▶ The Scroll Buddy arm-lift system by Best Wood Tools Corp. uses a heavy counterweight.

ufacturers of these devices. Both are designed to be easily mounted using existing holes and threaded openings of the saw's housing. One spring-operated type is available from Jim Dandy Products, Downer's Grove, Illinois. The second type, which utilizes a four-pound adjustable counterweight, is available from Best Wood Tools Corp. of St. Petersburg, Florida.

Seyco's Excalibur arm lift (**3–12**) is an aftermarket, pedal-operated mechanism that lifts the top arm of the Excalibur saw, leaving the operator's hands free to guide the blade or workpiece when threading to cut inside openings.

3–12. ▶ The top arm lift for the Excalibur saw is a foot-operated device invented, manufactured, and sold by Seyco for its "top-down" blade-threading system.

BLADE CLAMPS

Seyco's blade clamps (**3–13 to 3–18**) are another aftermarket product developed to upgrade the difficult and frustrating blade-clamping-and-tensioning systems found on many economy-model Eastern imports and older saws. Designed to fit various arm-end designs, including the examples shown in **3–14**, these conversion parts can be installed relatively easily. Usually one or two bolts fit existing holes or the holes just need simple enlarging. It may be necessary to saw off a little of the arms or file a larger table opening for the blade, depending upon the quality of saw marked for upgrading.

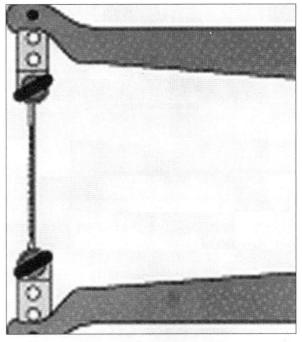

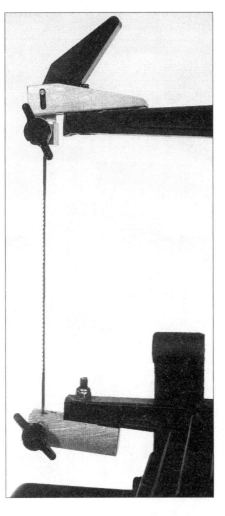

3–13. ▶ Seyco's Quick Clamps/Flip Tensioner attach to these straight scroll-saw arms with just two bolts. Notice the toolless blade clamps.

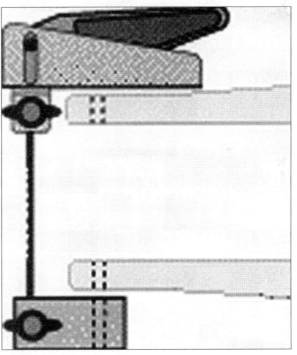

3–14. ▶ Two of several types of scroll-saw arm that Seyco can upgrade with its Quick Clamps/Flip Tensioner.

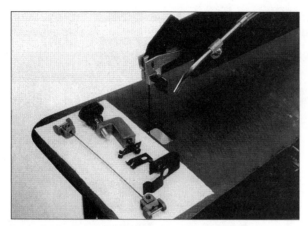

3–15. ▶ The parts shown on the table have been removed from an older, imported scroll saw.

3–16. ▶ When the lever is flipped down, the tension is released; flipping it up applies tension.

3–17. ▶ The Seyco Quick Clamps/Flip Tensioner components.

3–18. ▶ This older-style Eastern-import, bench-top saw has been upgraded with Seyco's quick-acting-blade-clamps-and-tension system. A generic floor-stand accessory makes it an economical floor-model machine for the hobbyist.

ABOVE-TABLE TILT SCALES

Above-table tilt scales are simple, inexpensive table accessories that make reading the precise degree of table tilt easier and more accurate. Very few scroll-saw manufacturers provide precise scales. Individuals with vision problems or who wear bifocal glasses will appreciate devices that can be read above the table rather than under it. Three popular types of this device are shown in **3–19 to 3–21**.

3–19. ▶ **An old-fashioned metal protractor works perfectly for making table-tilt adjustments to within one-half of a degree.**

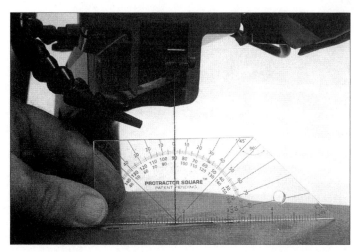

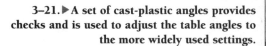

3–20. ▶ **This acrylic protractor square is also used to set the table to the desired angle to the blade.**

3–21. ▶ **A set of cast-plastic angles provides checks and is used to adjust the table angles to the more widely used settings.**

SANDING AND SHAPING ACCESSORIES

There are a number of abrasive devices for the scroll saw that will handle a variety of light-duty sanding jobs. Three different types are shown in **3–22 to 3–25**. All can be used to smooth miscuts, remove burn marks from sawn edges, help shape scroll-sawn slot-and-tab openings, and fit halved joints (**3–26**). *Tip:* You can make your own narrow sanders by gluing abrasive strips, emery boards, or fingernail files to dull pin- or plain-end blades as needed (**3–27 and 3–28**).

3–23. ▶ **Super Sanders from Jim Dandy Products are available in ⅛-, ¼-, and ⅜-inch widths and grits between 100 and 300. They mount into the blade clamps of scroll saws like plain-end blades.**

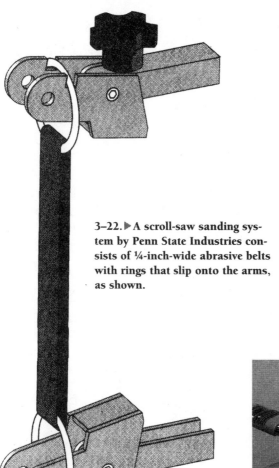

3–22. ▶ **A scroll-saw sanding system by Penn State Industries consists of ¼-inch-wide abrasive belts with rings that slip onto the arms, as shown.**

3–24. ▶ **Scroll Sanders are strips of cloth-backed abrasives of various widths and grits made with plastic mounts on each end. They install on the scroll saw like pin- or plain-end blades and can be used on most but not all scroll saws.**

3–25. ▶ **A Scroll Sander, shown in use with a shop-made platen clamped to the table, ensures square-sanded edges.**

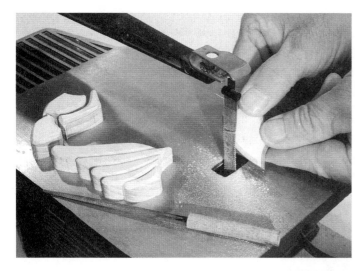

3–26. ▶ Scroll Sanders in use to shape and smooth a convex surface for an intarsia project.

3–27. ▶ Glue emery boards to dull saw blades to make your own scroll-saw sanders.

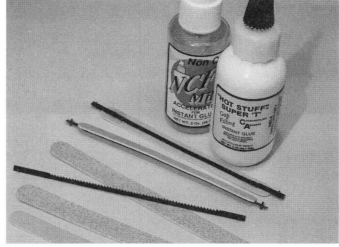

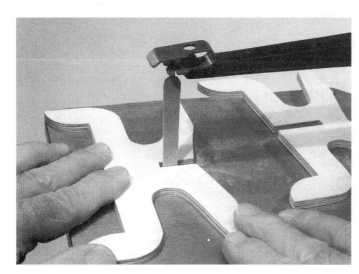

3–28. ▶ A shop-made scroll-saw sander with a fingernail file glued to an old blade to straighten cuts and widen the openings of mating slip (halved) joints.

Files

Hand files (**3–29**) are sometimes used to correct imperfect cutting. If your saw performs adequately and you saw with reasonable skill, filing and sanding should be very minimal because most saws cut very smoothly.

The *Electro-File power file* (**3–30**), made by Precision Hobby Tools of Hubertus, Wisconsin, is a useful accessory for model work and light woodworking. Available in either corded or battery-driven versions, these tools have a straight-line reciprocating action. This useful shop tool can be used with a set of needle files (refer to **3–29**) as well as with small saws and abrasive accessories. The unique chuck accepts both round shanks as well as flat blades and sanding paddles. *Tip*: The Power File could be fitted into a shop-made table such as one similar to that of a small router table. The Power File can be held in place with a hose clamp to create a power-filing workstation in your shop.

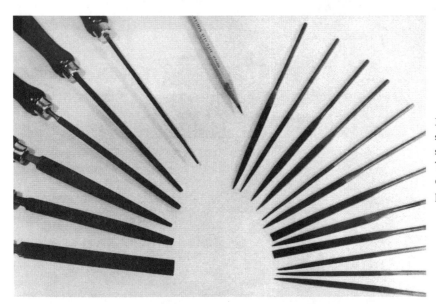

3–29. ▶ **Hand files of various shapes are often useful for smoothing sawing imperfections. The set of needle files on the right can be used with the Electro-File power file.**

3–30. ▶ **The Electro-File in use. This tool delivers up to 2,700 strokes per minute and features a special chuck that accepts both round and flat shanks/ accessories.**

Rotary Tools

High-speed rotary tools (**3–31 and 3–32**) have numerous uses for the active scroll-sawer. These versatile tools can be used as drills to make holes for small screws and nails in assembly work. When fitted with routing or forming cutters (bits with various edge-cutting shapes such as roundovers, coves, chamfers, rabbets, ogees, etc.), they shape scroll-sawn edges or segmentation and intarsia pieces quickly. When used with small, rotary sanding drums, they also cut surprisingly fast (**3–33**). These tools can also be used in small router tables.

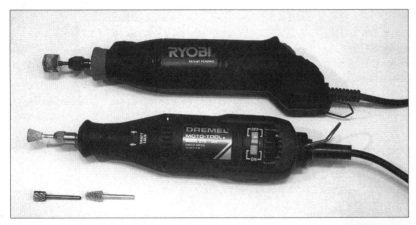

3–31. ▶ Ryobi, Dremel, and similar brands of rotary tool carry an endless variety of cutting, shaping, and drilling tools. They have collets from $\frac{1}{32}$ to $\frac{1}{8}$ inch in diameter and rotate at speeds up to 30,000 rpm.

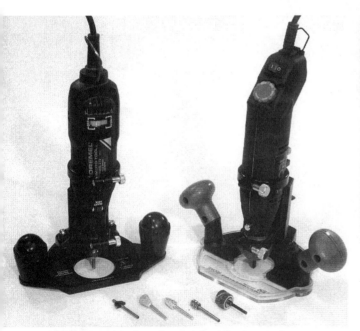

3–32. ▶ Rotary tools, when used with a router-base accessory, are ideal for rounding the edges of small scroll-saw work.

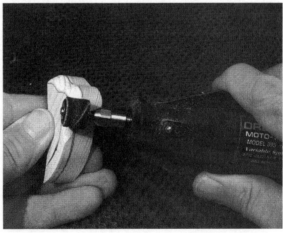

3–33. ▶ Here the rotary tool, with a drum-sander accessory, is used to shape a piece for a segmentation project.

Trim Routers

Small trim routers (**3–34**) are perfect for rounding the edges of thicker scroll-sawn shapes, as shown in **3–35**. Even relatively small pieces often required for segmentation and intarsia work can be rounded over when supported on top of a nonslip router pad (**3–36**).

3–34. ▶ A small trim router with a clear, shop-made plastic base. Notice the roundover bit and the zero-clearance opening for it in the base that permits safe routing of small and narrow parts.

3–35. ▶ Rounding over scroll-sawn edges of ¾-inch stock.

3–36. ▶ Rounding over the edges of small pieces for a segmentation project.

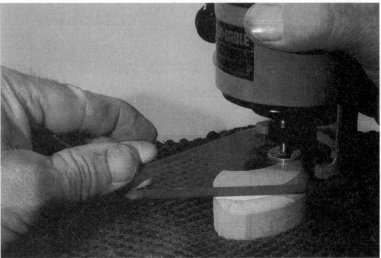
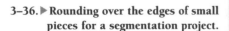

Sanding Drums and Flutter Wheels

Sanding drums and flutter wheels are useful to scroll-sawers making segmentation and intarsia projects. (Refer to **3–1** on page 111.) Small sanding drums are used to shape little pieces (**3–33 and 3–37**) and to smooth curved edges. Some drum sanders have flexible surfaces that conform to three-dimensional contours. One type, called a pneumatic sanding drum, is inflated with air in accordance with the amount of surface flexibility desired (**3–38**). Drum sanders of this type are available in various sizes.

Flutter wheels are abrasive strips crisscrossed on an arbor and driven by power-drilling tools. They are great for removing "fuzz" from the underside of fretwork, softening sharp edges (**3–39**), and smoothing contoured surfaces.

3–37. ▶ A small-diameter sanding-drum accessory is being used to make a concave surface on this segmentation part.

3–38. ▶ A sanding drum with a soft, flexible surface mounted to a used motor makes a good wood-shaping-and-smoothing setup for segmentation and intarsia work.

3–39. ▶ A drill-press-mounted flutter wheel softens the sharp edges of this fretted overlay glued to a box.

Surface Sanders

Flat surface sanders of either the hand-held oscillating pad or belt type are useful for smoothing stock prior to scroll-sawing. Small ⅛- or ¼-sheet pad sanders are wonderful for sanding small parts and leveling marquetry and inlays (**3–40**).

AUXILIARY MACHINES

Few auxiliary machines are needed to do scroll-saw work. There are, however, some machines that certainly help to extend the woodworking scroll-sawer's overall potential. A *drill press* (refer to **3–39**) ensures that vertical holes will be perfectly drilled, and it drives other accessories such as drum sanders. A *router table* designed for light-duty work is very useful for shaping the edges of scroll-sawn pieces (**3–41**). A *disc sander* with a tilting table (**3–42**) is especially good for fitting all kinds of miter joint. A *combination belt/disc sander* is well worth considering. The narrow one-inch belt of these machines cuts fast and is good for freehand-shaping and rounding over edges. Finally, a *thickness-sanding machine* or *surface planer* is excellent for preparing your own stock. The sander shown in **3–43** is ideal for the scroll-sawer because it can safely machine small stock as short as 2¼ inches in length and pieces just ¹⁄₁₆ inch thick.

HAND TOOLS

Miscellaneous hand tools found in most home shops are frequently needed. Items such as scissors, screwdrivers, hammers, clamps, measuring tools, squares, knives, chisels, etc., are essential for the serious scroll-sawer. Safety items such as dust masks, goggles, and hearing protectors should not be overlooked. Finishing needs can be very basic or involve a selection of brushes, spray and safety equipment, and related supplies. Additional tools and supplies are introduced throughout the various chapters of this book as they apply to specific techniques.

3–40. ▶ A small finishing sander used to level and smooth a segmented ornament.

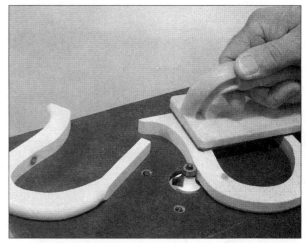

3–41. ▶ A small router table such as this shop-made version, designed to hold a trim router, is ideal for shaping the edges of scroll-sawn pieces.

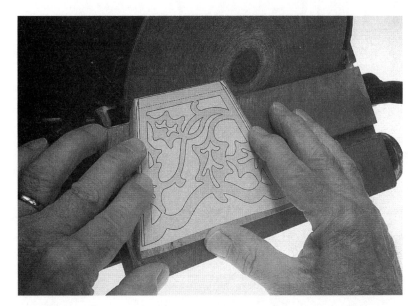

3–42. ▶ **Using a disc sander to prepare mitered edges on pieces to be scroll-sawn and assembled into a fretwork basket.**

3–43. ▶ **The Performax model 16–32 thickness sander consists of a horizontal drum 5 inches in diameter with a conveyor-bed power feed. This model will handle pieces as short as 2¼ inches and as thin as ¹⁄₁₆ inch, and larger work up to 16 inches in width.**

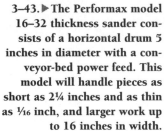

SELECTING A SCROLL SAW

If you are planning to buy your first scroll saw, or if you are somewhere between a scroll-sawing hobbyist and a professional and are thinking about upgrading, you will need to make some prudent decisions. Discreet spending is always important. Keep in mind, however, that the pleasure and satisfaction derived from owning a quality machine will far outlast the "sting" of paying a little more than you thought you could afford.

If money is your only consideration, there are plenty of inexpensive saws available, but buyer beware. Likewise, just spending a lot of money doesn't necessarily guarantee a good saw for your specific needs and expectations.

Before you can make any sense from this chapter, you need to review the Introduction and Chapters 1 and 2. You should have a good idea of the many things that can be done with the scroll saw, and which of those areas are most important to you.

There are many very good scroll saws available. The goal is to select the one that best matches your over-all needs—both current and projected.

Following are several factors to consider when determining which type of scroll saw to buy.

SPACE AND PORTABILITY

Space and portability considerations may be dictated by the size of your shop, its setup, or the primary end use of your saw (**4–1**). Weight also becomes a factor if you have to move and store your machine after each use, or if you haul it to cut at craft shows. Incidentally, more weight does not necessarily mean a better value. Extra weight is one way manufacturers hide poor engineering to counteract machine vibration.

4–1. ▶ **Two saws of the same size on stands that require comparatively different floor space.**

BENCH OR FLOOR SCROLL SAW?

Stands can be purchased to accommodate almost any brand of bench-top saw and easily convert it to a floor machine. The stands of some floor-model saws are an integral part of the overall design of the machine and cannot be separated from it. Also, some brands do not operate smoothly unless mounted to their specially designed stand.

TYPE OF BLADE YOU WILL BE USING

The type of blade you will be using is an important factor in saw selection. Do you want one of the low-priced, more restrictive saws that carry only pin-end blades? Or, do you want a more versatile saw that permits the use of a greater variety of exclusively plain-end blades? In short, the better saws carry only plain-end blades and don't even bother to offer provisions for installing pin-end blades.

Pin-end blades are similar to training wheels on a bicycle—no one wants to use them once they learn to ride. If you have a saw that carries both blade types, I can almost guarantee that once you start using plain-end blades, you are not likely to use pin-end blades again. That is, unless the provision for installing plain-end blades in your saw is so cumbersome you become frustrated and stop using them, which indeed would be very unfortunate. Does a beginner need to start with pin-end blades? Definitely not!

BLADE SUSPENSION

Blade suspension relates to the way the clamps function at the end of the arms and react throughout the stroke. Parallel-arm saws especially, and most other types as well, must provide a hinging or pivoting blade action. Otherwise the blade, if held with a "stiff connection"—that is, if installed into a clamp that is not hinged or if allowed to pivot on the ends of the arms—will kink or bend near the clamps, causing strain and metal fatigue at this point. Premature or frequent blade breakage is the certain result (**4–2**).

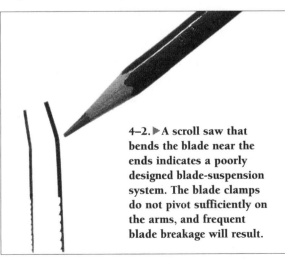

4–2. ▶ **A scroll saw that bends the blade near the ends indicates a poorly designed blade-suspension system. The blade clamps do not pivot sufficiently on the arms, and frequent blade breakage will result.**

BLADE CLAMPS

Blade clamps of various designs have been discussed in Chapter 2. Fast and easy blade installation is probably the single most important feature of a saw, and is associated with both pure scroll-sawing pleasure and total exasperation.

There are questions the scroll-sawer has to answer regarding blade installation and scroll-saw selection. Does he/she want to use blade clamps that are permanently fixed to the ends of the arms or loose clamps that are removable from the saw? Will special jigs or devices be needed to hold the clamps steady during blade changes? Are the thumbscrews large enough and ergonomically designed for weak or arthritic fingers?

Be sure to understand entirely what advertising terms such as "quick" or "fast-acting," "toolless," "hassle-free," and the like really mean for each specific saw. These terms are often used loosely to describe the installation of just the pin-end blades or may refer only to the upper blade clamp. Quick, easy, and convenient operation of both the top and the bottom blade clamps is essential and should be affordable and efficient on most medium- to high-priced saws.

BLADE-THREADING CAPABILITY

Blade-threading convenience for cutting inside openings is not related only to the quickness of getting the blade in and out of the clamps, but also to the general design of the arm, hold-downs, guards, etc. On most good saws, it is relatively easy to thread the blade through all small and thin workpieces. It is also important to check how easy or difficult it really is to thread a small plain-end blade through a small hole in the center of a very large piece of stock—about 1½ inches thick and 30 × 30 inches. It may shock the salesperson if you ask for a demonstration.

BLADE TENSION

Certain materials or techniques such as the sawing of any thick wood or stack-sawing of wood or plastic often require more than the usual recommended amount of blade tension to complete the task effectively. Can the arms withstand the extra strain? Do the blades slip out of the blade clamps when additional tension is applied? These are important questions to have answered if you intend to cut thick stock.

BLADE ACTION

The path of the blade during its up-and-down stroke may be important. By and large, a true, on-the-spot vertical movement is considered best for very precise cutting. A blade that moves into the work on the downstroke cuts more aggressively. You will find this to be more extreme with C-arm saws. Overall, a slight backward movement on the upstroke and a slight movement into the uncut wood on the downstroke is the preferred saw action. This does three things: 1, it reduces friction and tooth wear on the noncutting upstroke; 2, it minimizes chatter or stock-lifting tendencies on the upstroke; and 3, it provides a rasping, recutting, or polishing action to the sawn surfaces that makes them so smooth they seldom require sanding. Illus. **4–3 and 4–4** show how to make a "fingerprint" of the front-to-back blade action of a scroll saw. The steps are as follows:

1. Install a medium-to-large blade following the manufacturer's exact recommendations for blade installation.

2. Tension the blade well—slightly more than usual.

3. Place a thick block of wood with a clean, smooth edge lightly against one side of the blade and clamp it to the table.

4. Raise the blade to the full height of its stroke. Hold it there, and draw a fine line on the wood, following the back edge of the blade with a sharp pencil.

5. Lower the arm so the blade is now at the very bottom of its stroke, and draw another line with the block still clamped at its original position.

The two lines should give you a very acute V-shaped mark, merging to almost a single line. A single, perfectly vertical line is preferred, but the way present saws are designed, except for the oscillating-loop (Eclipse) saws, it is mechanically impossible.

Excessive front-to-back blade action will present the tendency to overcut at inside corners and intersections when doing very fine fretwork, marquetry, or inlay work. Excessive blade tilting from front to

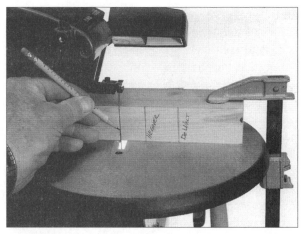

4–3. ▶ Check the front-to-back blade action by establishing the blade's position at the top and the bottom of the stroke.

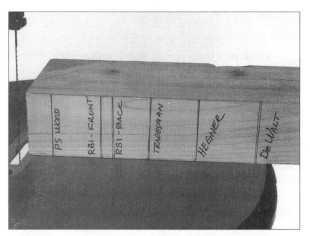

4–4. ▶ Recording the front-to-back blade action of various saws.

4–5. ▶ What happens when a blade breaks? It could be dangerous to the operator or damage the work as shown.

the upper arm lifts or the blade-reciprocation action automatically stops when a blade breaks. This is a much safer option.

SAW VIBRATION

Just like a smooth ride in a luxury car, you will appreciate a quiet, smooth-operating machine with minimal vibration. You can do average scroll-sawing with a vibrating machine. This condition, however, sends a warning that there may be some poor engineering or careless workmanship, or that parts are being stressed that could cause serious problems later (4–6).

4–6. ▶ Standing a coin on its edge on the table with the power on is one way to compare vibration levels.

back throughout the stroke may also create a bulge or "bellied" cut that will be out of square when cornering and sawing curves in thick material. In theory, a blade with no front-to-back action whatsoever would likely produce rougher sawn surfaces with ridges similar to those cut with a band saw, because there would be no rasping or smoothing blade action.

BLADE BREAKAGE DANGER

C-arm and parallel-link scroll saws present the hazard of a broken blade end possibly striking the operator's fingers or damaging the surface of the workpiece, as shown in 4–5. With other types of saw,

SPEED ADJUSTMENTS AND CONTROL LOCATIONS

Speed adjustments and control locations are fairly important considerations. Some machines, however, may offer extremely desirable "up-front" locations and convenience in this regard, but have other performance problems. Other machines may provide an excellent cutting performance, but don't have switches and speed controls conveniently located. You will have to decide if certain conveniences are more important than cutting performance. Variable speeds are becoming an increasingly standard feature on many saws, which makes speed adjustment easy.

The need for quick and easy speed changes depends upon the work you're doing. Production-cutting of the same material may seldom, if ever, require speed changes, whereas a model- or jewelry-maker cutting a variety of materials will change speeds more frequently.

HOLD-DOWNS, GUARDS, AND DUST BLOWERS

As mentioned earlier, experienced scroll-sawers seldom use the guard or hold-down, but every scroll-sawer appreciates a good blower that keeps the cutting line free of sawdust. A good hold-down is one that can be raised and swung out of the way when not desired or needed, but still be quickly brought into use without obstructing the operator's feeding and manipulation of the workpiece. Some saw manufacturers create a problem whereby the airline is connected to the hold-down in such a way that the hold-down/guard cannot be removed without affecting the use of the blower hose.

Hold-downs and guards are by and large recommended in schools for youngsters and beginners of all ages. Shrouds—the bodies of saws that enclose the moving upper arm and enclosures—are also important considerations. They guard the moving arms and prevent the user from pinching his fingers or hands between the moving arm and the workpiece. Some scroll saws do not have shrouds.

TABLES

Tables are available in many sizes and shapes, as are the openings in them for the blade. Table-tilt adjustments with positive stops and accurate, easy-to-read tilt scales are important to some scroll-sawers (such as those who do a lot of bevel-sawing) and almost never used by others, depending upon the nature of their work. Be aware, too, that some machines have tables that essentially tilt only in one direction. Some saws do not tilt a full 45 degrees, and others may not allow the bevel-cutting of thick stock because the upper arm doesn't provide enough clearance at the bottom of the stroke.

THROAT CAPACITY

This consideration is definitely based upon the kind and size of work intended. Remember, one can always cut small pieces on a large saw, but you can't cut larger pieces with a small machine. Those who make large clocks, furniture, and lawn and garden ornaments will appreciate a saw with a large throat capacity.

MOTORS AND BEARINGS

Motors and bearings should also be examined, especially for those planning on continuous production-cutting of tough hardwoods or other materials like thick plywoods. Induction motors are generally considered to be the most reliable type available, but they are the most expensive. Some variable-speed motors have electronics that lose power when the rpm is decreased.

Bearings at pivot points will vary in size, type, and quality. Saws may have sealed or sleeve-type ball bearings of bronze or nylon. Better saws have needle bearings that authorities claim to have a longer life than ball bearings. Some bearings require frequent lubrication from the operator, and other systems have drip or automatic lubrication.

ENGINEERING AND WORKMANSHIP

Engineering and workmanship can be evaluated with careful observation and visual inspection. With the power off, check both arms for side-to-side movement as shown in 4–7. There should be none. Any movement indicates bad or cheap bearings or improper assembly, either of which will likely contribute to premature part replacements. In the meantime, the owner will suffer a needless high frequency of blade breakage.

Check for *blade wobble*, another condition that results in frequent blade failure. Simply hold a white

4–7.▶ Check the arms for side-to-side movement.

4–8.▶ Visually check the blade for side-to-side wobble by holding a light paper (business card) behind the blade with the power on.

business card behind the blade as shown in **4–8**. Turn the power on and inspect the reciprocating action from the operator's position. If the blade appears not as a single, sharp line but as a blur, the machine needs to be either adjusted, if it has such a provision, or eliminated from your selection. Delta's newer machines, for example, have an adjustment provision that moves the lower blade clamp either right or left to bring it into alignment with the upper clamp.

If the scroll saw has small and/or poor-quality thumbscrews, levers, knobs, clamps, electrical cords, and plugs, and does not have a good-quality finish, smooth table surface, or deburred or softened metal edges, chances are the nonvisible parts will also be less than reliable. Check the owner's manual. Does it tell you how to properly adjust the saw and maintain it? Does it provide a "troubleshooting" guide and offer some tips about how to use and handle the machine?

SERVICE AND WARRANTY

Should you buy locally or via mail order? It may depend upon where you get the best price or service and the value you place on each. If your new saw is going to be the heart of your business and in use every day, then fast, reliable service is essential. You want assurances about long-term availability of replace-

ment parts, shipping costs, and warranty provisions. Warranties will vary in substance and duration. What is the company's return policy should you later determine that you are not happy with the scroll saw?

HANDS-ON TEST

Request the opinions and recommendations from fellow scroll-sawers and find out what their experiences have been. Take all this information into consideration while remembering that you want to satisfy your own needs (**4–9**). Do not allow yourself to be rushed into buying. The salesperson should allow you sufficient time to make a thorough inspection and a series of test cuts using various sizes and kinds of material.

4–9.▶ The saw's capability to make precise, accurate cuts, coupled with your own skills, will determine the eventual quality of your work. Here, for example, the cutting and fitting of a dovetail joint requires not just skill but a quality saw as well.

CHAPTER FIVE

BLADES, SPEEDS, & FEEDS

I n just about every scroll-sawing process, the primary objective is to achieve a cut surface that is so smooth it needs no subsequent sanding or polishing of any kind (**5–1 to 5–4**). Imagine the difficulty and frustration involved attempting to smooth the edges of highly detailed fretwork or to polish the sawn edges of the plastic and brass samples shown in **5–3 and 5–4.**

Efficient and skillful scroll-sawing of any material, by and large, depends on the relationship of three factors: 1, selecting the best blade; 2, sawing at the appropriate blade speed (strokes per minute); and 3, employing the optimum feed rate (speed of advancing the work into the blade). (If you have a single-speed saw, the major considerations involve blade selection and feed rate.) A properly functioning scroll saw must also be factored in to achieve the optimum sawing experience (**5–5**). Scroll-saw blades must be made from a material that allows for sufficient flexibility and yet be hard enough to provide sharp, lasting teeth without being too brittle (**5–6**).

Skillful sawing not only results in the smoothest possible finish, but the work is also completed in the shortest time with the least "wear and tear" to the machine and the operator. With each new scroll-sawing experience, it becomes easier to coordinate all of the related factors.

5–1. ▶ Matching the best blade to the job at hand is crucial to successful scroll-sawing. Here are just a few kinds and sizes of blade, with some so fine it is difficult to see the small teeth with the naked eye.

5–2. ▶ The resulting scroll-sawn edges on this piece of poplar are so smooth they actually shine.

5–3. ▶ This ⅜-inch acrylic eagle, cut by Bill Pickens, has polished-like edges produced directly by a scroll saw, as do the author's test cuts in ½-inch clear acrylic at the left and the two ⅜-inch pieces stack-cut below.

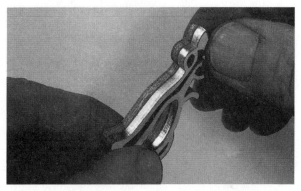

5–4. ▶ One-eighth-inch brass, temporarily bonded to a plywood waste backer, has sawn edges that appear almost polished.

5–5. ▶ This simple demonstration shows the interacting elements important to successful sawing: the tensioned blade bends slightly from feeding pressure; the blade clamps must pivot; and the arms of the saw must also bend slightly because the blade does not stretch.

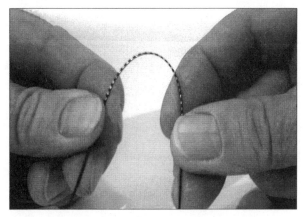

5–6. ▶ Blades must be made from materials that are both hard and flexible.

Some years ago, there were many small manufacturers of scroll-saw blades, all producing a few standard blades. Today, because of mergers and corporate partnerships, there are now only a few large companies that provide a wider choice of blades, and many are packaged with private labels for distributors around the globe.

It has been said that there are less than a half-dozen major scroll-saw blade manufacturers remaining worldwide. The author knows of two companies in Germany, one in Switzerland, one in Japan, one in Taiwan, in addition to a well-known United-States manufacturer, Olson Saw, which has been a leading producer of scroll-saw blades since 1918.

The number of brand names on the market, however, has grown substantially, as many small, new suppliers offer blades under their own labels. Upon reviewing various sources, you will see names such as Apollo, Crown Tooth, Dutchman, Eberlee, Fix, Flying Galaxy, Gottfried, Mach, Mascot, Niqua, Olson, Online, Penguin Silver, PGT, Polar, Scroll America, Shark, Super Sharp, Tiger Tooth, Top-Cut, and Woodrunner, among others. Those are all blades just for wood! Metal-cutting blades carry names such as Antelope, Escargot, Expert, Golden Eye, Goldsnail, Hercules, Laser Gold, Record, Rio, Supra, and others.

Improved scroll saws, the growing list of available materials that can be cut with a scroll saw, and the demand for better cutting performance have led to a wider selection of blade types and sizes. The good news, however, is that in spite of new and improved woodcutting designs and the large number of different brands available, there are actually a comparatively small number of different kinds of blade to choose from. There are even fewer choices in the metal-cutting and specialty-blade categories.

Scroll-saw blades cost around 15 cents to 20 cents each, with higher-quality blades in the 40- to 50-cent range. Buying blades by the gross generally saves you 20 to 25 percent. Be wary of blades offered at very cheap prices. Because of shoddy workmanship, they may prematurely dull or break, track poorly, and leave rough or burned edges (**5–7**).

BLADE SPECIFICATIONS

Blades are specified according to their length, thickness, and width; whether they have plain or pin ends; and the type and spacing of their teeth (**5–8 to 5–12**). (Tooth spacing is referred to in terms of teeth per inch, or "tpi.") These factors are discussed below.

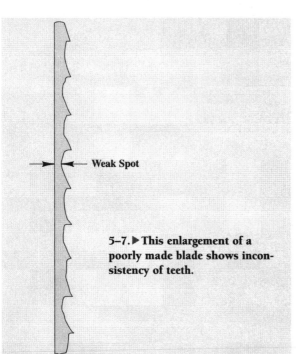

5–7.▶ This enlargement of a poorly made blade shows inconsistency of teeth.

Weak Spot

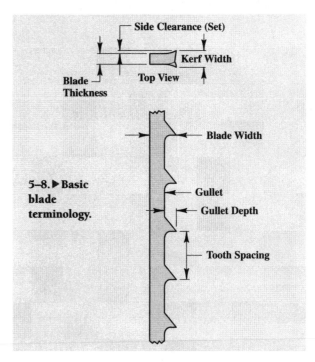

Side Clearance (Set)

Kerf Width

Blade Thickness

Top View

Blade Width

5–8.▶ Basic blade terminology.

Gullet

Gullet Depth

Tooth Spacing

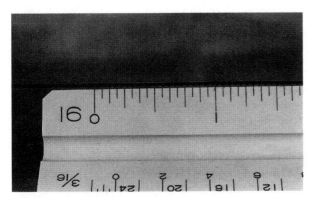

5–9. ▶ Tooth sizes of a blade are specified as the number of teeth per inch (tpi). Here is a No. 2 skip-tooth blade with 20 teeth per inch.

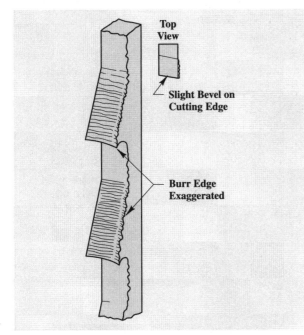

5–10. ▶ This enlarged sketch shows a sharp, microscopic burr along the right edge of the blade resulting from material flow incurred by the method of manufacturing. This causes the blade to track unevenly.

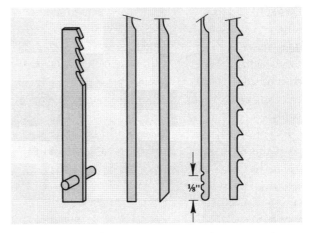

5–11. ▶ The first four blades shown, from left to right, have different ends: pin, square, pointed, and round (an experimental end designed to thread easier through entry holes; the notches identify the bottom of the blade). The blade on the far right is a continuous-tooth blade.

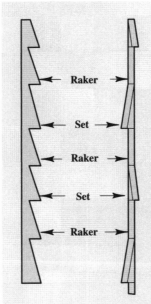

5–12. ▶ Some blades have a mechanical set to provide side clearance. Shown here is an unusual set pattern on a new blade sold by P.S. Wood Machines. Most pin-end blades and stamped or notched blades larger than 1/16 inch have every tooth set in a left, right, left, right pattern.

Blade Lengths

Most plain-end blades are 5 inches in length, but some blades labeled as 5 inches are as much as ¼ inch longer or shorter. Japanese-made Apollo blades are generally 6 inches long, and they also have their own numbering system. Blades this long can be used simply by snipping off the ends to adjust the length as needed. Most manufacturers size blade thickness and width by a nonstandardized generic numbering system that starts at 3/0 (the smallest) up to a No. 12, which is the largest size.

Tooth Size

Coarse-cutting blades have fewer teeth per inch. Larger teeth have bigger gullets that effectively carry out the sawdust; this permits faster feeds, but generally results in rougher sawn surfaces. Coarse blades may splinter thin wood and leave sharp burrs when metal-cutting (**5–13**). Conversely, finer blades with many small teeth cut smoother and require slower feeding rates because they are not only more prone to breakage, but sawdust removal is also slower and less efficient.

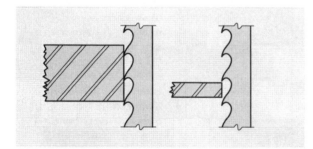

5–13.▶As a general rule, two or more teeth should always be in contact with the workpiece as shown at the left. With one tooth, bottom tear-out and blade breakage is likely.

It is always best to try several sizes and different types of blade for the cutting job at hand. Then select the largest blade that cuts the detail required while still producing the smoothest cut surface in the least time.

In many cases, you will not be able to visually detect smoother surface cuts produced by a No. 5 blade versus a cut made with a No. 7 blade. If you can cut the detail you want, it's a good idea to use the larger blade. It will cut faster and last longer.

Blade Types

Pin-end blades (refer to **5–11**) are available with skip or regular teeth. Regular teeth have a 5- to 10-degree hook angle on the tooth face and a small, round gullet for more aggressive cutting. All pin-end blades have a tooth set for side clearance and rapid chip evacuation. This prevents burning and provides a medium-to-smooth surface finish, depending upon the number of teeth per inch.

Essentially there are only three major types of blade to choose from that will handle most wood-cutting jobs. These are the standard "skip-tooth," the "double-tooth," and the "ground skip-tooth" designs (**5–14**).

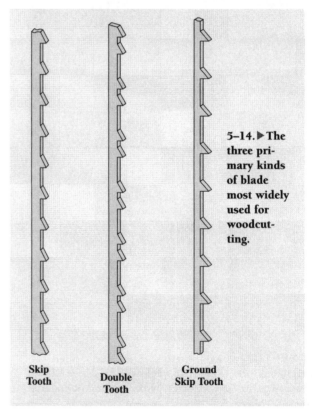

5–14.▶The three primary kinds of blade most widely used for woodcutting.

Skip
Tooth

Double
Tooth

Ground
Skip Tooth

Skip-tooth blades cut fast and provide smooth surfaces. *Double-tooth blades* generally perform about the same as skip-tooth blades, but some scroll-sawers find that the double-tooth configuration has better chip removal, and many insist that the small 3/0 to No. 3 sizes are the best for sawing wood veneers.

Ground skip-tooth blades are regarded by many experts as the sharpest and longest-lasting blades available. They have a unique tooth design with widely spaced gullets that provide good chip removal. They are cool-cutting and minimize or totally eliminate burning when cutting difficult hardwoods. They cost about 34 cents each, compared to about 18 cents for skip-tooth blades. Ground skip-tooth blades are made from high-quality carbon steel and involve a more costly manufacturing process. *Ground double-tooth blades* have recently become available.

Blades are made by one of three different processes, i.e., punched (stamped) or notched, milled, or ground.

Punched or notched blades are made with punch presses using pretempered (already-hardened) steel. Blades of this type have alternately set teeth to provide blade clearance in the kerf during cutting. These blades cut a comparatively wide kerf; depending upon the blade thickness, total tooth-set range is .013 to .029 inch, just a few thousandths under ⅟₃₂ inch in width. Available with plain and pin ends and 5 or 6 inches in length, they generally provide medium-to-smooth finishes on cut surfaces. Incidentally, all narrow scroll-saw blades up to the No. 12 size do not require set for clearance, radius scroll-sawing, and burning prevention..

Milled blades have teeth formed with milling cutters in soft steel. They are then heat-treated for optimum hardness and spring-back flexibility. This manufacturing method causes a "material flow" (in one direction only). Usually, this creates a slight burr along one edge of the blade that causes it to "track" slightly to one side (refer to **5–10**). This kind of blade requires some compensation in direction when feeding to make a straight cut. (See page 135.) Milled blades come in a variety of tooth shapes, including skip, reverse-skip, double-tooth, spiral, crown-tooth, and metal-cutting. These are economical blades that cannot be made with pin ends.

Ground blades are the best-performing blades. Their teeth, formed in hardened, high-carbon steel, are made with a double pass of a stone-grinding wheel. The raw material begins as round steel wire (not slit sheet steel) that is flattened to size and then

hardened and tempered. The grinding process ensures that every edge of the tooth (face, tip, and gullet) is very sharp. Known as PGT blades (in the Olson brand), they have reverse lower teeth. Because there is little-to-zero material flow, these teeth cut ("track") straighter and produce sand-free, polished sawn surfaces on most woods (**5–15**).

5–15. ▶ Comparative cuts in ¾-inch pine (above) and oak (below). Left: Surfaces sawn with a German-made double-tooth blade without reverse teeth. Right: Smooth, polished surfaces with no bottom tear-out that were cut with Olson's No. 5 ground blade with lower reverse teeth.

Ground blades are the most expensive, but generally last three to four times longer than other blades. Currently, ground blades are only available in sizes Nos. 5, 7, and 9 in skip-tooth and double-tooth designs. Smaller sizes of ground blade may be available in the near future. *Note*: Do not confuse "precision-milled blades" with "precision-ground blades." There is a major difference in quality as well as cost.

The reverse teeth located on the lower end of various types of blade (**5–16**) are a concept developed by Olson Saw Co. in the early 1950's to eliminate tear-out and splintering on the underside of scroll-sawn wood. The first reverse-tooth blades were made in response to a request from Playskool, Inc. to develop a blade that would cut clean edges without splintering as the blade exits the wood. Now, reverse teeth are found on many kinds and brands of saw blade used worldwide. Finer blades have a greater number of reverse teeth than coarse blades.

---

*This information is taken in part from Olson's scroll-saw blade catalog, copyright 1999

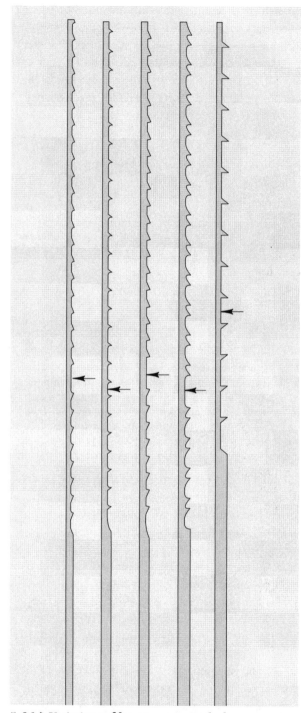

5–16. ▶ **Variations of lower reverse teeth shown enlarged 200 percent. Left to right: Niqua's Fix No. 7, five-inch skip-tooth blade; Olson's PGT No. 7, five-inch skip-tooth blade; Mascot's Woodrunner No. 7, five-inch skip-tooth blade; Scroll America's five-inch double-tooth blade; and Apollo's No. 3 six-inch blade.**

Blades with reverse teeth have to be installed so they work favorably. If cutting thin material, for example, all of the sawing may be done using only the reverse teeth; this, however, causes splintering on the top surface. For most material you want just one or two of the reverse teeth above the table when the saw is at full upstroke (**5–17**). To accomplish this may require a more careful installation in the lower blade clamp—either raising the blade slightly or snipping off the end slightly if too many teeth remain above the table. Each scroll saw has a different table height, so give this the appropriate attention if you want the reverse teeth to function effectively.

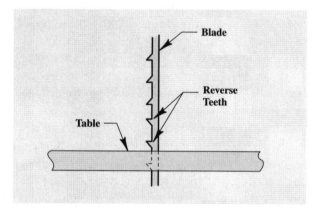

5–17. ▶ **Correct positioning has one or two reverse teeth coming through above the table surface, as shown, when the lower arm is at the full upstroke position.**

Two-way-cutting blades (**5–18 and 5–19**) are designed to cut on both the upstroke and downstroke. Olson's crown-tooth blade and Niqua's Top Cut blade are two examples. Blades of this type are excellent performers for certain jobs, which draws praise from some scroll-sawers and a negative response from others.

The advantages of the crown-tooth blade are its ability to make smooth, splinter-free cuts in a variety of materials. It can cut acrylic plastics, soft woods, and even layers of stacked fabrics sandwiched between cardboard very well. Another advantage is that when the teeth dull, you can simply turn the blade end over end in the saw for a new set of teeth.

Critics of the two-way-cutting blades claim they are slower cutting, they tend to lift the stock, and they

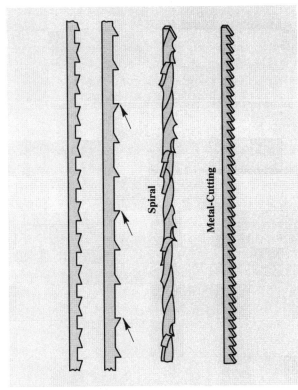

5–18. ▶ Special blades, from left to right: Olson blade with crown-tooth design; Niqua's Top Cut blade, with every third tooth reversed; and spiral and metal-cutting blades.

5–19. ▶ Recent blades from Olson Saw Company, shown from left to right: a precision-ground No. 9, double-tooth blade; a No. 9, crown-tooth blade; and the Thickwood blade.

leave a "fuzz" not only on the bottom but also on the top of the workpiece. And, two-way blades tend to pull more sawdust up from the kerf, which obscures the cutting line.

Spiral blades (**5–18 and 5–20**) are simply regular-tooth blades that have been twisted. Spiral blades are designed to cut in all directions, so there is no need to rotate the workpiece to make a curved cut. They have few uses for the serious woodworking scroll-sawer because they cut considerably slower and leave much rougher sawn surfaces than other blades. Spiral blades *do not* cut smooth flowing curves easily. The blade tends to follow the grain of the wood rather than the intended line of cut. Large-radius curves and straight-line cutting are more easily done with regular blades.

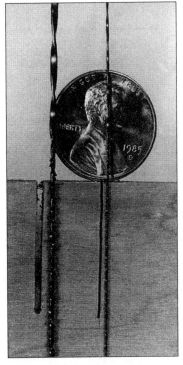

5–20. ▶ Spiral blades and the kerfs they cut. At left is a No. 6 blade, and at right is a 2/0. Notice the roughness and torn fibers visible in the kerf at the left.

Spiral blades are useful when the workpiece is too long or large to rotate on the saw. They cut a comparatively large kerf, which, depending upon the job, may or may not be an advantage (**5–21**). Jewelry-makers often use spiral blades to cut hard-wax models.

Spiral blades traditionally have twisted ends that make installation difficult or impossible on some saws, and the twisted ends cause chuck-retention

5–21. ▶ **This wide kerf-line art was cut through the wood with a No. 6 spiral blade.**

problems. Olson Saw Co. has recently introduced spiral blades with flat ends for easier installation and improved retention.

Thickwood blades (refer to **5–19**) are another new blade configuration from Olson Saw Co. These are coarse blades that have seven hook teeth per inch. They are designed essentially to cut soft- and hardwoods up to two inches in thickness. This blade is a good choice for production scroll-sawers who stack-cut multiple layers at once. The sawn surfaces are usually remarkably smooth, and users claim that tough-to-cut wood such as 1½-inch-thick oak and 2½-inch-thick sugar maple can be cut relatively easily with a medium/smooth finish. Only available in one size, this blade was not given a generic number. It is wider than a No. 12 blade (it is actually .080, or about 5/64, inch in width), which limits tight radius-cutting.

Olson's Thickwood blades are cut from continuous coils made in manufacturing. That is why they have full-length teeth and no reverse lower teeth. The blade also has moderately alternating set teeth, for added clearance.

Metal-cutting blades (refer to **5–18**) are designed and manufactured especially for use in power-driven scroll saws. They have more regular-type teeth per inch than other blades and are less brittle than the jeweler's or metal-piercing blades commonly used in handheld frames. Olson's metal-cutting blades are available in Nos. 1, 5, 7, 9, and 12. A No. 5 metal-cutting blade has 36 teeth per inch, compared to just 12½

teeth on a No. 5 skip-tooth woodcutting blade.

Although Olson also offers metal-piercing and jeweler's saw blades, it does not recommend them for power-driven scroll saws because they are too brittle and present a serious hazard when they break. Some suppliers, however, do sell German-made jeweler's 5¼-inch blades for use in scroll saws, but they generally do not recommend using anything finer than a 4/0 size, which is a very fine blade (depending upon the manufacturer, a blade this fine may have as many as 72 teeth per inch).

Mach blades. Olson Saw Co. has recently introduced a new series of blades with reverse teeth that have widely spaced teeth, like its ground blades. However, the Mach blades are milled, not ground. They are less expensive, made of annealed steel, and are available in Nos. 3, 5, 7, and 9 sizes. Since Mach blades are milled, they will track to one side because of the burr resulting from the milling process (refer to **5–10**).

GENERAL BLADE-SELECTION GUIDELINES

Table 5–1, on pages 148 and 149, gives recommended blades for cutting various kinds and sizes of material. There are many variables that can affect the cutability of a material, so there may be situations where a different size or blade configuration than the one recommended may actually perform better. Furthermore, blades with the same specifications may vary from manufacturer to manufacturer. Eberle double-tooth blades, for example, tend to be larger than Olson-made blades of the same generic number. A No. 5 blade from one company may be closer to a No. 7 blade from another company.

3/0, 2/0, and No. 2 blades are used for very fine and delicate cutting of veneers and all thin woods up to 3/16 inch thick. *Nos. 4, 5, and 7 blades* are best for general-purpose hard- and softwood-cutting, including average fretwork and tight-radius patterns in some softwoods 1 to 1¼ inches in thickness. *Nos. 7, 9, and 12 blades* are for heavier and faster cutting of softwoods up to 1½ inches thick and hardwoods ¾ to 1 inch thick.

MODIFYING SCROLL-SAW BLADES

Sometimes, you may find it to your advantage to alter the way certain blades have been manufactured. This may allow you to perform an otherwise impossible cutting job or improve the cutting action or performance of a particular blade. Blade modification usually involves altering the ends, back, or side of the blade, but not the face or tooth edge.

Changing Blade Length

Snipping off one or both ends of the blade to shorten it can be done for a couple of reasons. The most obvious need to reduce blade length is to make it fit into the saw. Use wire nippers or side-cutting pliers. Some blade clamps have vertical stops, so each new blade is inserted in exactly the same position as the previous blade. Since this does not usually provide any tolerance for inserting the blade at different heights within the clamps, the blade may need to be shortened to make reverse teeth function efficiently. Too many reverse teeth exposed to the work may cause "tear-out" on the top surface or "chatter"—the lifting of the workpiece with every upstroke.

90-Degree Twist

This technique (**5–22**) changes the cutting direction of the blade, so you can feed the stock into the blade from the side rather than from the front of the machine. Sawing in this band-saw fashion may allow you to make certain kinds of cut in long stock that otherwise might be restricted because of the scroll saw's throat capacity.

Most blades are not tempered at the ends, so they can be bent without breaking. Remember, however, that all saws have some front-to-back blade action that, if excessive, is less than ideal. The blade will have a side-to-side motion and rub on the walls of the kerf. This may cause overheating and breakage, particularly when fine blades are used.

Reducing and Adding a Point to Blade Ends

Sometimes your favorite blade may be too wide to insert through an entry hole to cut a small opening or to make fine veining and detail cuts. Carefully grinding down the flat ends and/or shortening the length of pins on a pin-end blade may permit threading it through a smaller-than-usual entry hole (**5–23 to 5–27**).

5–22. ▶ Use a vise or two pairs of pliers to twist the blade ends 90 degrees to make longer cuts than otherwise permitted on your saw.

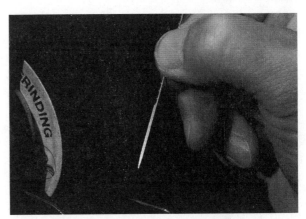

5–23. ▶ Reducing the end width and producing a pointed blade end on a grinder.

5–24. ▶ Unmodified blade on the left. The same modified blade on the right permits drilling smaller-size blade-entry holes.

5–25. ▶ Pin-end blades normally require ³⁄₁₆-inch-diameter blade-entry holes. Reducing the blade-end width and pin lengths permits using much smaller drill sizes, as shown above.

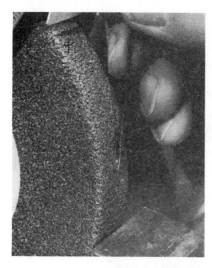

5–26. ▶ Reducing the width of a pin-end blade.

5–27. ▶ Grinding the pin shorter.

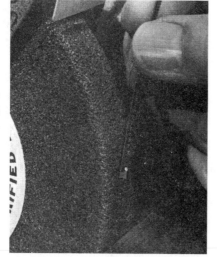

Honing the Blade's Back and Sides

Honing the back and sides of certain blades (**5–28**) allows a wider blade to make tighter or sharper radius cuts, minimizes burning, and improves tracking. Improved tracking means making straight-line cuts without any angular compensation by feeding the stock directly into the blade so the cutting line is in line with the arm(s).

5–28. ▶ Rounding and/or reducing the thickness of the blade behind the teeth allows the sawing of tighter turns with a wide blade and often improves the finish on difficult-to-cut materials such as cherry, maple, and acrylic plastics.

Because milled blades come with a burr on one side of the tooth (refer to **5–10**) as a result of the manufacturing process, they actually cut crooked, that is, they track more easily to one side than to the other. To correct the "crooked-cut" phenomenon, you must either make a slight compensation in the feed direction or simply remove the burr with a flat abrasive, hone, or file (**5–29 to 5–31**).

Honing the back of a blade using an abrasive can also improve blade performance. With the power on, gently apply a file or stone to the blade so as to round the back edges. When cutting plastics and other difficult-to-cut materials, it may be advantageous to reduce the thickness of the blade by removing material on each side behind the teeth as shown in **5–28**. (Chapter 19 contains information on selecting and modifying blades when cutting plastics.) Remember that many blades, such as ground blades, do not have a burr along one edge.

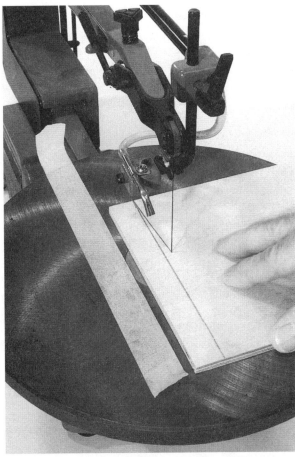

5–29. ▶ The "crooked-cut" phenomenon. A length of tape on the table parallel to the upper arm indicates how the burr edge on milled or stamped blades tracks to the right, off the intended line of cut.

5–31. ▶ The same blade with the burr removed can now cut straight without tracking.

Painting Blades

Painting blades (5–32) does not improve blade performance or the surface quality of the cut, but in many cases it makes the sawing experience much less stressful for those with vision problems. Simply apply a light coat of a brightly colored spray paint to the entire blade except at the ends. Painted ends will slip in the blade clamps.

Sometimes the silver color of a blade against a light or gray-shaded pattern or a blued blade against a black pattern line is difficult to distinguish if one's eyesight is not perfect. A painted blade is helpful, therefore, in providing good visual contrast to the pattern lines, making them easier to follow more precisely. The paint will quickly wear away from those teeth engaged in the wood, but the teeth above the stock will remain highly visible.

5–30. ▶ Removing the burr as shown takes just seconds. Use a fine file, hone, or aluminum-oxide abrasive glued to a block as shown here.

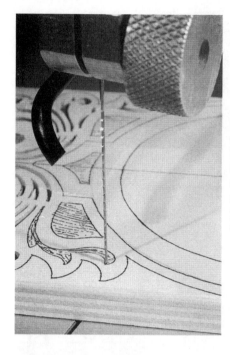

5–32. ▶ Scroll-saw blades spray-painted bright, fluorescent colors are easier to see and help you cut more accurately.

Lubricating Blades

Special lubricants are available that are claimed to prolong blade life and enable blades to make smoother cuts and saw faster. Lubricants are used in various wood industries to resist pitch buildup and to generally improve cutting-tool efficiency. They are also worth trying on your scroll-saw blades for the same reasons. Saw-blade lubricants are available as a wax stick or in a water-based, liquid form that is applied with a hand-pump misting spray.

BLADE SPEED AND FEED RATE

The optimum combination of blade speed and feed rate is essential to achieve the best cuts. Each is discussed below.

Speeds

Machine speed (strokes per minute) is actually not as important as the rate or speed at which the operator advances the material into the reciprocating blade. Different feed rates mean different-quality cuts. Common sense regarding feed rates can prevent problems that might arise when using a single-speed machine. For almost all wood-sawing, the highest machine speed is best, anyway. The only times slower speeds are important are when cutting unusu-

ally hard or difficult-to-saw materials like very hard woods, metals, and plastics. And slower speeds are normally best for controlled sawing of thin wood, veneers, soft metals, bone, ivory, rubber, and laminated plastics.

Most machines have top blade speeds of 1,300 to 2,000 cutting strokes per minute. Simple profiles in hardwoods, softwoods, hardboard, plywood, and paper products over ¼ inch thick can generally all be cut at the higher speeds. This covers about 95 percent of the general cutting jobs of most woodworkers. Medium machine speeds (700 to 1,000 spm) may be an advantage for cutting ⅛- to ¼-thick softwoods, for making puzzles, and for some inlay work. Cutting marquetry work and thicker plastics and jewelry-making are often best done at slower speeds, from less than 100 to 600 or 800 spm. Remember, for efficient cutting, as the material thickness increases, select wider blades with fewer teeth per inch.

Feeds

If you occasionally cut materials such as soft metals or thin veneer-like wood and slow cutting speeds are recommended, you can often get by just slowing the feed rate. As a general rule, slower feed rates result in a smoother finish on the cut surface. The best blade for the material being cut is one that not only produces smoothly cut surfaces, but also is the most efficient as far as time and control are concerned.

Since feed rate is related to time and quality or smoothness of cut, let us look at a few examples. Illus. **5–33** shows a cut surface across the grain on a ¾-inch-thick piece of white pine. A No. 9 skip-tooth blade with 11½ teeth per inch was used. The first inch of pine at the left in the photo was cut at a rate of 10 seconds per inch of feed. The remainder of the cut was made at more than double that speed—at the rate of four seconds per inch. Notice the obvious difference in surface quality. Incidentally, pine is not one of the smoothest-cutting woods. Walnut can burn at high cutting speeds with skip-tooth blades, whereas poplar, a softwood, cuts smoothly and doesn't burn at high speeds.

Illus. **5–34** shows three different finish qualities on hard maple. The first inch of hard maple at the left

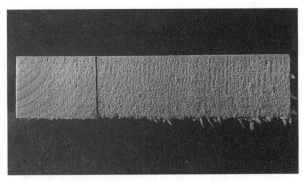

5–33. ▶ **Three-quarter-inch pine cut at different feed rates. The inch of pine at the left was cut in ten seconds; the remainder of the cut was made at a rate of four seconds per inch of cut surface. Notice the bottom tear-out.**

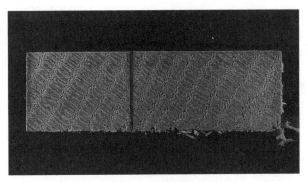

5–35. ▶ **Two cuts on ¾-inch oak. The left cut was made with a feed rate of 10 seconds per inch; the remaining cut was made at a feed rate of four seconds per inch.**

5–34. ▶ **Different cuts on hard maple. The left cut was made at one-third the speed of the center cut. The cut on the right was made on a band saw.**

was cut with a No. 9 skip-tooth blade with 11½ teeth per inch at a feed rate of 12 seconds per inch. The next inch was cut with the same blade, but at three times the feed rate (4 seconds per inch). The final inch at the right was cut slowly, but on a band saw using a ¼-inch skip-tooth blade.

Illus. **5–35** shows ¾-inch red oak that was cut at two dramatically different rates. There was not a great deal of difference in the appearance of its surface qualities. However, tear-out on the bottom was greater at the faster feed rate, and the same will happen with other woods. Slowing to a feed rate of about six or seven seconds per inch increased surface quality considerably. A reverse-tooth blade is recommended to eliminate or minimize bottom tear-out or feathering. The old saying, "haste makes

waste" is usually very true when it comes to fine scroll-saw work. Remember to relax and let the blade do the cutting.

SAWING VARIABLES

Everyone likes rules and charts that provide guaranteed results. There are, however, so many variables in the scroll-sawing process that it is impossible to establish entrenched rules. What works in one situation may or may not work in another. First, there are the many variables of nature, in that no two pieces of wood are exactly the same. From the same tree may come a board sawn from the center *heartwood*, which is denser and tougher than one from the softer outside *sapwood*. The surface grain may be plain- or quarter-sawn. The moisture content of wood from different sources can vary dramatically. All these factors play a role in how sucessful you are when scroll-sawing wood.

Then there are the mechanical and human variables to consider. Various brands and sizes of scroll saw have different performance characteristics in the blade and stroke actions, speed ranges, etc. Blade designs themselves are becoming more specialized, which is great, but there are no uniform industry standards. One manufacturer's No. 9 blade may be closer to a No. 5 or 7 blade sold by another manufacturer, thus making precise blade-size recommendations difficult.

Scroll-sawers have different levels of physical strength, eye-hand coordination skills, and feel or touch for feeding the workpiece. Motivations are also mixed: some scroll-sawers enjoy the challenge of making the perfect cut; for others, getting the job done quickly means making money.

Through the collective efforts of scroll-saw and blade manufacturers and scroll-sawers themselves, there are helpful tips and tricks for solving previously problematic cutting jobs. Many of these tips are found randomly throughout the book, located where they best apply to specific techniques.

BLADE STORAGE

Most hobbyist scroll-sawers tend to specialize in certain kinds of project. Generally, most do not need a huge supply of different sizes and kinds of blade necessary to cut a variety of different materials. A few select blades can do a fairly wide range of cutting jobs.

An organized storage system becomes more important as your arsenal of blades increases. A strip of magnetic tape or a small magnet mounted somewhere conveniently on your saw or stand will keep a few of your more widely used blades handy. If you do jobs that require switching blade types or sizes frequently, you may want to purchase some extra lower blade clamps and keep them "preloaded" with frequently used blades so you can quickly grab a blade already partially installed (**5–36**). Quantities of blades are best stored in labeled plastic tubes available from scroll-saw supply firms. Or make them yourself using ½-inch PVC plastic pipe with end caps (**5–37**) or cork plugs.

Lazy-Susan Blade-Storage System

A lazy-Susan blade-storage system (**5–38 to 5–40**) can be custom-made for your needs. It will compactly hold up to 68 plastic blade-storage tubes, if needed, and can be made to include space for extra blade clamps. Enlarge the patterns 200 percent. Color-code the labels or caps of the plastic tubes to identify certain types of blade such as red for ground blades, green for skip-tooth, yellow for double-tooth, black for metal-cutting blades, etc.

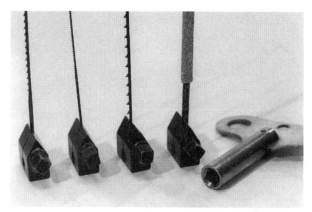

5–36. ▶ In some cases, it saves time and is convenient to have extra blade clamps "preloaded" with frequently used blades to speed blade changes.

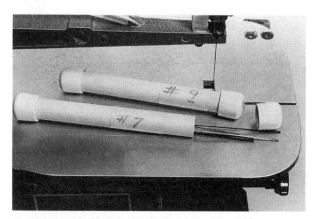

5–37. ▶ One-half-inch PVC pipe and end caps make good blade-storage containers.

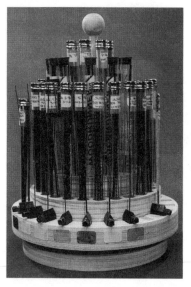

5–38. ▶ Lazy-Susan blade storage is compact and convenient.

5–39. ▶ A blade-storage carousel made from layered discs of plywood with holes that hold blade-storage tubes.

5–40. ▶ Scroll-saw blade organizer.

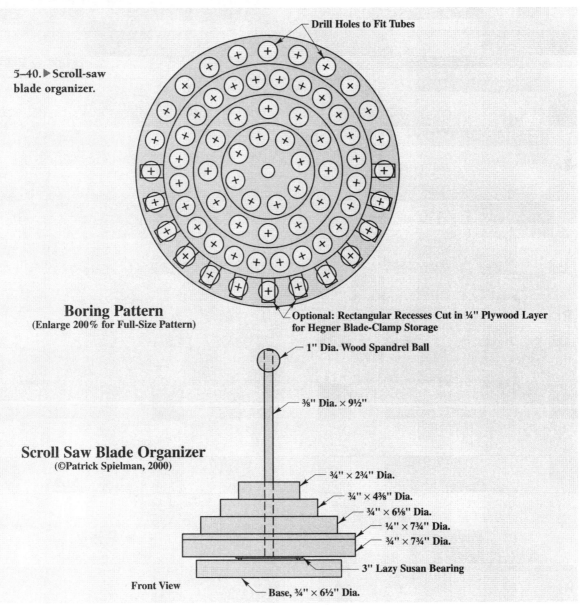

Drill Holes to Fit Tubes

Boring Pattern
(Enlarge 200% for Full-Size Pattern)

Optional: Rectangular Recesses Cut in ¼" Plywood Layer for Hegner Blade-Clamp Storage

1" Dia. Wood Spandrel Ball

⅜" Dia. × 9½"

Scroll Saw Blade Organizer
(©Patrick Spielman, 2000)

¾" × 2¾" Dia.

¾" × 4⅜" Dia.

¾" × 6⅛" Dia.

¼" × 7¾" Dia.

¾" × 7¾" Dia.

3" Lazy Susan Bearing

Front View

Base, ¾" × 6½" Dia.

Blade Selection Chart*

KEY

Recommended=R
Usable=U
Not Recommended=X

Skip Tooth
(Cuts fast, smooth finish)

Reverse Skip Tooth
(Eliminates Underside Tear-Out)

Double Tooth
(Cuts Fast, Smooth Finish)

					HARD WOOD ½"-¾"	HARD WOOD TO 1½"	SOFT WOOD ½"-¾"	SOFT WOOD TO 1½"	VENEER, WOOD TO 3/16"	PLYWOOD	MDF	PARTICLEBOARD	CORIAN	PLASTIC	NONFERROUS METAL	ALUMINUM	SMOOTH	SPLINTER-FREE	MEDIUM
No.	Width	Thick.	T.P.I.	Entry Hole															
Skip Tooth																			
3/0	.022"	.008"	33	1/32"			U		R								X		
2/0	.022"	.010"	28	1/32"			R	U	R								X		
2	.029"	.012"	20	3/64"			R	U	R	U				U			X		
4	.035"	.015"	15	1/16"			R	R	U	U	U	U		U			X		
5	.038"	.016"	12.5	1/16"	U	U	R	R		U	U	U		U			X		
7	.045"	.017"	11.5	1/16"	R	U	U	R		U	U	U		U			X		
9	.053"	.018"	11.5	1/16"	R	R	U	R		R	R	R		U			X		
12	.062"	.024"	9.5	5/64"	R	R	U	R		R	R	R					X		
Reverse Skip Tooth																			
2/0	.022"	.010"	28	1/32"			R		R								X	X	
2R	.029"	.012"	20	3/64"			R	U	U								X	X	
5R	.038"	.016"	12.5	3/64"	U		R	R		U	U	U					X	X	
7R	.047"	.017"	11.5	1/16"	R	U	U	R		R	R	R					X	X	
9R	.054"	.019"	11.5	1/16"	R	R	U	U		R	R	R					X	X	
12R	.062"	.024"	9.5	5/64"	R	R	U	U		R	R	R					X	X	
	1.00"	.022"	9.5	1/8"	R	R	U			R	R	R					X	X	
Double Tooth																			
3/0	.023"	.008"	33	1/32"			U		R								X		
2/0	.023"	.011"	37	1/32"			R	U	R								X		
1	.026"	.013"	30	3/64"			R	U	R								X		
3	.032"	.014"	23	3/64"			R	R	U	U	U	U	U	U			X		
5	.038"	.016"	16	1/16"	U	U	R	R		U	U	U	U	U			X		
7	.044"	.018"	13	1/16"	R	U	U	R		U	U	U	U	U			X		
9	.053"	.018"	11	1/16"	R	R	U	U		R	R	R	U	U			X		
12	.061"	.022"	10	5/64"	R	R	U	U		R	R	R					X		

MATERIAL   FINISH

*Adapted from Information Provide by Olson Saw Company ©2000

Blade Selection Chart

KEY

Recommended=R
Usable=U
Not Recommended=X

Category	No.	Width	Thick.	T.P.I.	Entry Hole	HARD WOOD ½"–¾"	HARD WOOD TO 1½"	SOFT WOOD ½"–¾"	SOFT WOOD TO 1½"	VENEER, WOOD TO 3/16"	PLYWOOD	MDF	PARTICLEBOARD	CORIAN	PLASTIC	NONFERROUS METAL	ALUMINUM	SMOOTH	SPLINTER-FREE	MEDIUM
Crown Tooth (Cuts on Up and Down Stroke)	2/0	.024"	.011"	20	1/32"			R		R				1/8"	1/8"			X	X	
	2	.026"	.013"	20	3/64"			R		R				1/8"	1/8"			X	X	
	3	.032"	.014"	16	3/64"			R	U	U	U			1/8"	3/16"			X	X	
	5	.038"	.016"	16	1/16"			R	U	U	U	U		1/8"	1/4"			X	X	
	7	.045"	.017"	11	1/16"	U		U	U		U	U	U	1/8"	3/4"			X	X	
	9	.053"	.018"	6	1/16"	R	U	U	R		R	R	R	1/8"	3/4"			X	X	
	12	.065"	.024"	6	5/64"	R	U	U	R		R	R	R	1/2"	3/4"			X	X	
Ground Skip, With Reverse Teeth (Smoothest Finish)	5RG	.045"	.018"	12	1/16"	U		R	R		U	U	U	1/8"	1/8"	U	U	X	X	
	7RG	.047"	.018"	10	1/16"	U	U	R	U		R	R	R	3/8"	3/8"	U	U	X	X	
	9RG	.049"	.018"	8	1/16"	R	R		U		R	R	R	1/2"	3/4"			X	X	
Ground Double Tooth (With Reverse Teeth)	5RG	.045"	.018"	12	1/16"	U		R	R		U	U	U	1/8"	1/8"	U	U	X	X	
	7RG	.047"	.018"	10	1/16"	R	U	R	U		R	R	R	3/8"	3/8"	U	U	X	X	
	9RG	.049"	.018"	9	1/16"	R	R		U		R	R	R	1/2"	3/4"			X	X	
Spiral (Cut in All Directions, Rough Finish)	0	-	.032"	46	3/64"			U	U										X	
	2	-	.035"	41	5/64"	U	U					U	U						X	
	4	-	.041"	36	7/64"	U	U					U	U						X	
Thickwood (Cuts Wood Up to 2" Thick)	-	.080"	.018"	7	3/32"		R	U	R		R	U	R					X	X	X
Metal-Cutting	7	.041"	.019"	30	1/16"											R	R			X
	9	.049"	.022"	25	1/16"											R	R			X
	12	.070"	.023"	20	5/64"											R	R			X

CHAPTER SIX

SAFETY
TECHNIQUES &
GUIDELINES

he first priority of every scroll-saw user should be to prevent injury and to exercise every possible caution to ensure long-term good health. The scroll saw is considered the safest of all power-driven woodworking machines. Everyone, however, must respect it and be aware of its potential dangers. In addition to using the obvious safety devices such as eye and ear protection, guards, and hold-downs, you need to be concerned about a more serious and threatening hazard—dust, which scroll saws generate profusely.

The chapter will provide some specific guidelines for safe operation of the scroll saw. You will also be alerted to some related health issues and will be provided with suggestions for dealing with wood dust.

SAFETY RULES

Here are some general safety rules that apply to scroll saws specifically and power tools in general:

1. Read and study the owner's manual to become acquainted with the mechanical features, adjustments, and general instructions for operating the saw.

2. Dress properly. Do not wear loose clothing or dangling jewelry. Contain long hair and wear a dust mask, goggles, and some form of hearing protection if the machine and/or shop vacuum is loud (**6–1 to 6–3**).

3. Do not move scroll saws by lifting them by the upper arm unless a special carrying handle is provided. Lift with the base or stand.

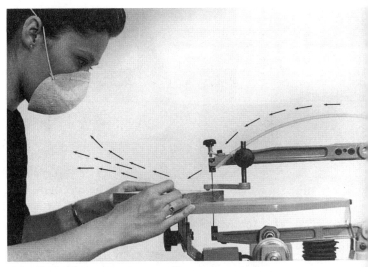

6–2. ▶ **Some saws still have poorly designed blowers that direct sawdust toward the operator—a very unhealthy situation.**

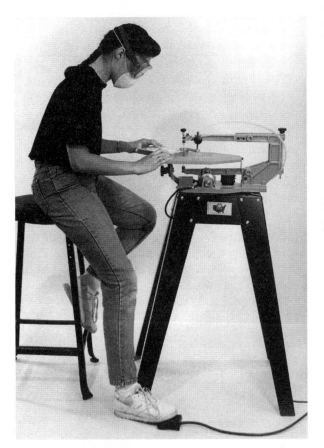

6–3. ▶ **A shop-made system that, like many of the newer adjustable sawdust blowers, directs dust particles away from the operator.**

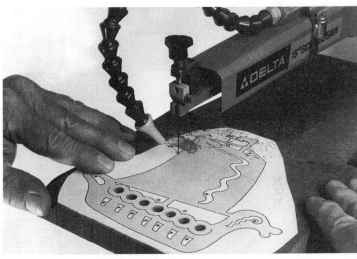

6–1. ▶ **A demonstration of good safety techniques: the woodworker's hair is pulled back and her back is straight; there is no loose clothing or jewelry; goggles, a dust mask, a hold-down, and a foot switch are being used; the stool is at a comfortable height; and the work area is clean and well lit.**

4. Make sure the saw is properly grounded.

5. Be sure the blade is inserted with the teeth forward and pointing down toward the table.

6. Do not use dull or bent blades.

7. Be sure the blade is properly tensioned before operating the saw.

8. Always release the tension before loosening the blade clamp.

9. Use properly adjusted hold-downs and guards as appropriate (**6–4**).

10. Remove keys, wrenches, etc. before starting the power.

11. Exercise extreme caution when sawing round material such as dowels. They tend to roll uncontrollably into the blade, causing it to jam and possibly break. Use a V-block to support round dowels, etc.

12. Ensure that the table-lock clamp is tight before starting the machine.

13. Use extra precautions when sawing very small pieces. (See pages 196 to 201 for tips and suggestions.)

14. Never reach under the table while the machine is running.

15. A foot switch is a recommended safety feature (refer to **6–1**). Be very cautious of it, however. Do not accidentally step on it during noncutting jobs such as when changing or threading blades, making adjustments, or cleaning.

16. Do not place fingers in the line of cut (**6–5**). *Tip:* Use the eraser end of a pencil rather than your fingers when necessary to reach in close to the blade.

17. Do not force the machine. If it's not cutting as fast as you think it should, a new or larger blade may be needed.

18. Recognize the sound and feel of a good cutting machine. Stop immediately and investigate any unusual sounds or sensations.

19. Stop if you smell or see smoke rising around the blade and investigate.

20. If a work light and/or magnifier are used on a parallel-arm saw, be sure they are positioned so that in the event of blade breakage, the accessory lamp is not struck by the sudden, automatic lift of the upper arm.

21. Do not use brittle jeweler's or metal-piercing blades in power-driven saws. They may shatter.

22. Exercise caution when sawing thick stock (**6–6 to 6–8**). It is easy to become mesmerized by the cutting action and forget that you might pinch your fingers between the arm and the workpiece, especially if you have the habit of placing your hands behind and close to the sides of the blade.

23. If using a C-arm or double-parallel-link saw, remember that blade breakage can be hazardous because these saws do not have the instant lifting provision of the upper arm when a blade breaks.

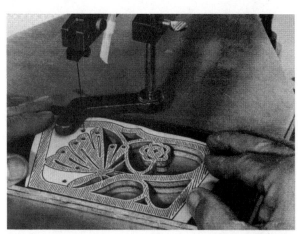

6–4. ▶ **Operator's view of fretwork in progress. Notice the use of the hold-down and the safe hand positions.**

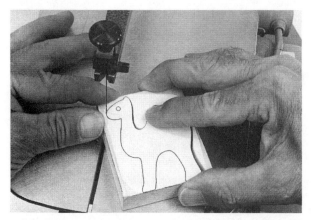

6–5. ▶ **When it is necessary to have fingers close to the blade to hold and control the work, keep them to the side or rear, as shown, and never in front of the blade.**

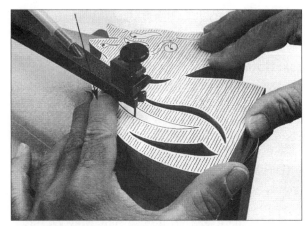

6–6. ▶ **Be especially cautious when sawing thick stock. Hands and fingers can become wedged between the upper arm and the workpiece, as shown here.**

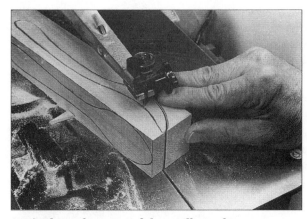

6–7. ▶ **Always be aware of the oscillating levers or knobs that, on some saws, extend from the blade clamps over the workpiece.**

6–8. ▶ **Some saws have guards or enclosures that protect the operator from contact with a moving upper arm.**

24. Slack off the tension at the end of the day and when the saw will not be used for a period of time.
25. Do not operate machines while under the influence of drugs, alcohol, or medications, or when fatigued.
26. Keep observers and visitors at a safe distance.

HEALTH CONCERNS

Good physical posture is important when sawing for extended periods of time. Back, shoulder, and neck strain should be avoided (**6–9**). When standing, try to keep your back straight, bending at the waist. If the saw is too low, raise it with blocks; if the saw is too high, make a platform to stand on. A floor mat is recommended when standing on concrete. The generally recommended table height is about level with the elbows or slightly lower. Consider the advantages of using a stool. Or, another good option is to attach your machine to a low stand designed for use with a chair. An office-type chair with wheels provides comfort and mobility. (See Illus. **3–2** on page 111.)

6–9. ▶ **Standing for long periods hunched over the saw may cause back, shoulder, and neck strain. Notice the use of goggles, dust mask, hold-down, and floor switch.**

Carpal Tunnel Syndrome

Carpal tunnel syndrome may develop in the wrists of serious scroll-sawers who have removed their hold-downs or beginners who have trouble keeping their work from jumping up and down on the saw table. If you subconsciously and consistently apply downward pressure with your arms, you may be causing serious wrist strain and exposing yourself to the incipient stages of the nonreversible condition known as carpal tunnel syndrome. If you press to the point of tiring your hands or if your fingers start to tingle after excessive sawing, then ease up and use the hold-down whenever possible.

Dealing with Wood Dust

More and more research is revealing the serious health risks associated with wood dust. Scroll saws are miniature dust factories. Dust created by the small teeth of scroll-saw blades is too often given less than sufficient concern. Just dust in itself can be annoying. Inhaling dust from any kind of wood can be risky, but dust from certain species poses more serious health threats than others. Individuals also react differently, with some people having immediate adverse reactions and others not recognizing symptoms until years afterward, when it is too late.

Some of the more commonly used woods known to be hazardous in various levels of intensity are alder, ash, beech, birch, cedar, cocobolo, Douglas fir, ebony, elm, hemlock, iroko, limba, mahogany, makore, mansonia, maple, myrtle, oak, opepe, padauk, pine, poplar, purpleheart, sassafras, satinwood, spruce, walnut, wenge, willow, and yew.

Resin Dust and Plastic Fumes

Many scroll-sawers cut Baltic birch and other plywoods, medium-density fiberboard (MDF), particleboard, and other man-made products bonded or coated with adhesives, plastic resins, and chemicals. It is common sense to avoid breathing dust from these products. Inhaling dust and fumes from scroll-sawing plastics and other materials may have serious health consequences. One expert warns that fumes may be toxic. He advises the use of a shop vacuum with a long hose located close to the cutting action to pull and direct fumes away from the operator. Check with your plastics and other material suppliers about such hazards.

Reactions to Wood Dust

Reactions to wood dust vary in severity. Some people become increasingly sensitive to certain woods the more they are exposed to them. Skin irritation, nausea, watery eyes, headaches, and sneezing are some typical warning signs. Serious respiratory problems and cancer of the nose, throat, or lungs are much more serious conditions, as are adverse reactions to the digestive and nervous systems and heart—all of which may be traced, to some extent, to wood dust. If you are a smoker, your risks are compounded.

One of the worst scenarios is using a scroll saw with a nonadjustable blower that directs sawing dust directly toward the upper body of the operator (refer to **6–2**). Using a dust mask and retrofitting your saw with an adjustable blower accessory that directs the sawdust to the side or away is only a partial solution. Adjustable dust blowers simply move the dust elsewhere. The seriousness of the dust problem is compounded by the fact that one cannot see the fine microparticles of dust that hang in the air for hours and even days that need to be removed. Both visible and invisible dust is best handled when it is properly vacuumed away or collected in a suitable air filter.

Devices for Alleviating Dust

Fans, Filters, and Vacuum Systems

Fans, filters, and vacuum systems used alone or in combination with each other are solutions to alleviating dust problems (**6–10**). One popular and economical setup is to use fans and a furnace filter to gather airborne dust (**6–11**). This same system also works well next to hand and power-driven carving and sanding stations.

Shop Air-Filtration Devices

Shop air-filtration devices (**6–12**) are being added to workshops by woodworkers concerned about dust problems. These operate quietly and filter the air several times per hour, depending on the shop size, the filter efficiency, fan and motor sizes, and the CFM (cubic-feet-per-minute) ratings.

6–10. ▶ Safety accessories: eye, dust, and hearing protection. Notice the Power Visor shown in the rear. This highly recommended product has a battery-powered fan that draws in air and filters it before it flows over the face.

6–11. ▶ A double-fan setup creates an airflow that carries dust to the furnace filter taped to the larger, square household fan at the right.

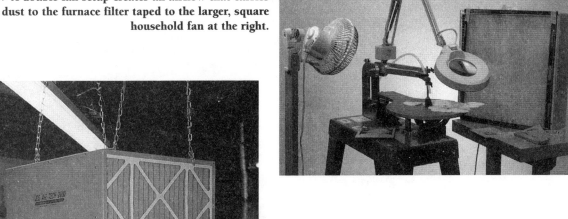

6–12. ▶ This ceiling-mounted air-filtration system quietly filters the shop air several times per hour, removing invisible and dangerous dust particles.

Vacuum Systems

Many saw manufacturers are adding special ports and dust-collecting enclosures to vacuum away falling sawdust from under the saw (**6–13**).

The Hegner saws have a "dust-removal-system" accessory that provides vacuum collection both above the workpiece and below the saw (**6–14**). Although there are some minor inconveniences associated with using a vacuum tube positioned close to the blade, the trade-offs are minimal. Occasionally, the suction lifts small areas of the pattern or brings up small waste pieces from the cut that obstruct the tube entrance.

The problems with using most portable shop vacuums to collect sawdust at the scroll saw is their loud noise and that they often must run all the time. Newer shop vacuums are available, however, that operate

6–13.▶ This bench-top saw features a lower vacuum port.

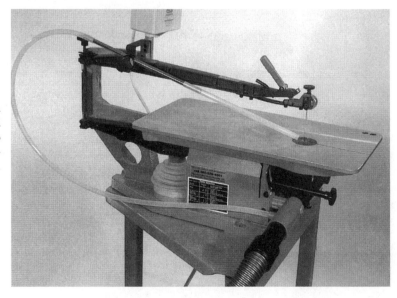

6–14.▶ Hegner's vacuum system removes dust through a tube located behind the blade. The dust is carried to a large under-the-table port that connects to a shop vacuum.

very quietly. Many can be switch-activated from the scroll saw (even with a foot switch) (**6–15 and 6–16**), so they only run when the scroll saw is turned on. More importantly, some shop vacuums can now be fitted with filters that deliver a 5.0- to 1.0-micron filtration. Typically, shop vacuums remove only 50 microns, which is roughly the smallest particle size visible with good eyes.

6–16.▶ **The automatic switching feature on this Fein vacuum operates the scroll saw and vacuum simultaneously with the saw's foot switch.**

6–15.▶ **A Hegner saw equipped with its dust-removal system, and a Fein shop vacuum with a 5.0 micron-filtration capability.**

CHAPTER SEVEN

PATTERNS & LAYOUT

atterns are drawings that outline the shape of the object to be cut (7–1 to 7–4). Layout refers to directly marking the work with lines that locate joints, holes, or areas that are to be cut. The eventual quality of work produced on the saw depends upon the accuracy of the pattern or layout. Sharp, crisp, and smooth flowing lines are essential.

There are thousands of patterns available today in one form or another. Pattern quality ranges from very poor and incomplete to excellent with all details and fabricating instructions. This chapter will examine some typical patterns and discuss ways of enlarging or sizing them to satisfy your specific needs. Tips for finding and developing your own patterns are also included, along with information about transferring and bonding photocopies of the pattern to the workpiece.

7–1. ▶ Samples of high-quality patterns. Notice the light shading, fine outlines, and smooth, flowing curves. The line shading (lower left and right) usually suggests which way to orientate the pattern to the grain direction of the wood.

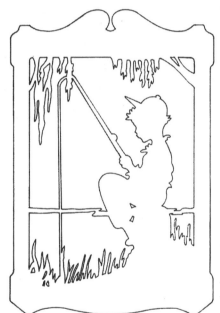

7–2. ▶ Fretwork patterns—unshaded at left and shaded at right.

7–3. ▶ Fully blackened patterns such as these are less desirable than patterns with light gray shading. With patterns of this type, it is hard to distinguish the dark saw blade from the pattern.

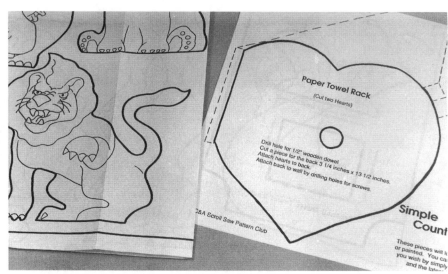

7–4. ▶ Be wary of crude patterns such as these. Notice the thick, irregular, and sloppy line work, the lack of shading, and uninteresting designs.

PATTERN TYPES AND SOURCES

Patterns can be obtained from a variety of sources, including:

1. Books filled with patterns that can be traced, copied, or enlarged. (See Scroll-Saw Books by Patrick Spielman on pages 344 and 345.)

2. Mail-order pattern companies that sell one or more patterns at a time.

3. Magazines.

4. Your own designs or computer-generated art.

Layout aids such as a compass, rule, square, and special templates are often helpful. A template is a purchased or shop-made, trace-around pattern made of a thin, stiff material such as cardboard, plastic, or thin plywood. Illus. **7–5 to 7–7** are examples of several kinds of purchased template made from thin plastic.

Simple shapes are easily and more quickly laid out using templates, especially when making many identical pieces (**7–8**). Depending upon the complexity of the design, templates are easy to make and use. More complex patterns can be converted to reusable templates by simultaneously sawing template material along with a pattern-guided cut (**7–9 to 7–13**).

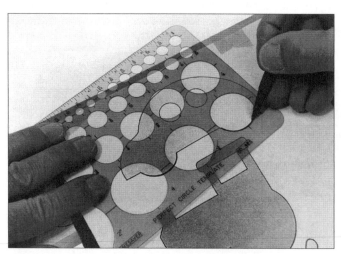

7–5. ▶ A circle template helps to lay out perfect arcs and circles.

7–6. ▶ A stencil type of template.

7–7. ▶ Trace-around plastic-letter templates.

7–8. ▶ Shop-made templates such as these are ideal for laying out simple shapes quickly.

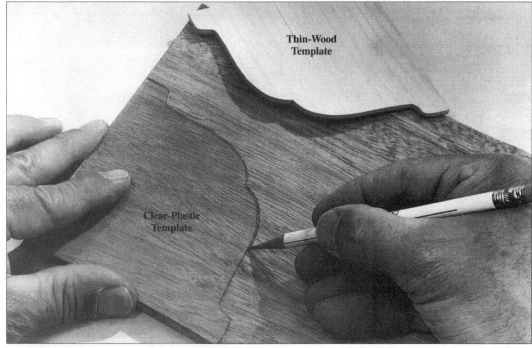

Thin-Wood Template

Clear-Plastic Template

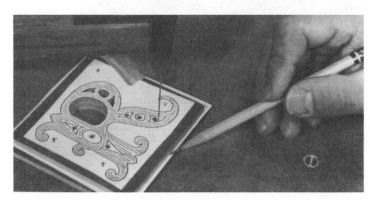

7–9. ▶ A stiff piece of tagboard or file-folder material inserted between two pieces of wood that have been tacked together will provide a reusable template when the original pattern is sawn.

7–10. ▶ The finished template.

7–11. ▶ Tracing the template.

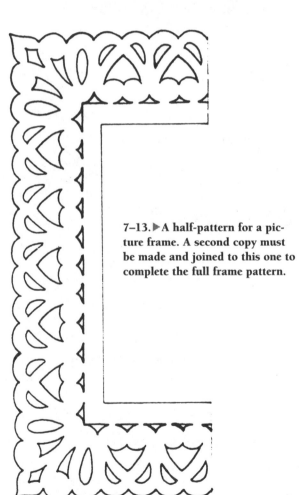

7–12. ▶ A template that was simultaneously sawn with a wooden part preserves the design for future use.

7–13. ▶ A half-pattern for a picture frame. A second copy must be made and joined to this one to complete the full frame pattern.

ENLARGING OR REDUCING PATTERNS

Enlarging or reducing patterns is best accomplished with the help of the modern office photocopy machine (**7–14**). Good photocopiers are capable of enlarging up to 200 percent in one-percent increments. Many local libraries have enlarging copiers for public use, as do office and copy shops located in most municipalities. Check your Yellow Pages for the nearest location.

One word of caution about making exceptionally large photocopies from small originals: some machines will distort the copy somewhat if enlarging over 200 percent. This is especially critical when enlarging clock, furniture, or other patterns that have interlocking or multiple parts that must fit together.

7–14.▶ An office copy machine with enlarging and reducing capabilities is a tremendous help for today's serious scroll-sawer.

Sizing Patterns with a Proportional Scale

A proportional scale (**7–15**) is an inexpensive device that is used to determine precisely how much to enlarge or reduce a pattern on a copy machine to get it at a specific, predetermined size. It eliminates all guesswork in trying to make a photocopy a certain size, thereby saving time and expense. A proportional scale is easy to use, and every scroll-sawer should have one. These are readily available at art-supply stores and via mail order. Illus. **7–15 to 7–18** show how to use a proportional scale to enlarge a letter pattern to a specific new size.

Tip: Sometimes a nice piece of wood that is just a little small for the intended pattern can be used by reducing the pattern slightly. Use the proportional scale to determine the percentage of reduction that allows for fullest use of the stock.

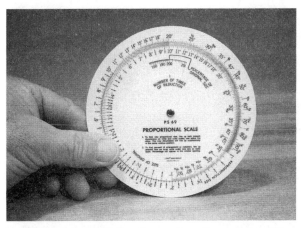

7–15.▶ A proportional scale consists of two discs with a common pivot. Scaled divisions are marked around the outside of each disc.

7–16.▶ The problem: An original pattern of a letter design measures 1¹¹⁄₁₆ inches high and has to be enlarged to 3 inches.

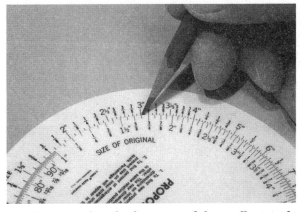

7–17.▶ Step I: Align the dimension of the small original pattern on the inner disc with the dimension you want (3 inches) on the outer disc, as shown.

7–18. ▶ **Step II: Read the percentage given in the window, which in this case is 180 percent. Step III: Set the photocopier and make the enlarged copy. Notice the new 3-inch pattern shown to the left.**

PROJECT DESIGNS

Designing your own scroll-saw projects is often easier than one might expect. The creative scroll-sawer can find near ready-to-use designs from various sources such as wallpaper, coloring books, stickers, and decals (**7–19**), gift wrapping, greeting cards, and books that give profiles of animals, plants, fish, cars, etc. Designing *original fretwork*, however, requires some artistic talent. An easy place to start is to create connecting, geometrical designs, as shown in **7–20**. Included here are just a few fundamental techniques for those who might want to design fretwork patterns themselves and some basic guidelines to help the fretsawer recognize well-designed patterns and fretwork.

7–19. ▶ **Decals applied directly to the wood make quick, colorful puzzles for children.**

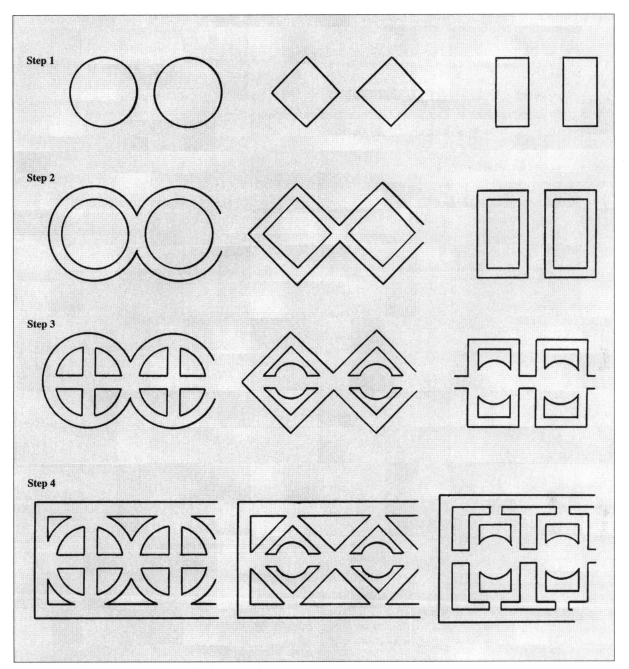

Step 1

Step 2

Step 3

Step 4

7–20. ▶ Steps to develop geometric fretwork patterns.

Start an idea by sketching simple, single-line geo-metric forms (refer to **7–20**). Then progress to double lines and include an internal profile. The idea can be expanded by repeating or continuing the design side by side indefinitely. You can reduce basic, familiar profile shapes to their simplest forms, and then embellish them by tactfully creating internal openings (**7–21**). Notice how a simple silhouette of a swan (**7–22**) can provide the inspiration for a stylized version. The same princi-ple applies when developing a stencil-like pattern, which is nothing more than a simple shape fragmented into pierced, open spaces (**7–23**).

Very ornate designs involving foliage, stems with veined leaves, and flowers demand a higher level of artistic talent. Observe and study actual flowers, leaves, etc., to draw the designs as accurately as pos-sible. It will also help if you analyze the designs of fretwork pieces shown in books and pattern catalogs. You will notice through careful observation that larger pieces are made when certain key elements, lines, and forms are repeated over and over. Also, don't forget to use an enlarging and reducing copy machine to your advantage when creating designs.

Ties

Fretwork is more often intended to be ornamental than functional, but this does not mean that it must be fragile. Designers often incorporate certain connec-tions into their pieces to strengthen otherwise highly delicate frets. One method is to simply surround the design on one or all edges with a frame composed of straight or appropriately curved lines.

7–21. ▶ **Above: Simple shapes transformed to double-line forms. Right: Examples of interior spaces divided with designs that can be as simple or as complex as desired.**

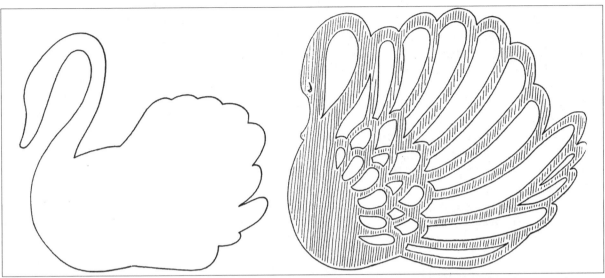

7–22. ▶ Left: Stylizing begins with simple profile shapes that establish essential realistic features. Then proportions can be enlarged, reduced, or modified to emphasize interesting features. Here the feathering detail was developed by single-line work and then converted to double lines, which creates the open space.

7–23. ▶ A stencil scroll-saw design is merely a fragmented plan of a familiar shape that provides pierced, open spaces in a solid background.

Wherever the design touches the border or frame, it is called a "tie" (**7–24**). Many designs would simply fall apart without ties, which bind the design together. They also strengthen the work and, when prudently used, can enhance or accentuate the look of the object.

There are various kinds of tie, but the two most widely used are the tangent and touching ties. Notice how the character of the curve of the tangent tie in **7–24** still remains, and that the straight border line remains unbroken. In the touching tie, also shown in **7–24**, the leaf tips touch the border naturally without distorting the leaf, giving strength as needed.

It is important when you are using a tie that you do not detract from the integrity of the design. You may have to enlarge, reduce, modify, or shift the fretwork piece to ensure that the touching tie looks correct.

Structural ties are ties that are added to connect the design; they are an integral part of the overall ornamentation.

7–24. ▶ Types of "tie." Above left: Tangent tie. Above right: Touching tie. Lower: Examples of structural ties.

Line Continuity

Line continuity (**7–25 and 7–26**) is a reference to the uninterrupted trueness of a line. When straight lines and long curves are broken by different types of tie, the lines really are parts of cutouts, each of which must be drawn individually. This results in a number of successive shorter lines, but you must remember to focus on the integrity of the entire length. Illus. **7–26** depicts line continuity not only in straight and flowing, curved lines but also in the irregularly curved lines of the stems. Before beginning to saw out a project using a purchased pattern, be sure to check the lines for continuity (**7–27**).

Circles and Ovals

Circles and ovals are important and frequent forms for many scroll-saw projects, including picture frames, hand mirrors, signs, plaques, and silhouettes.

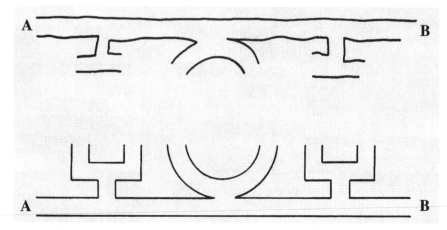

7–25. ▶ Above: Exaggerated imperfections in line continuity. Below: Accurate, crisp line work and perfect line continuity.

7–26. ▶ Another look at good line work. Notice that lines A-B and C-D are crisp and appear continuous, while the other elements of the design have smooth, flowing curves.

7–27. ▶ The excellent visual impact of this work by Jim Reidle typifies the importance of pattern quality and line continuity.

Lay circles out directly onto the wood with a compass in a sharp, crisp line. Ovals, on the other hand, are more complex to draw and are more difficult to lay out. Do not draw any part of a true oval with a compass—even though some drafting textbooks offer a technique known as the "approximate four-center ellipse."

You can draw a true oval, or perfect ellipse, by following the easy steps demonstrated in **7–28 to 7–32**. Although these illustrations do show a compass being used, it is used only to set off distances (as one would use a divider or ruler). It is not used to draw any part of the line that comprises the profile of the ellipse.

Some common oval sizes that are good for picture frames, mirrors, and similar projects are as follows (in inches): 2 × 3, 3 × 5, 5 × 7, 8 × 10, and 11 × 14. *Tip:* Keep oval patterns on file. The proportions may be useful later and they can be quickly enlarged or reduced as needed with a photocopy machine.

Transferring Pattern Lines

The pattern lines can be transferred to the workpiece in several ways. One conventional technique is to hand-trace a pattern placed over carbon or graphite paper (**7–33**). Always check to be sure all lines are traced and transferred to the wood before removing or shifting the position of the pattern. Graphite transfer paper is better because it can be cleaned off the wood more easily than the "greasy" carbon papers. White and dark graphite papers are available in various sizes from arts and crafts supply stores (**7–34 and 7–35**).

When tracing with transfer papers or making layouts directly onto the wood, use circle templates, a compass, or a straightedge to ensure accurate layouts. Freehand tracing is simply not a good way to transfer accurate lines for sawing (**7–35**).

The fastest, most accurate, and easiest way to apply a pattern to the surface of the wood is to tem-

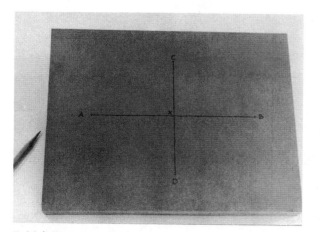

7–28. ▶ **Drawing a true oval. Step I: Lay out the major and minor axes. A-B equals the major diameter and C-D the minor diameter. Both are laid out perpendicular to each other, as shown.**

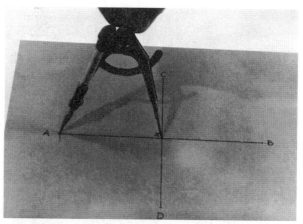

7–29. ▶ **Step II: Set a divider or compass to half the major diameter as shown.**

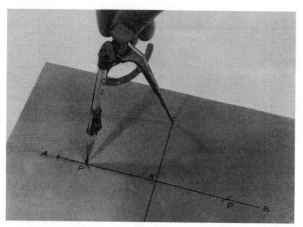

7–30. ▶ **Step III: With C as the base center point, set off P-P on line A-B. C-P is equal to A-X (that is, it is one-half the distance of the major diameter).**

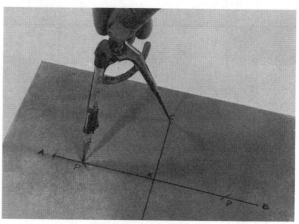

7–31. ▶ **Step IV: Set nails, tacks, or pins at P-P and point C. Pull a string tightly around these three points and tie it securely. Remove the pin or tack at point C.**

7–32. ▶ **Step V: Keeping the string as taut as possible with the pencil, draw a perfectly true oval as shown.**

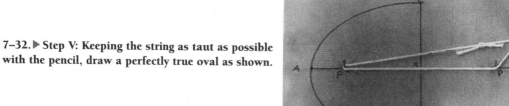

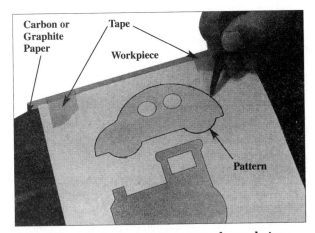

7–33. ▶ **Transferring a pattern copy to the workpiece involves freehand-tracing over carbon or graphite paper, as shown.**

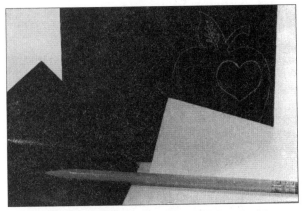

7–34. ▶ **A pattern transferred onto dark wood with graphite paper (left) is more visible when white graphite paper is used as shown on the right.**

7–35. ▶ **The pattern traced freehand with graphite paper at left is not as true or perfect a cutting guide as is a photocopy applied directly to the wood with spray adhesive, as shown at the right.**

porarily bond it directly to the workpiece (**7–36 to 7–38**). Two kinds of adhesive are commonly used: rubber cement and a special spray adhesive with temporary bonding qualities. The author prefers the latter.

Caution: There are many kinds of spray adhesive available, and some have a much more aggressive tack than others. In fact, some scroll-sawers use a permanent spray adhesive that requires a solvent or heat to remove the pattern from the workpiece. This also often leaves a difficult-to-remove residue on the surface that inhibits good finishing.

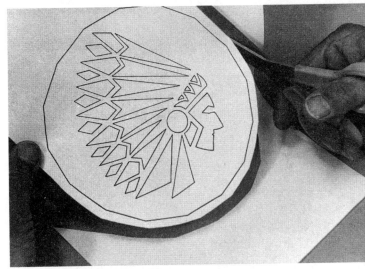

7–36. ▶ **Cutting roughly around the outside of the pattern with scissors to remove excess paper.**

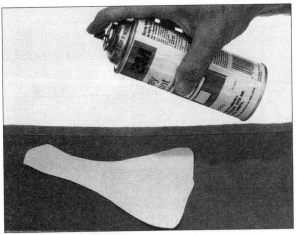

7–37. ▶ **Apply a very light mist of temporary-bond spray adhesive to the back of the pattern.**

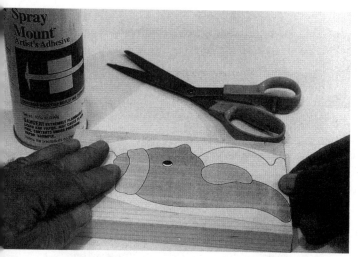

7–38. ▶ **After a few seconds, press the adhesive-coated pattern onto the workpiece. Notice that the bottom straight edge of this pattern is aligned with the previously sawn straight edge of the wood.**

Qualities of a good, temporary-bond spray adhesive are:

1. It delivers a fine, uniform mist rather than "globs" of adhesive.

2. It requires only a very light coverage to get sufficient tack.

3. It holds throughout cutting and allows the sawing of patterns or shapes with very close parallel lines that do not come loose or lift.

4. It allows the pattern to be easily removed upon completion of sawing, as shown in **7–39**.

Here are some helpful tips for using temporary-bond spray adhesives:

1. Sand surfaces and completely remove all dust particles with a tack cloth or compressed air before applying the pattern.

2. Apply adhesive only to the back of the pattern.

3. Make a practice test when using a new adhesive.

4. Strive for thin, uniform coverage.

5. Bring wood and spray adhesive up to room temperature (at least 65° F) before using them.

6. If you still have trouble removing your pattern, apply it to a piece of cardboard and then tack the cardboard to the top of the workpiece. *Tip*: Use empty cereal-box cardboard.

Using a Transfer Tool

A new, inexpensive tool has been developed to transfer photocopied patterns and artwork to wood (**7–40**). Any image in black and white or color that is reproducible with a photocopy machine can easily be permanently applied to a smooth wood surface. This means woodworking patterns of any kind and photos, greeting cards, announcements, and artwork in almost any printed form can be incorporated into special projects in just a matter of minutes. This 16-watt electric tool performs marvelously for transferring highly detailed scroll-saw patterns (**7–41 and 7–42**).

This tool eliminates all of the problems associated with trying to work with glued-on patterns or messy

7–39. ▶ **Patterns should hold sufficiently during sawing, yet remove easily upon completion without leaving any residue on the surface.**

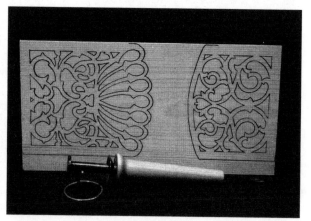

7–40. ▶ **An electric tool is available to transfer smaller-size photocopied patterns and artwork in black and white or color to wood surfaces.**

7–41. ▶ **The pattern is taped to the workpiece surface.**

7–42. ▶ **The tool is moved in a slow, straight line or in small circular motions over the back of the pattern, transferring the image to the wood.**

work with computer printers, depending upon the type of toner used.

The transfer tool has endless possibilities in the woodworking crafts and arts. Photocopies of family portraits or snapshots can be used to personalize special woodworking projects (**7–43 and 7–44**). The tool can also be used to transfer wood-burning designs and to decorate leather and many fabrics. Oil stains (in light tones) and polyurethane and acrylic topcoats can be applied over the wood-transferred images to protect the art and the project. Artists can use the transfer tool to put down pattern lines for decorative painting.

A personalized three-initial accessory is available from the manufacturer that will convert the transfer tool into a small branding iron (**7–45**). The transfer tool is available from woodworking- and craft-supply mail-order companies.

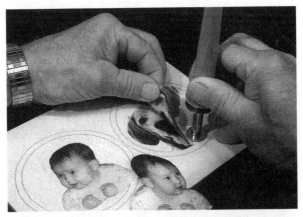

7–43. ▶ **Photos and artwork copied on a black-and-white or color photocopier can be transferred to wood.**

and time-consuming tracings with carbon or graphite papers. The result is a pattern on your workpiece that is as true, sharp, and crisp as the original. It is, however, somewhat time-consuming if used to transfer large patterns.

All you need to do is make a good copy. Place the copy facedown on your workpiece and apply heat to the back with the tool as shown in **7–41 and 7–42**. Move the tool in a circular motion or a straight-line ironing action as you slowly peel back the original to check for a complete transfer. The tool is designed to provide just the right amount of heat concentration to activate the toner delivered to the pattern by the office copy machine. The process may or may not

7–44. ▶ **Samples of personalized ornaments made with a copy machine, transfer tool, and scroll saw.**

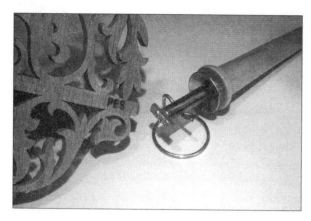

7–45. ▶ **This inexpensive, interchangeable accessory for the transfer tool can brand three initials just ³⁄₁₆ inch high.**

Pattern Placement

Placing patterns on the workpiece prudently can often save material and sawing time. Generally, for maximum strength, it is best to apply the pattern so the longest dimension of the design runs with the grain of the wood (**7–46**). Since good wood is scarce and expensive, always look for ways to conserve stock. (See **7–47 and 7–48** for two ideas.) Where patterns have outside straight edges, it is usually a good idea to place the pattern edge so it is aligned to the edge of the wood.

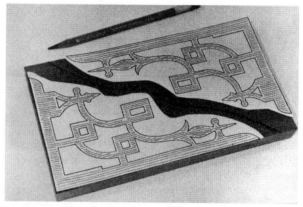

7–47. ▶ **Conserving stock by "nesting" two shelf-bracket patterns to mate each other. Notice that the patterns are aligned with the square corners and straight edges of the board.**

7–46. ▶ **Work ready for sawing. Above: Patterns arranged so the longest dimension runs with the grain. Below: Small cutouts arranged around knots and positioned so that the bottom edges of the pattern are aligned to the straight edges of the board.**

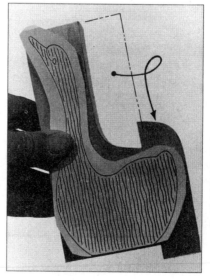

7–48. ▶ **Making a narrow board wide to receive the pattern. Here the waste area of the above right was cut free and glued to the lower portion before applying the pattern.**

Copying Scroll Work

Copying one of your own scroll-sawn pieces to replace a lost pattern or to copy another design can sometimes be done just by placing the actual piece directly onto the copy machine. Another technique is to make a "rubbing," as shown in **7–49**. Use the side, not the point, of a soft lead pencil or charcoal with the paper taped down so it does not shift.

A final note: Be sure to respect the copyright privileges afforded by law to designers and publishers when considering copying patterns. Some designs can be reproduced only for personal, one-time use, and cannot be mass-reproduced or reproduced for resale. In the latter case, be sure to obtain appropriate permission before proceeding.

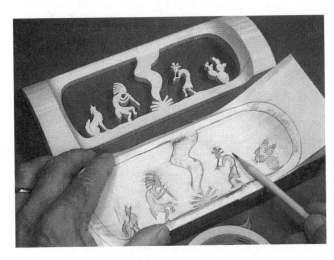

7–49. ▶ Copying an existing piece of scroll-saw work by making a "rubbing" using paper and a soft lead pencil.

CHAPTER EIGHT

SCROLL-SAWING BASICS

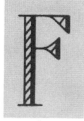 undamental scroll-sawing techniques can be mastered fairly quickly, with accuracy being the early key objective. Once you learn to consistently produce true cuts, the speed of cutting will increase naturally. This chapter provides a discussion of basic but essential techniques that in time will become unconsciously routine.

PREPARING THE SCROLL SAW

Getting the machine ready for use includes many of the obvious details, such as selecting the best blade and installing and tensioning it (8–1). Review the description of the saw you intend to use in Chapter 2. That chapter and the owner's manual should provide all the necessary information about adjustments and instructions.

Blade Tensioning

The proper blade tension is a matter of "feel," which will be discussed in this chapter. Follow the saw manufacturer's instructions. Heavier blades will allow higher levels of tensioning. The sound of a free-running machine will quickly indicate insufficient tension. The saw will make a clattering sound not heard with a properly tensioned saw.

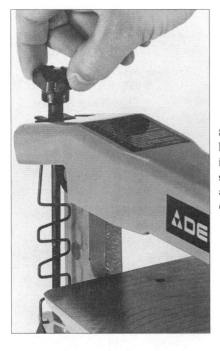

8–1. ▶ With the best blade installed, tension it with the appropriate control.

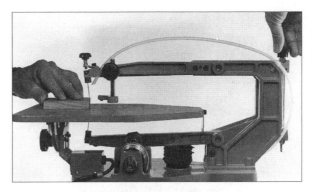

8–3. ▶ Checking blade tension (with the power off) by exerting moderate pressure against the front of the blade. Medium-to-large blades should deflect ⅛ to ³⁄₁₆ inch.

If a blade breaks prematurely, it's likely that there is too much tension. If the blade "drifts" or wanders away from the line of cut and tends to follow the grain, there is insufficient tension.

Most scroll-sawers test for tension with the power off by either "plucking" the blade as one would a guitar string (8–2) or pushing a scrap block against the front of the blade (8–3). When properly tensioned, the plucking produces an appropriate sound. Sound plus feel indicate the best tension level.

Squaring the Saw Table

All of the basic cuts discussed in this chapter will be done with the table adjusted precisely at 90 degrees to the blade. One way to do this is to read the tilt scale and tighten the clamp at the zero setting (8–4). However, you can trust the scale markings on very few machines.

There are two other ways that are much better and more certain. Simply align the table to the blade with a good square (8–5). Another very quick method is done with a piece of thick scrap wood. Make a shallow cut, just deep enough to mark the wood (8–6). Turn the stock end for end and bring it up behind the blade. If the blade lines up with the cut, the table is square (8–7). If it does not, adjust the table slightly (about half of what is off) and repeat the procedure.

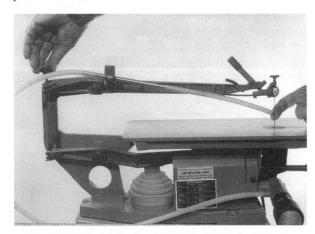

8–2. ▶ Plucking the blade with one's finger to determine resistance and listening to the sound it makes are ways to check for proper tension.

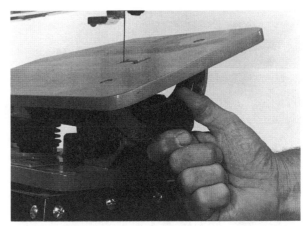

8–4. ▶ Use the table-tilt control knob to clamp the table square to the blade.

8–5. ▶ Check ing the table adjustment with a square.

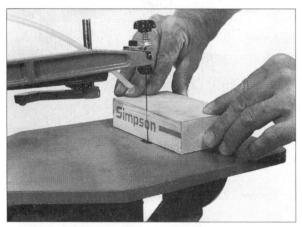

8–6. ▶ Checking table squareness. Cut a shallow test kerf into a thick scrap piece as shown.

8–7. ▶ Rotate the test piece, keeping the same surface on the saw, and bring it and the test kerf to the back of the blade as shown. The table is square when the blade and the test cut align perfectly.

Adjusting the Saw Parts

Adjust the hold-down (**8–8**), dust blower, light, and safety devices as appropriate. Most of the sawing techniques that are shown in the following pages depict the hold-down either raised out of the way or totally removed from the saw. This not only makes close-up and technique photos clearer but also shows how most experienced scroll-sawers actually cut—and that is without a hold-down. The hold-down, however, is strongly recommended for beginners and those with arthritic or weak hands.

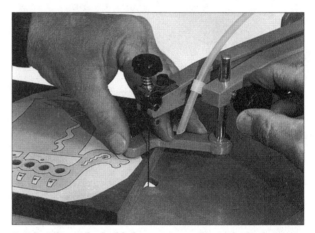

8–8. ▶ Adjust the hold-down to match stock thickness.

SAWING TECHNIQUES

Roughing Out

If your project is to be cut from a large board, apply your pattern close to an end or side and make a roughing cut to give yourself a workpiece that is of a size that is more manageable (**8–9**).

Hand Positions

Hand positions during sawing must be such that you can maintain a relaxed but continuous downward pressure on the workpiece while controlling the direction and speed of feed (**8–10 and 8–11**). To minimize strain, apply only as much downward pressure as required by the nature of the work, which can vary. Since you have two hands and ten fingers, you can alternately move hands (and/or fingers) so one hand controls the work-piece as the other is moved to a new position.

8–9. ▶ Rough-cutting the workpiece from a large board to make it a more workable size.

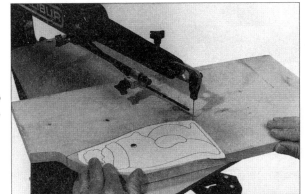

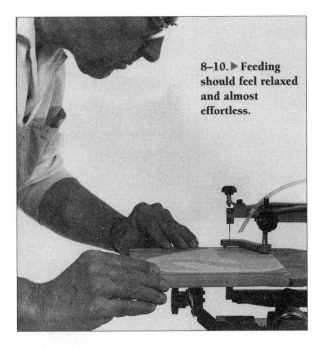

8–10. ▶ Feeding should feel relaxed and almost effortless.

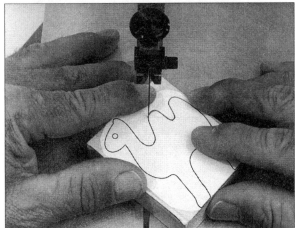

8–11. ▶ Typical hand placements. The thumbs steer the workpiece directly into the blade, while the fingers hold it down and provide pivot points for turning.

Every scroll-sawer will develop holding and feeding techniques he or she is comfortable with. I, for example, feel more in control hooking the thumb of my feeding hand over an edge or end when possible. I feel that I really am not in control when I attempt to feed the work with all fingers on the top surface of the workpiece.

Starting Points and Grain Direction

The best place to start a cut of any design is at a point or corner. Take a simple heart shape, for example; begin the cut so you come into the pattern at the point of the heart (8–12). This is a much better starting point than beginning the cut on the side (8–13). When you came around and met the starting point, it would be difficult to make that part of the cut a flowing curve that intersected smoothly with the start (8–14).

When cutting out a circular shape like a disc or toy wheel, it is best to come into the pattern layout line in a crosscutting (across-the-grain) direction, rather than a ripping (with-the-grain) direction. It is, however, far better to have a starting point on an outside curve, as in 8–14, than an inside curve. It is easier to sand away any knobs or wavy lines that result when "coming around" and meeting up with the starting point.

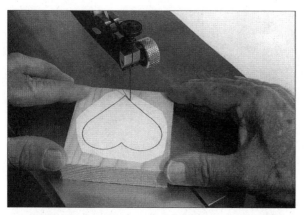

8–12. ▶ **Starting a cut at a point is usually better than beginning it on a curve.**

8–13. ▶ **With solid wood, this is not the best location for starting the cut, because it is on a curve and with the grain.**

8–14. ▶ **The problem arises when coming around to meet the starting point; it is difficult to connect in a smooth, continuous flowing curve.**

Scroll-sawing solid wood is more difficult than sawing plywood because sawing characteristics change as grain direction changes. You'll cut faster with the same feed rate across the grain than with it. Consequently, you always need to know where you are grain-wise, and, when cutting curves, you must be aware of constantly changing resistance that affects cutting speeds. Beginners will also have more difficulty sawing thin materials without slowing the blade speed. By and large, it is best to make practice cuts on cheap softwoods ½ to ¾ inch thick using No. 5 or 7 blades.

Following Cutting Lines

It is a good idea, from early on, to decide whether you will saw on the inside, outside (**8–15**), or exactly on the line (**8–16**) and then try to be as consistent as possible. Later, as your experience grows, you will be able to saw on either side of the line as you wish, or in fact split the line at will. Given the choice, I recommend that beginners always saw on the outside— or, as it is often referred to, the "waste side" (throwaway part)—of the workpiece.

8–15. ▶ **Making a cut following the outside (or waste side) of the line. Saving the line provides an opportunity to sand and reduce the size if necessary without making the object smaller than required. Notice how this cut was started across the grain.**

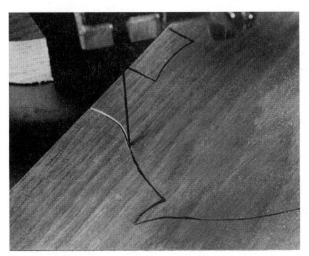

8–16. ▶ Sawing directly on the line is often necessary where the dividing of parts is required and there is no one part designated as a waste side.

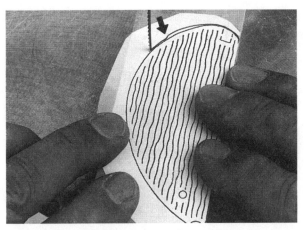

8–17. ▶ Cutting a gradual curve. The arrow indicates how the blade gradually strayed away from the line and then the scroll-sawer abruptly corrected the feed direction.

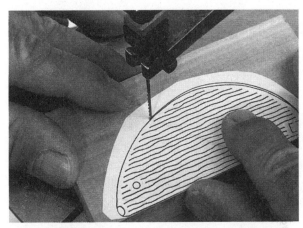

8–18. ▶ "Fairing" a miscut. Gradually bringing the line of cut back to the pattern line (rather than abruptly, as shown in 8–17) produces a shape that is more pleasing to the eye, and, in most cases, the miscut will never be noticed in the finished product.

Sawing Irregular Curves

Sawing irregular curves is much easier than sawing straight lines and true circles or ovals. Practice sawing some gradual curves drawn on scrap stock. When comfortable sawing one-way curves, progress to some gradual S-shaped curves. Finally, practice tighter curves such as those shown in **8–11**. Concentrate on feeding speeds and, if you have a variable-speed machine, slow the spm to coincide with the sharpness of the curves. You must feel confidently in control, but don't be discouraged if, at first, you sometimes wander away from the line of cut. If you do, simply compensate the feed gradually (rather than quickly) to bring the blade back on course.

Learn to use your index finger(s) as a pivot point for rotating the stock into the blade. This is shown in **8–17 and 8–18**, which also present a technique known as "fairing out" a cut to produce a smooth flowing outline that is pleasing to the eye. Remember that even though you are sawing curves, you still must feed the work directly forward into the *front* of the blade. Most beginners and many more experienced scroll-sawers have difficulty correcting a sideways feeding habit that not only causes miscuts but also burning and a higher rate of blade failure.

Sawing True Circles, Arcs, and Ovals

Sawing true circles, arcs, and ovals (**8–19 to 8–21**) requires a fine, sharply drawn pattern line and an unusually high level of sawing skill and patience. It is important to note that many enlarging copy machines distort slightly and will not provide a copy with a true circular shape when enlarged substantially. It is best to make the layout of the desired size circle directly on the workpiece using a compass. Select the widest blade usable and a safe, slow blade speed for optimum control. Start at a point where the cut will be across the grain (**8–19**). Do not allow the blade to cut inside the layout line. Instead, feed the workpiece slowly and directly into the front of the blade, sawing the entire layout line all around (**8–20 and 8–21**).

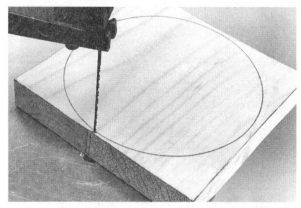

8–19. ▶ **Start circular cuts in solid wood in a cross-grain direction.**

8–20. ▶ **When the cut comes around to the starting point, a small dimple may remain as shown.**

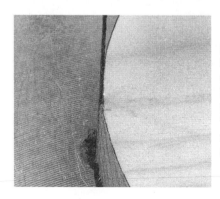

8–21. ▶ **Carefully use the side of the blade as a file to rasp and "fair" the cut, removing the dimple.**

Sawing Straight Lines

The scroll saw is not particularly designed nor is it usually expected to make perfect, true, and long straight-line cuts. Don't use the scroll saw if other machines such as a table saw are available to handle the crosscutting and ripping jobs at hand. There are times, however, when you must use what you have, and most scroll-sawing jobs, like it or not, include a variety of short straight-line cuts that must be made either directly across the grain (crosscutting), with the grain (ripping), or obliquely to the grain (**8–22 and 8–23**).

By and large, it is best to cut straight lines freehand, following a true layout line as when cutting curves. Guide fences and other stock-guiding devices used on band saws, table saws, and other machines do not work effectively on scroll saws. The narrower blade of the scroll saw tends to follow the wood's grain. And, as you know, some blades (for example, milled and stamped blades) cut or lead to one side. (Refer to Chapter 5.)

The keys to straight-line cutting are:

1. Use a wide blade when possible.

2. Use a ground blade or one with equal set on both sides of the blade.

3. Compensate feed direction two to five degrees when using milled or stamped blades (refer to **8–22 and 8–23**).

4. Use controllable feed rates and blade speeds that match the material being cut.

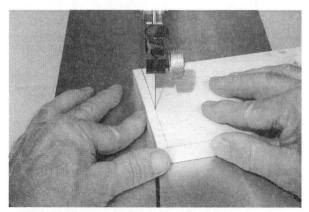

8–22. ▶ **Making a straight-line cut parallel to an edge or end. Here a milled blade is used; this type of blade requires a slight angular compensation in the feeding direction.**

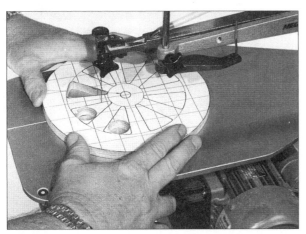

8–23. ▶ Scroll-sawing the straight-line spokes of a plywood wheel.

Cutting Sharp Outside Corners

Producing clean, sharp corners when called for is another benchmark of scroll-sawing craftsmanship. To cut sharp outside corners easily, make a looping cut into the waste area (**8–24**).

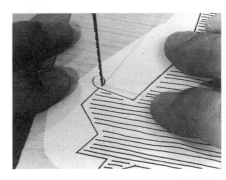

8–24. ▶ Completing a looping cut into the waste area and advancing in a new direction as shown produces a sharp outside corner.

Making Sharp Inside Cuts

Sharp inside cuts (**8–25**) can be made in various ways. One of the easiest and surest methods is:

1. Saw into the corners (**8–26**).

2. Stop, back up about ⅛ to ¼ inch, and advance again slightly, widening the kerf on the waste side (**8–27**).

3. Stop the feed, turn the work, and advance it in the new direction (**8–28**).

Sometimes, however, the job may be such that there is no waste area to cut into. Typical examples are when cutting puzzles or making segmentation projects where there is no waste. In such cases, you must exercise an "on-the-spot" sharp turn. (Refer to pages 186 and 187.)

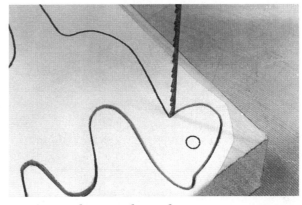

8–26. ▶ Stop the cut at the inside corner.

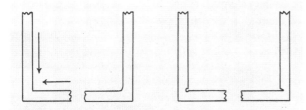

8–25. ▶ Examples of inside corner cuts. The best one, on the far left, is made by sawing inward from two directions or properly employing an on-the-spot technique. All the other corners show common faults.

8–27. ▶ Back up and widen the kerf, stopping again at the line.

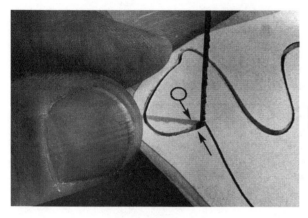

8–28. ▶ **With the kerf widened, reposition the workpiece and advance it, cutting in the new direction.**

Making Inside Cutouts

Making inside cutouts (**8–29 and 8–30**), also known as piercing- or internal-cutting, is a very fundamental scroll-sawing procedure. Essentially, the very same sawing techniques are employed as when making outside cuts. The only difference is that each inside cut begins from a hole drilled into the waste area through which the blade has been threaded. The starting holes are also called "saw-gate," "blade-entry," "pilot," "access," or "piercing" holes.

Exercising some basic logic when deciding just where to drill layout holes in the waste area can save

8–30. ▶ **Sawing narrow inside openings.**

8–29. ▶ **Threading the blade to saw an inside opening. Notice the location of the blade-entry hole. A layout made with red pencil is easier to follow than a black line.**

sawing time and provide the best starting point (**8–31**). Basically, it is best to start at a corner or point. When sawing round holes and the like, it is again best to start the cut in a cross-grain direction (refer to **8–29 and 8–31**). When perfectly true holes or a series of true round openings is required, it is best to drill or bore them to the finished size if possible (**8-32**).

Caution: Certain woods and some plywood will tear the grain when drilling, so be sure to take appropriate cautions:

1. Do not drill too close to the layout line.

2. Drill with higher bit speeds (rpm's) and slower feed rates to get cleaner holes.

3. Use a waste backer held tightly under the workpiece for support and to minimize bottom tear-out.

4. Use a drill press to ensure true vertical holes.

5. Finally, remove any bottom feathering or tear-out fibers with sandpaper as shown in **8–33** before starting to saw.

Saving the inside cutout is sometimes required such as when making puzzles and when doing segmentation, intarsia, and other techniques. In such cases, you need very small entry holes that are best drilled right on the line in corner areas, or at the most inconspicuous locations possible (**8–34 and 8–35**).

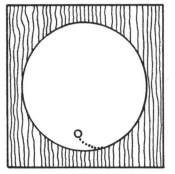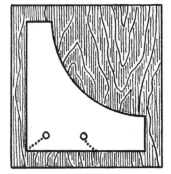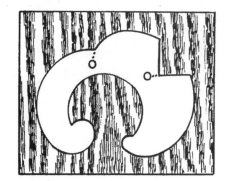

8–31.▶ Various internal openings and suggested starting-hole locations.

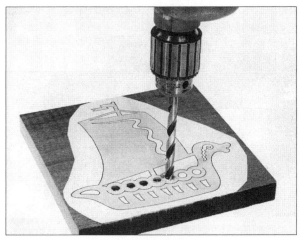

8–32.▶ Drilling or boring round inside openings is often faster than sawing them, and the results will be more consistent in size and shape.

8–33.▶ Removing exit-side grain tear-out or splintering to ensure the workpiece will rest flat on the saw table.

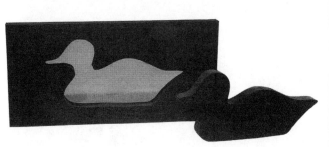

8–34.▶ Here, "positive" and "negative" shapes have been sawn simultaneously with no waste.

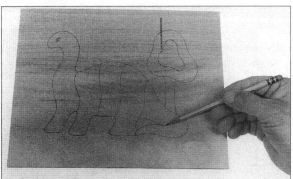

8–35.▶ This tray-type puzzle pattern requires two very small blade-threading holes drilled on the line because there is no waste.

On-the-Spot Turns and Cornering

On-the-spot turns and nonstop cornering are skills that require practice. An on-the-spot turn is the ability to spin the workpiece on a very small radius that actually equals just one half of the blade's width. On-the-spot turns can be used to saw both inside and outside corners when cutting thick or thin stock. Blade widths, however, should be relatively proportional to the thickness and kind of stock being cut, but the cleanest corners are made with narrower blades rather than larger-size blades.

Spinning the workpiece around on the blade is a new experience and technique for woodworkers accustomed to conventional band-sawing techniques. Instead of making the "spin" (turn) slowly, which is the usual way, hold down on the work while turning it as quickly as you can. (Study **8–36 to 8–38**.) Don't become alarmed if the first time or so the blade catches in the workpiece and chatters up and down on the table. Practice sharp corner cuts using a hold-down. Continue practicing 180-degree on-the-spot turning as shown in **8–36 to 8–38** until you can do it with confidence. The ability to make on-the-spot turns permits sawing sharp inside or outside corners nonstop.

An example of a simple job requiring sharp corner cuts is shown in **8–39**. The cuts are made nonstop from start to finish. Illus. **8–40** shows a sawing imperfection caused by using a wide blade to make a sharp on-the-spot turn in softwood. This defect is sometimes referred to as a "turn mark" or "spin gap." If you must use a wide blade, it is best to make this cut with two inward cuts, as shown in the photo.

Another technique is to intentionally saw a radius, rounding the corner and then "cleaning it up" later. Illus. **8–41 and 8–42** demonstrate this technique. Sawing sharp outside angles or corners such as shown in **8–43** can result in broken-off points when you have short cross-grain. This is true with plywood as well as solid wood. In this example, it is best to cut from point A to point C, rather than from point C to point A.

The "backing-in" technique is a very useful trick to employ when sawing acute inside angles, exterior scallops, and similar tight cuts. This technique saves sawing time, but more important, it is a good alternative to on-the-spot cornering that will eliminate blade-turning (or spin) marks. To effectively employ this technique, the saw table must be adjusted perfectly square to the blade.

8–36. ▶ **Practicing on-the-spot turns. Here the feed is stopped and pressure is applied to the left side of the blade as the work is spun quickly around the blade. The left finger acts as a pivot point.**

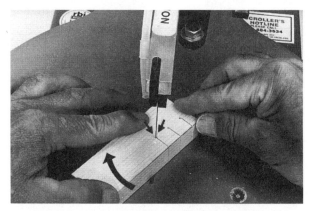

8–37. ▶ **Continuing an on-the-spot turn. The pressure is shifted from the side to the rear of the blade as the stock is spun quickly around the blade.**

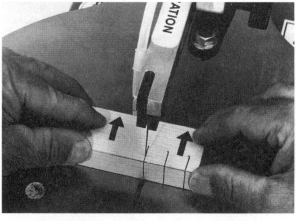

8–38. ▶ **Completing an on-the-spot turn. Here the blade exits on the inbound cut.**

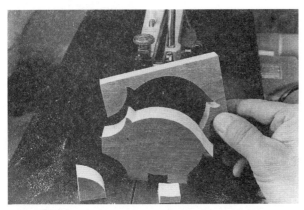

8–39. ▶ Sharp, on-the-spot, quick cornering completes this cut-out project in just seconds.

8–40. ▶ Above: A serious defect, called a "turn mark," results when an excessively wide blade is used to make an on-the-spot turn in softwood. Hardwood will likely show a burn. Below: A cleaner angle is achieved using the same blade but with two inward cuts.

8–41. ▶ Rounding a sharp turn that will be cleaned up later. Notice how here the feed must be carefully controlled to avoid an overcut as the waste is freed.

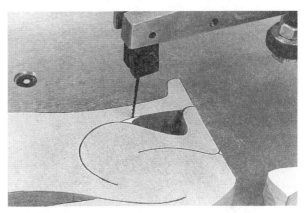

8–42. ▶ "Cleaning up" the sharp inside corner with two short, inward cuts.

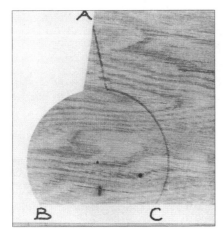

8–43. ▶ To prevent chipped or broken points on sharp, exterior angle cuts such as this, complete the cut sawing into the point from A to C rather than from C to A; the latter would break off the point because the wood becomes weaker as the cut continues toward the point.

The essential "backing-in" steps are:

1. Saw into the corner (**8–44**).

2. Back up slightly and spin the work 180 degrees on the spot with the teeth of the blade toward the waste area (**8–45**).

3. Back the blade all the way into the corner (**8–46**).

4. Continue sawing in the new direction (**8–47**).

SAWING PROBLEMS AND TIPS

Even though the basic cutting techniques are performed as recommended and the resulting sawn shapes are perfect, the quality of the sawn edges may be less than desirable. Typically, some softwoods tend to have rough-sawn edges, and certain hardwoods may yield burned or charred cut surfaces. Either condition is not good since it affects subsequent finishing and is perceived as poor workmanship.

Basswood, butternut, cedar, some pines, redwoods, and other softwoods require extremely sharp tools to sever their grain fibers cleanly. Slow feed rates are usually directly proportional to the quality of cut. The tendency for the fibers to bend or tear out below the line of cut is much more likely at higher feed rates, as shown by the top test piece in **8–48**. The fibers of wet wood will not cut as cleanly as material properly dried. Modifying the blade to provide more side clearance by and large has little effect on improving the cut-surface quality of most softwoods. *Tip:* When starting a project, make some test cuts on the scrap side of the cutting line and inspect the sawn edges. If they are not what you want, slow the speed and try other blades in other sizes and styles.

Cherry (**8–49 and 8–50**), maple, birch, and oak can char and even burn severely on the sawn edges. This condition is indeed extremely frustrating and almost

8–44. ▶ Saw along one "leg" of the angle, all the way to the point or corner.

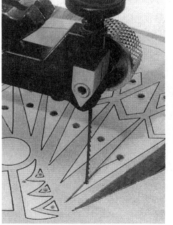

8–45. ▶ Back up a short distance and make a 180-degree on-the-spot turn with the teeth facing the waste side of the line.

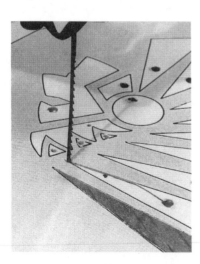

8–46. ▶ Back the blade completely into the apex of the angle.

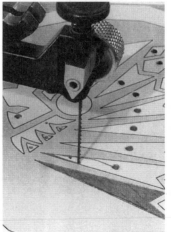

8–47. ▶ Continue sawing in the new direction.

impossible to remove once it happens. Always make test cuts when using these materials (**8–49**).

Cherry seems to be the worst of these materials, with the highest tendency to burn. Modifying the blade's side clearance helps considerably. (Refer to page 142 for more on modifying blades.) Still, however, you must always feed directly into the front of the blade and avoid any side pressure during feeding that causes the blade to rub against the side(s) of the kerf. Sometimes even a hesitation in the feed can cause a line-like burn. Obviously, use sharp and coarse blades when possible.

The *packaging tape technique* (**8–50**) has a sensational effect on the scroll-sawing process and virtually eliminates all of the burning tendencies described

above. When inexpensive clear or colored plastic packaging tape is applied over the line of cut, it somehow cools the cutting action. It is unbelievable how effective this technique is! Even if the blade is loaded with a charred, pitch-like residue, the wood cuts cleanly as soon as the tape is applied over the cutting line(s). Incidentally, duct and masking tape have similar results and may be worth testing on problem woods if they are on hand.

When using tape, it is usually desirable to apply the tape directly to the wood and the pattern over the tape. Thus, you can use pattern adhesive and create a more aggressive bond of the pattern to the tape. The tape removes easily and cleanly from the wood's surface.

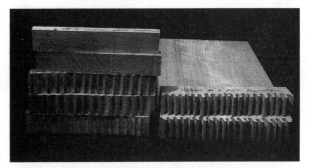

8–49. ▶ Test cuts in cherry. The left top piece was rip-cut with a regular Olson No. 9 skip-tooth blade. The second piece on the left was crosscut with same blade. The third piece shows tight radius cuts made with Olson's No. 9 PGT blade, unmodified. The fourth piece shows tight radius cuts made with Olson's No. 9 regular skip-tooth blade, unmodified. The bottom piece shows tight radius cuts made with Olson's No. 9 double-tooth blade, unmodified.

The pieces on the right show cuts made with an Olson No. 9 PGT blade that was modified for additional side clearance; it clearly made the cleanest cuts.

8–48. ▶ Crosscuts in butternut, all from the same board. The top left piece was cut with a No. 9 Olson double-tooth blade at a feed rate of 1 linear inch per 15 seconds. The top right piece was cut with the same blade, but with a feed rate of 1 linear inch per two seconds. The center piece was cut with a modified No. 9 Olson double-tooth blade. The bottom piece was cut with a No. 9 crown-tooth blade and a slow feed rate.

8–50. ▶ The dramatic effect of the "packaging-tape technique." Three pieces of ⅞-inch cherry from the same board, all cut with the same blade, Mascot's Woodrunner No.7 reverse-tooth, unmodified blade. The top cuts were made with packaging tape, but only on the top surface. The center piece was cut with the same blade, but without any tape. The bottom piece was cut with the same unaltered blade, but packaging tape was applied to the top surface.

CHAPTER NINE

STACK-CUTTING & CUTTING THICK WOOD

tack-cutting is the process of holding two or more pieces of material together, one on top of the other, and sawing them all at once. This technique may also be called "plural-" or "pad-"sawing.

Sawing one thick piece of wood (9–1) and cutting a stack of thinner wood (9–2 to 9–4) often involve similar preparations and concerns. Successful stack-cutting is obviously an important technique for production scroll-sawers working for profit. A number of identical pieces can be made with little more time and effort than required to make just one piece.

Not all stack-cutting, however, involves sawing major thicknesses. Often, a scroll-sawer needs just two or more identical pieces sawn from thin stock (⅛ to ¼ inch thick). Stack-cutting is still the most practical method and is often employed in thin veneer, inlay, and marquetry work.

9–1. ▶ Sawing a piece of 2½-inch-thick butternut on a scroll saw. Cutting wood this thick involves the same preparations and concerns as when stack-cutting.

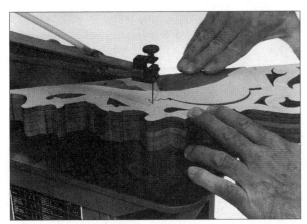

9–2. ▶ Stack-cutting six layers of ¼-inch-thick solid walnut for the project shown in 9–3.

9–3. ▶ Cutting the six identical parts for this hanging plant holder all at once is essentially six times faster than sawing the pieces one at a time.

9–4. ▶ The identical shelf brackets and the fretted sides of this decorative wheelbarrow are typical projects involving stack-cutting.

This chapter will discuss some important precautions and considerations related to sawing materials that are generally considered thicker than usual. A number of methods and tips for holding layers of material together to be stack-sawn are also discussed and illustrated.

SAWING REQUIREMENTS

Sawing wood materials of a thickness that challenges the cutting capacity of your saw can cause unpredictable problems. Most scroll saws cannot effectively saw hardwood equal to the thickness capacity listed or advertised. The machines are just not built sturdily enough. Light- and medium-duty machines that specify a two-inch thickness-cutting capacity will, as a rule, not handle hardwood or plywood stock of this thickness, and even cutting softwoods of this size will be a challenge.

When stack-cutting for production and profit, it is important to evaluate how effectively your saw cuts at full thickness capacity. Various materials will be cut differently, with hardwoods and plywoods being the most difficult. You are likely to find it easier and faster to cut consistently sawing fewer pieces rather than pushing your saw to its limit.

The essential requirements for successful stack-cutting and cutting thick woods are:

1. The table must be adjusted perfectly square to the blade and remain at that position during cutting. If the table is not square to the blade throughout the stack-cutting operation, the bottom piece(s) may end up being sawn smaller or larger in size than the top pattern. The end result is a waste of expensive material and valuable time.

2. A wide, sharp blade with some side clearance and deep gullets to carry out the sawdust has to be used. (Refer to Chapter 5.) When you saw stock that is thicker than the stroke length of your saw, not all of the sawdust is ejected with each stroke. This accumulation of sawdust in the kerf creates more friction and requires a slower feed rate to allow the sawdust to clear out.

3. The saw should be capable of maintaining a higher-than-normal blade tension, and the blade clamps should not allow the blade to slip. If a blade slackens during the cut, the damage may be done before it's detected.

4. The blade action of the scroll saw has to be true. If the blade is not vertical in the cut, has an excessive front-to-back action, or moves in an arc as typical of C-arm saws, the resulting cut may bow out or be nonvertical. Finally, remember that sawing with the grain will be much slower than sawing across the grain. Therefore, the feed should be slowed accordingly without forcing it (**9–5 and 9–6**).

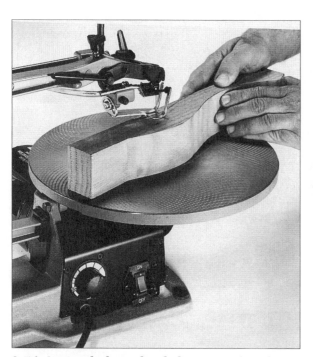

9–5. ▶ **Sawing thick wood with the grain such as this is generally much slower than crosscutting and cannot be forced. Use a high speed, a coarse blade, and a perceptive feed rate.**

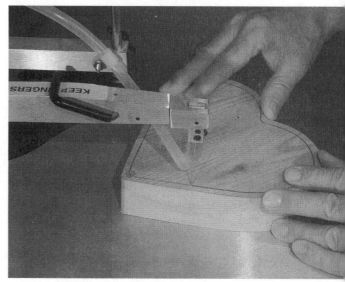

9–6. ▶ **Sawing two-inch-thick butternut.**

STACK-CUTTING GUIDELINES

Stacking woods of unlike colors can cause the sawn edges of lighter woods to take on the color of darker woods. Sawing walnut or padauk with maple in the same stack, for example, will often give the maple dirty-looking edges that are difficult to clean up.

Keeping stacked layers together during sawing can be done in numerous ways. Illus. **9–7** shows a few methods. In all situations, it is important that the layers do not shift. Each layer must be flat and tight to the next without any gaps in between layers. Open spaces between layers may generate interior grain tear-out or chipping when drilling blade-entry holes and when sawing. If the pattern is fairly large and the layers are thin, it may be necessary to apply some sort of pressure or a fastener to the central area to keep the entire surface of the stack tight.

Nails, brads, and tacks are the quickest and easiest fasteners to use. Nailing is not a problem when stacking thicker material, and stacks of thin wood material can be nailed in two different ways. Stacks of thin veneers and ⅛-, ¹⁄₁₆-, or ¹⁄₃₂-inch plywood can be nailed by simply adding a thicker waste piece to the bottom (**9–8 and 9–9**), which is a good idea anyway to minimize bottom tear-out. Another technique I especially like is nailing stacks together over a flat steel surface. This is an especially good technique when stacking layers of exceptionally thin material

9–7. ▶ **Some ways to hold layers of wood together for stack-cutting. From left to right: staples, tape, beads of hot-melt glue on the edges, and brads or nails.**

9–8. ▶ **Here, six layers of ¹⁄₁₆-inch plywood are fastened to a ¼-inch-thick scrap backer with brads.**

9–9. ▶ **Six identical parts cut from thin plywood.**

such as ¹⁄₁₆- or ¹⁄₃₂-inch stock. Simply drive the brads or nails completely through the stack until the points strike the steel plate below (**9–10**). The steel will peen the nail points on the bottom side, securing the bottom layer without worry of the protruding points scratching the saw-table surface (**9–11**).

Other stack-holding methods are staples, double-faced tape, and dots of glue. A staple gun can often be used to secure the edges of thicker stock (**9–12 and 9–13**). Staples can also be driven through the surface when stacking a small number of thin materials (refer to **9–7**).

Double-faced tape is tricky. It is best applied only to waste areas of the work, but it is not necessarily limited to that. In general, use less double-faced tape than you think is necessary. If it is applied correctly to smooth, dust-free surfaces, it can be very difficult to remove. It is especially tricky when holding areas of the work that are highly delicate.

Glue, like tape, should be used conservatively.

Thicker and heavier work gives you more fastening options, providing you have a scroll saw capable of making square cuts in thick stock (**9–14 and 9–15**). To be sure, always make a test cut on stacks of like scrap material. Press the layers tightly together so there are no gaps between layers. Tight layers are more difficult to achieve with double-faced tape and drops of hot-melt glue than with nails. Nailing, however, does not work well for stacking plastics, in which case tape or adhesives may be a better choice.

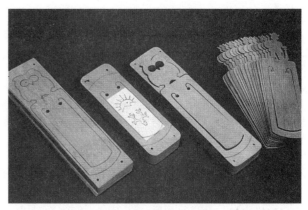

9–11. ▶ **As many as 17 to 20 layers of ¹⁄₃₂-inch Baltic birch are tacked together and stack-cut to produce large quantities of bookmarks.**

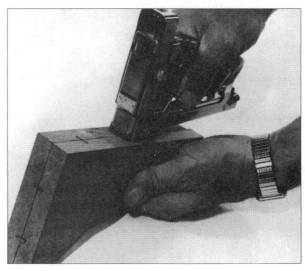

9–12. ▶ **Staples driven into the edges as shown hold these two pieces together for stack-sawing.**

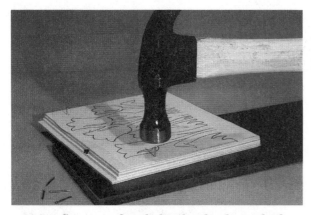

9–10. ▶ **A flat piece of steel placed under the stack of four ¹⁄₁₆-inch layers of plywood will flatten points of brads or nails when they are driven through the bottom plywood layer.**

9–13. ▶ **Removing the staples from the sawn stack.**

9–14. ▶ Stack-cutting thick layers is an important process for making Victorian gingerbread pieces such as this corbel.

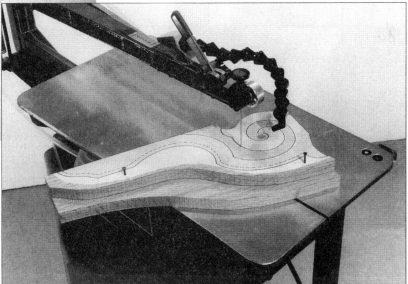

9–15. ▶ Stacking two thick bracket pieces that will become the outsides of a heavy, laminated corbel.

CHAPTER TEN

SAWING THIN &
SMALL STOCK

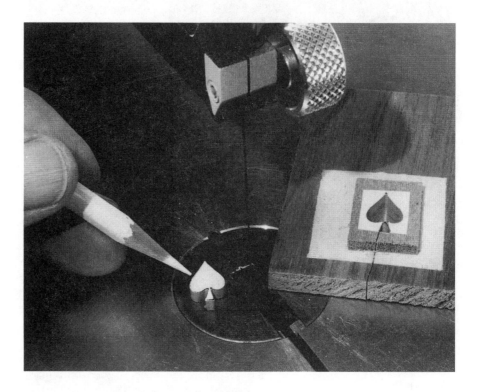

 iniatures (**10–1 to 10–3**), models, jewelry, and thin overlays and inlays are typical scroll-saw projects that involve the cutting of small and/or thin parts. All of this work is relatively similar in nature and a reasonably safe scroll-sawing activity. There are, however, a few precautions, preparations, and tips offered in this chapter that will be helpful to the novice. In addition to sawing veneers and tiny wooden parts, these same techniques can be applied to cutting other small and thin materials, including metals, plastics, paper, leather, and fabric.

Thin, soft sheet metals such as copper, brass, and aluminum can be cut on a limited, short-term basis using fine, skip-tooth woodcutting blades. The edges may be ragged unless precautions are taken. When doing more extensive work, use metal-cutting blades from a No. 1 size and upward as appropriate for the thickness of metal being cut. Thin veneers can be sawn with skip- and double-tooth blades in the 3/0 to No. 2 sizes. Use 2/0 to No. 2 crown-tooth blades for plastics up to ⅛ inch thick. (Review Chapters 19 and 20 if necessary.)

In addition to selecting the best blades for the work at hand, other concerns are that the work over the blade opening of the saw table is supported (**10–4**); that the blade speed is slow and the feed rate is controlled; and that blade tear-out is minimized.

10–3. ▶ **Miniature gingerbread trim for a dollhouse by Kirk Ratajesak.**

10–1. ▶ **Comparing the size of this miniature clock by Kirk Ratajesak to a pencil.**

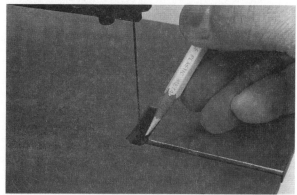

10–4. ▶ **The table openings on most saws are too large to safely support sawing thin stock and small parts that may tip or fall through the opening.**

10–2. ▶ **Miniature furniture by Kirk Ratajesak compared to tweezers used for assembly work.**

SAFETY GUIDELINES

Keep in mind that most serious woodworking accidents happen when attempting to cut parts too small to handle safely. Cutting very small parts on a scroll saw is considered a safe activity as long as a few simple precautions and commonsense safety techniques are practiced. Parts or scraps that drop into or become wedged in the table opening and the placement of fingers too close to the blade are unsafe situations when sawing small parts. Often, standard hold-downs are ineffective and do not work for sawing small parts. *Tip:* Use the eraser end of a wood pencil, not your fingers, when necessary to feed the workpiece or hold it down very close to the blade.

Other dangers include losing feed control or using blades that are too coarse on thin material. In the latter case, the blades catch the edge of the work, causing the stock to flop up and down. The material can bend, tear, or break because of lack of support around the blade area. It is very likely that you'll be using smaller blades than usual that will tend to break more frequently.

When sawing a considerable amount of thin material, adjust your machine to a shorter stroke if your saw has this feature. The short stroke increases efficiency and accuracy.

WORKPIECE SUPPORT AND AUXILIARY TABLES

Providing support under the workpiece as it passes over the table opening and support around the blade can be achieved in various ways, from simply taping down a business card over the table opening to making a special reusable auxiliary table. The business-card trick involves making a cut or punching a hole for the blade in the center of the card and then taping it over the saw-table opening. Illus. **10–5** shows the same idea in which a larger piece of thin plywood or plastic is used. The procedure is to simply drill a very small hole for the blade, thread and tension the blade, and finally tape the plywood or plastic to the table. Illus. **10–6** shows the blade extending through the auxiliary table, with near-zero clearance providing maximum workpiece support all around the blade.

10–5. ▶ **For a quick fix to support small pieces, tape a piece of thin plywood or plastic with a small blade hole to the tabletop.**

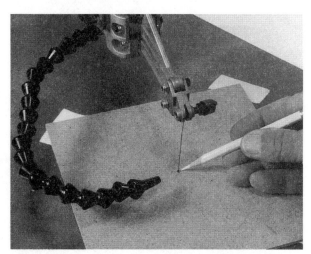

10–6. ▶ **This close-up shows support all around the blade provided by an auxiliary table held in place with double-faced tape.**

Zero-Clearance Table Inserts

Zero-clearance table inserts (**10–7**) are available for a number of scroll saws such as various Delta models. You can also make your own from thin plastic or plywood of appropriate thickness. Simply cut a slot or drill a very small hole for the blade and replace the standard insert with the zero-clearance one that will provide added support to the bottom of the workpiece.

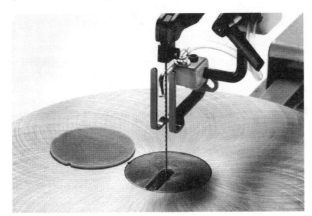

10–7. ▶ Blanks, as shown on the left, are available for making zero-clearance inserts for some machines such as this 20-inch Delta saw.

Reusable Auxiliary Table

Making a reusable auxiliary table that you can quickly pop on or off as needed is another option (**10–8 and 10–9**). You may also want to consider making your auxiliary table of a thicker material equal to or greater than the operating stroke length of your saw. This will bring new and unused teeth of the blade into use, thereby getting extended service from an otherwise dull blade.

BLADE SPEED AND FEED CONTROL

Sometimes thin, soft, or easy-to-cut materials cut so easily it is difficult to control feeding the workpiece and almost impossible to saw accurately. Always try to use a blade speed slow enough to allow for complete feed control. That may be as little as 50 or fewer strokes per minute. If you only have a single-speed saw, or your machine's slowest setting is still too fast, you need to create some counterresistance to slow the overly aggressive cutting action. This can be accomplished by including the workpiece in a stack along with some waste material to thicken the sawing work (**10–10**).

10–8. ▶ Making a reusable zero-clearance auxiliary table that can be quickly put on or removed. Using ⅛-inch or thicker oversized plywood, saw inward; then stop and mark the table shape all around the underside, as shown here.

10–9. ▶ Glue on wooden block stops to keep the table fixed in one location during use.

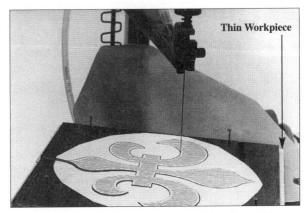

10–10. ▶ Sandwiching very thin material in between waste plywood as shown provides sawing resistance for better control, and the bottom layer minimizes tear-out.

SAWING VENEER

Sawing veneer obviously requires a fine blade (**10–11**). To get the least amount of bottom tear-out, the work should be supported on a waste backer. Even plain, corrugated cardboard support makes a noticeable difference (**10–12 to 10–15**).

10–11. ▶ **Cuts that demonstrate bottom tear-out when sawing veneer. The cut on the left was made unsupported with a No. 5 skip-tooth blade that was obviously too coarse. The center and right cuts were both made with a No. 2/0 blade, but the right cut was made supported on corrugated cardboard.**

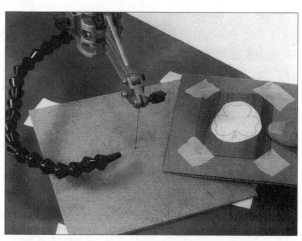

10–12. ▶ **Preparations to saw veneer cleanly. The auxiliary table provides support near the blade, and the workpiece is taped to a waste piece of cardboard.**

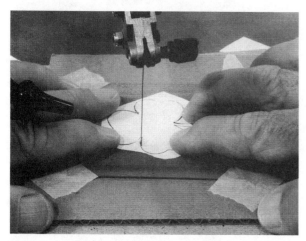

10–13. ▶ **Sawing veneer. Pressure must be cautiously and continuously applied close to the cut to prevent "fluttering" of the workpiece.**

10–14. ▶ **The resulting part is cut clean and splinter-free on the bottom surface.**

10–15. ▶ Sawing very thin peel-and-stick veneer. Bottom tear-out of cuts, from left to right: No. 2 blade with veneer supported on cardboard; No. 2 blade with veneer unsupported; No. 2/0 blade with veneer supported on cardboard; and No. 2/0 blade with veneer unsupported.

SAWING SMALL PARTS

Depending on the size of the work, use an auxiliary table or attach the workpiece to a larger waste piece that is easier to handle and control (**10–16**). With or without an auxiliary table, it will be easier and safer to handle the workpiece (**10–17**).

10–16. ▶ A small cutout is held to a waste piece with double-faced tape. This way, the work can be more easily controlled and cut with your fingers at a safer distance from the blade.

10–17. ▶ The completed cutout.

CHAPTER ELEVEN

COMPOUND-SAWING

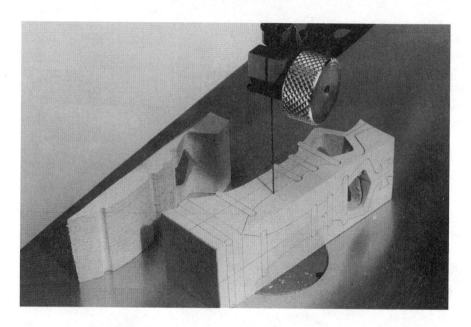

ompound-sawing, also known as double-cutting or three-dimensional sawing, is simply the process of cutting on two or more surfaces of a workpiece (*11–1 to 11–4*). Compound-sawing is one of the more fascinating scroll-sawing techniques. Today, there are at least four books devoted exclusively to compound-sawing techniques and patterns.

Compound-sawing is also a common band-saw operation. It is often employed to make the curved cabriole-styled legs of Queen Anne and Chippendale furniture. The band-sawing technique is also used by many carvers to rough-out larger carvings such as decoy blanks. The scroll-sawer can do much of the same kind of work, but is restricted to making works of a much smaller scale because of the limited thickness-cutting capacities of the scroll saw.

MATERIALS

Most compound-sawing projects require the cutting of thick material, so be sure to review Chapter 9 before undertaking this work. If the project involves very accurate or detailed sawing, you must also select wood that cuts easily. The woods used to make the chess pieces shown in *11–4,* for example, are sugar pine and mahogany. Most scroll-sawers use white pine and a No. 3 or 5 blade for detail-cutting or a Thickwood blade for shapes such as the fish shown in *11–1,* which has gradual curves.

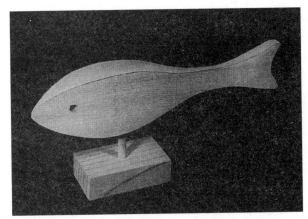

11–1. ▶ **This fish project was cut to shape by compound-sawing with the scroll saw.**

11–2. ▶ **Compound-sawn candlestick spindles.**

11–3. ▶ **Three-dimensional miniature cutouts by Diana Thompson.**

11–4. ▶ **Chess pieces in process by the author.**

SAWING TECHNIQUE

Two fundamental points to remember about compound-sawing are:

> **1.** Be sure the table is set square to the blade.
> **2.** Always be careful not to get your hand pinched between the upper arm and the work-piece (**11–5).**

Basic Technique

Compound-sawing simply involves laying out or applying a pattern on two adjoining surfaces (**11–6 to 11–9**). The pattern does not have to be the same shape on both surfaces. In fact, different-shaped designs are often used to create very interesting projects.

11–5. ▶ **Compound-sawing often involves sawing thick stock. Always be sure you don't pinch your fingers between the arm and the workpiece.**

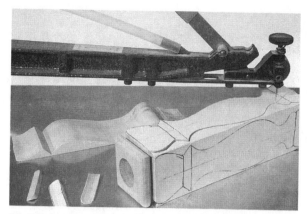

11–6. ▶ **Sawing the spindle for the candlestick project shown in 11–2.**

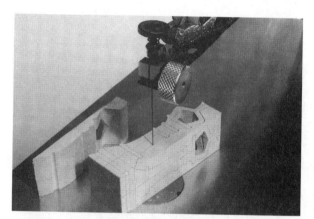

11–7. ▶ **Completing the second cut of a chess piece.**

11–8. ▶ **After the two outside waste pieces have been cut off of one surface, reattach them to the blank. Here, strategically placed spots of glue are applied in the waste areas, or wrap with tape to hold the sawn pieces together.**

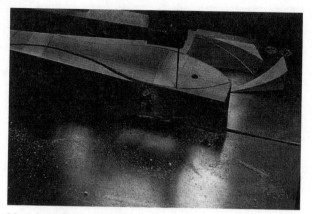

11–9. ▶ **Making the final cut of the fish project shown in 11–1. Notice the wrap of tape used to hold the pieces together.**

Once the workpiece is laid out with the patterns drawn or glued to both surfaces, you have to make a choice as to which of the two surfaces to saw first. Usually it will not make any difference, but sometimes you can save yourself some aggravation by thinking about the sawing sequence. Select the first profile cutting that will have the fewest free scrap pieces once it is cut. After the first profile is cut out, return the scrap or waste pieces to their original locations so you have a fairly complete prismatic shape to safely and effectively cut out to obtain the second profile.

The pieces have to be held secure without any slippage until the second profile cut is completed. Sometimes it is advantageous to drive small nails into the scrap areas, use drops of glue (**11–8**), or use tape to secure the waste pieces while cutting out the second profile shape, as shown in **11–9**. When using glue, strategically locate the drops on the waste pieces so no glue will contact the finished part. Use hot-melt, instant, or yellow glue, allowing it to set before sawing (**11–10 and 11–11**).

Compound-Sawing Piercing or Inside Cuts

Compound-sawing piercing or inside cuts adds to the variety of interesting designs produced by this sawing technique. Notice the inside openings of the chess pieces and the projects shown in **11–12**. Always saw the inside openings (**11–13**) before cutting the outside profiles.

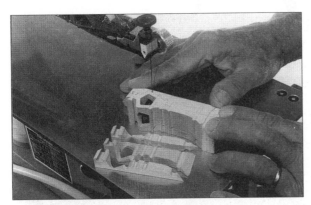

11–10. ▶ Making the final cut of a chess piece.

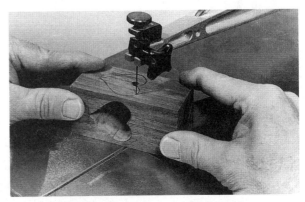

11–13. ▶ Compound-sawing an internal opening.

11–11. ▶ Sawing completed for the candlestick spindle. Also shown is the waste cut from each surface and the two extra square pieces prepared for the base.

Stack-Cutting Compound or Three-Dimensional Shapes

Compound or three-dimensional shapes can be stack-cut to some extent as long as the design is suitable and the stack thickness does not exceed the capacity of the scroll saw. The technique shown in **11–14** was developed by Burt Whitman. It allows him to produce two compound-sawn pieces at once—another timesaving and production-enhancing technique for the scroll-sawer.

11–12. ▶ Openings sawn through two surfaces create these interesting projects. The candle is in a metal cup insert

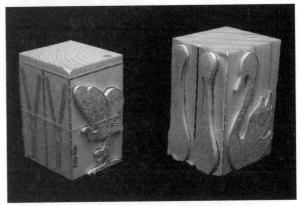

11–14. ▶ Material prepared for stack-cutting three-dimensional shapes. Notice the double pattern applied to one surface.

BEVEL-SAWING
BASICS

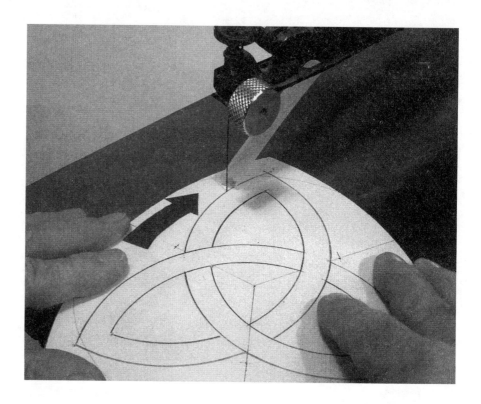

evel-sawing involves any kind of work in which the table is intentionally set so it is not exactly square to the tensioned blade (12–1). Whether the table is adjusted a full 45 degrees or merely 1 degree from a true perpendicular adjustment, the result is still a bevel cut.

This chapter discusses techniques that involve bevel-sawing just one thickness of stock at a time. Bevel-sawing two thicknesses at once is a basic procedure involved in inlay work, which is discussed in the next chapter. Bevel-sawing techniques are also employed in marquetry work and incise carvings, which are discussed in Chapters 14 and 15, respectively.

Depending upon the amount of table tilt, bevel-sawing means that you will be cutting more material than just the actual thickness of the stock. The greater the angle of table tilt, the more thickness of material you are actually sawing and the less intricate the overall shapes must be to minimize problems. A board that is ¾ inch thick, for example, will present almost 1⅛ inches of material to be cut when sawing with the table tilted to 45 degrees.

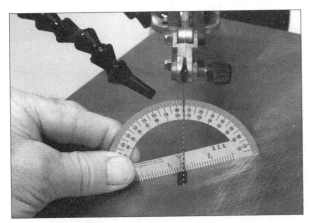

12–1. ▶ **A good protractor capable of checking the saw-table adjustment to within one-half-degree accuracy is necessary for some bevel-sawing jobs.**

SCROLL-SAW FEATURES

Some saws are not "user friendly" when it comes to sawing thick stock and heavy bevel-sawing jobs. There have been major brand saws sold in the past that did not permit 45-degree bevel-cutting, even though they had a 45-degree mark on the tilt scale. Their lower arm would strike the table when set at 34 degrees or more. On another scroll saw, there was only ¼ inch of clearance under the hold-down arm when the table was tilted 45 degrees. On yet another saw, if the workpiece extended over the edge of the table, it would strike the floor stand on the lower side, limiting the workpiece to a size smaller than the surface area of the table.

In addition to being able to make the bevel cuts to the angle you want, another feature to look for in a scroll saw is a hold-down that can be tilted to the same angle; some hold-downs cannot make that adjustment. Finally, you may need to set more blade tension than usual to keep the cut true. This requires good blade clamps, so the blade does not slip loose during sawing.

PROJECTS

The creative scroll-sawer will find a number of projects that involve bevel-sawing. One is just bevel-sawing outside edges of profiles of various-shaped cutouts. This work is best limited to gradual outside curves and straight-line cuts. Bevel-sawing is typi-cally employed when creating simple shapes for various project bases (**12–2 and 12–3**), wall plaques, or overlays, doing appliqué work for signs or artwork, and when sawing miter joints (**12–4**) and chamfering outside edges (**12–5 to 12–7**).

12–2. ▶ **The base for this simple project is bevel-sawn.**

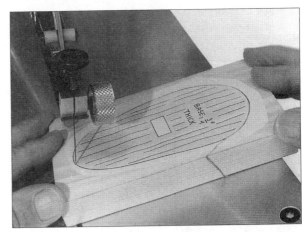

12–3. ▶ **Sawing a 15-degree bevel around the outside of a base.**

12–4. ▶ Making a full 45-degree bevel cut. When you are bevel-sawing, the slanting cut means more material is being sawn than just the thickness of the stock.

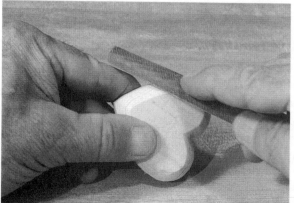

12–5. ▶ Bevel-sawing with the workpiece facedown to make a chamfered edge.

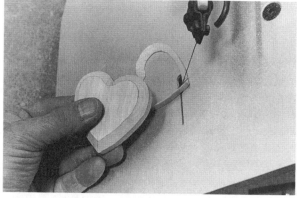

12–6. ▶ It is difficult to make a uniform and smooth chamfered surface like that made with a router, but on this small piece, the scroll-saw technique is safer.

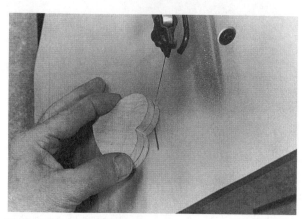

12–7. ▶ Smoothing a sawn chamfer or rounding over the edge with a hand file.

SAWING TECHNIQUES AND APPLICATIONS

Sharp Inside Corners and Curves

Sharp inside corners and curves will be impossible to bevel-saw cleanly because the blade overcuts into the lower portion of the cut edges. The best way to understand this is to refer to **12–8 and 12–9** and make some sharp, inside-corner trial cuts in scrap softwood with the table tilted. Using softwood may allow you to make a sharp inside turn, if you can accept the fact you are going to have some uncontrollable miscuts in the corners. If using hardwoods, the wood will burn and the blade may break.

The thicker the material, the greater the bevel angle, the harder the material, and the sharper the turn or corner of your pattern, the more unlikely making this type of cut becomes. In short, expect some limits to what you can do at inside corners. One solution is to change the pattern of a sharp corner to one with a small but workable radius.

Sawing with Spiral Blades

Bevel-sawing with spiral blades offers the unique advantage of making bevel-sawn edges in and all around a cutout slant in the same direction. One example is shown in **12–10**. The workpiece is not rotated at all during sawing. Remember that spiral blades make wide kerfs and the resulting cuts are very rough. As a rule, spiral blades have very little use in bevel-sawing.

On-the-Spot Turns

Making bevel-sawn on-the-spot turns will help you when cutting various designs. This technique is especially helpful when carving incised letters and other designs with a scroll saw as described in Chapter 15.

When an on-the-spot turn is made in stock supported on a tilted table, the result is a cone-shaped piece that comes out of the bottom or the downside (**12–11 and 12–12**). Practice a few of these cuts on scrap pieces, trying both clockwise and counterclockwise turning directions. With the table tilted to the left, you will probably find it easier to make the turn feeding the stock in one direction rather than the other. The reverse will be true with the table tilted in

12–8. ▶ **Bevel-sawing to produce letter cutouts with slanted edges. It is impossible to cut the inside corners cleanly because the blade overcuts into the lower portion of the slanted edge as you saw into the corner.**

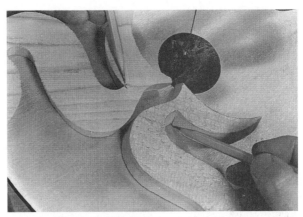

12–9. ▶ **Here are the overcuts as seen from the back of the workpiece at the left and from the front at the right.**

12–10. ▶ **This cutout, sawn with a spiral blade capable of cutting in all directions without rotating the workpiece, has all of its edges slanted to the right. Notice the roughness of cut produced by the spiral blade.**

12–11. ▶ Backing the blade out of the inbound kerf after making a 360-degree, on-the-spot turn with the table tilted.

12–12. ▶ The result of a bevel-sawn on-the-spot turn is this perfect cone-shaped waste removed from the bottom of the workpiece.

the opposite direction. Knowing how to control the workpiece when making bevel-sawn on-the-spot turns will be helpful to you when attempting some fairly sharp turns.

Inside Openings

Bevel-sawing inside openings is a simple process that just involves the added step of drilling a suitable blade-entry hole at an angle to start the cut (**12–13**). Often, the hole needs to be drilled at the same angle as the anticipated bevel cut.

The same general cutting procedures are involved when making beveled inside cutouts as normally done with the table square to the blade. There is, however, the unique situation whereby the waste of the two sawn pieces will separate from

each other in one direction only, i.e., either up or down. The waste piece will come free in one direction, but bind or wedge in the other direction. Illus. **12–13** compares a vertically sawn circular shape to a bevel-cut one; the vertically sawn circular shape can

12–13. ▶ Comparing bevel-sawing to a vertical cut. Notice how the circular bevel-sawn cutout binds or wedges when moved in one direction and not the other.

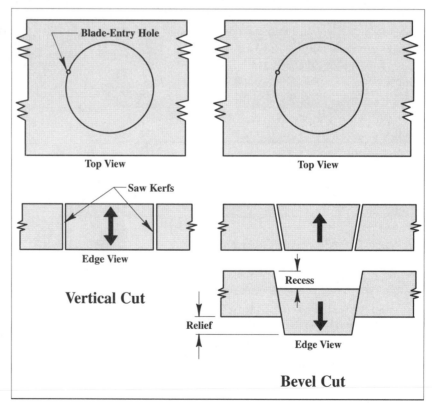

be removed in either an up or down direction, but the bevel-sawn shape can only be removed in one way.

The fact that bevel-sawn cutouts bind or wedge against the sides of the cut and eliminate or close the kerf is used to advantage to create some wonderful projects. Actually, what you end up with is a surface that on one face is recessed and on the other surface is raised in relief. Doing either intentionally can create some very interesting projects such as collapsible baskets, three-dimensional plaques, or vessels and bowls sawn from a single flat board.

Making Collapsible Baskets

Making collapsible baskets (**12–14 and 12–15**) involves both regular vertical sawing and making one continuous bevel cut in a spiraling path. The neat thing about these projects is that they are made from a single flat board so that, when completed, they pop open into a self-contained stand with a three-dimensional basket-like cavity. The "basket" part consists of bevel-sawn edges that wedge against each other (**12–16**). Well-known scroll-sawer, designer, and author Rick Longabaugh has designed and made

12–14. ▶ Side view of a collapsible basket in the "open" position. What appears as a group of gradually smaller-size individual rings is actually a continuous spiral form made with the table tilted several degrees. (Photo courtesy of Rick Longabaugh.)

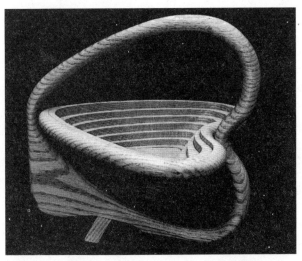

12–15. ▶ View showing the inside of a collapsible basket. (Photo courtesy of Rick Longabaugh.)

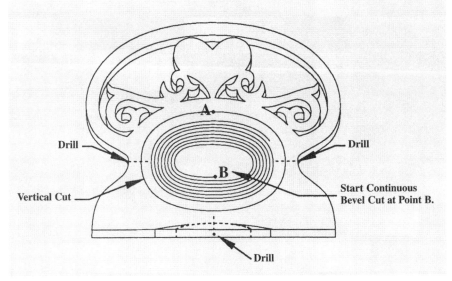

12–16. ▶ Typical spiral bevel-sawing plan (B) for the basket. Hole "A" begins a vertical cut to separate the "basket" and allow it to pivot into an "open" position. The drilled holes are screw pivot points.
(Drawing courtesy of Rick Longabaugh.)

hundreds of collapsible baskets and offers full-size, ready-to-cut patterns from his Centralia, Washington, mail-order business The Berry Basket.

Making Bevel Test Cuts

Making bevel test cuts in scrap stock before actually beginning work on your project is always necessary (**12–17 and 12–18**). The resulting height of the relief desired or the depth of a recess is determined by the angle of table tilt and the width of the saw kerf or the size blade used.

Remember, it is possible to saw more detail with sharper curves and produce higher relief the closer the table is adjusted perpendicular to the blade (**12–19**). Make test cuts at various angles using different sizes and/or kinds of blade; keep them on hand for future reference.

In general, a No. 9 blade with a 3½-degree table tilt works for fast sawing of the gradual curves in ¾-inch-thick stock when making collapsible baskets. A No. 5 or finer blade and a 2½-or 3-degree bevel work well for creating a ⅜-inch relief or recess depth in ¾-stock when making signs or decorative accents with more detail (**12–20**). Blade sizes vary from manufacturer to manufacturer, so make your own test cuts to be sure you know what you'll end up with before starting.

Also to be considered are the relationships between the direction of table tilt and the direction of feeding the stock into the saw, i.e., either clockwise or counterclockwise. To more easily understand these relationships, refer to **12–21 to 12–23**, which show examples sawn with the saw table tilted to the left. The results will be the opposite if sawn with the table tilted to the right (**12–24**).

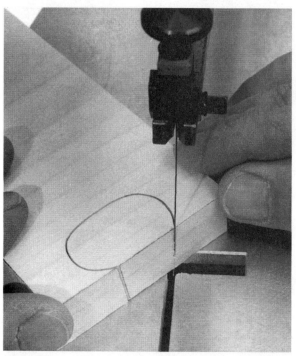

12–17. ▶ A test bevel cut can be made quickly by sawing a circular or oval shape near the edge of the stock as shown.

12–18. ▶ Bevel-cut samples. The greater the table tilt, the less the cut part can move vertically before being wedged tightly against the sides of the cut.

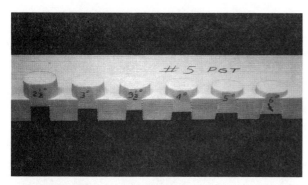

12–19. ▶ Here is one of the author's bevel-cut test pieces made at angles between 2½ and 6 degrees with a No. 5 ground blade. Notice the different results.

12–20. ▶ Pieces cut with designs raised in relief and recessed inward. The "S" on the bookend at the left appears as if it were router-engraved, but it was actually bevel-sawn with the scroll saw. (See 12–24.)

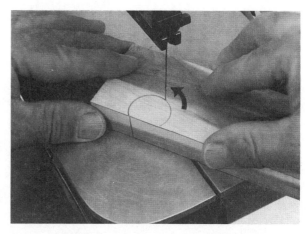

12–21. ▶ Bevel-sawing with the table tilted to the left and when feeding the workpiece into the blade in a counterclockwise direction results in a circular piece that is smaller at the bottom than at the top.

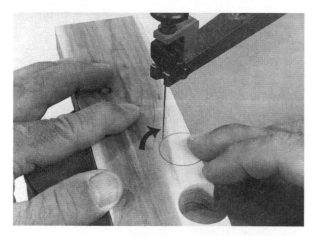

12–22. ▶ Bevel-sawing with the table tilted left and the workpiece fed into the saw blade in a clockwise direction creates a circular piece that is larger at the bottom than on the top. The cut pieces can be raised in relief to the surrounding background.

12–23. ▶ Two slight bevel cuts (3 to 5 degrees), each cut in a different feeding direction with a left table tilt, make these circular wedge-shaped pieces that bind against the sides of the cut when pushed in the direction of the arrows.

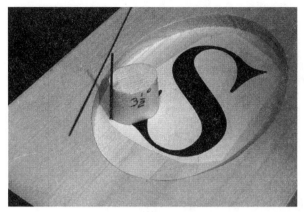

12–24. ▶ First, a recessed oval background surface was created, and then the "S" initial was raised in relief to make the engraved look shown in 12–20 on page 213. Be sure to drill angled holes in the right direction. Notice how the test-cut piece is used to guide the drill angle for the blade-entry hole.

Making Designs in Relief

Designs in relief are easy and fun to make once you understand the fundamentals of bevel-sawing. The examples shown in this section are very basic; however, there are scroll-sawers who have created some beautifully detailed wildlife scenes with various elements recessed and some set out in relief.

Depending upon the nature or complexity of the design, the edges of the piece or pieces raised in relief and/or the edges of the background can be rounded over (12–25 to 12–27). When done properly, relief cutouts look as if the background were entirely cut or carved away. The key is remembering which combination of table-tilt direction and feed direction is required to create the recess or relief where desired.

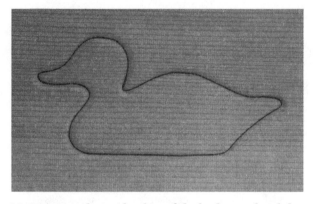

12–26. ▶ Here the inside edges of the background and the outside edges of the relief cutout have been rounded over.

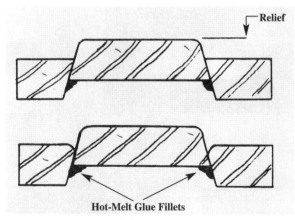

12–25. ▶ Using basic hand- or rotary-tool rounding-over techniques, some visually interesting designs can be created. These two techniques are shown in cross-section.

12–27. ▶ In addition to creating designs recessed or in relief with square or rounded corners, the individual pieces can be stained various colors before inserting them back into the background to create other visual options.

Rounded edges on relief-sawn work give projects added dimension and greater visual interest. Illus. **12–28 to 12–36** depict the pattern and steps involved in making a box that features a Celtic knot design. These include rounding over and shaping the bevel-sawn design and sawing thick wood to make the box.

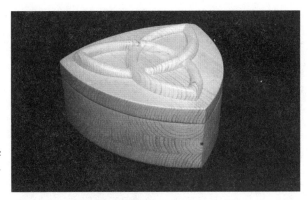

12–28. ▶ Bevel-sawn relief combined with simple roundover techniques made this Celtic knot design.

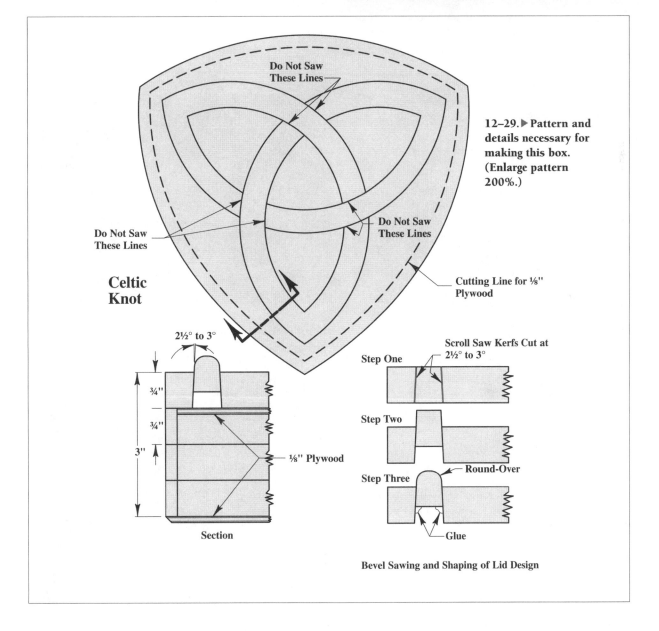

Do Not Saw These Lines

Do Not Saw These Lines

Do Not Saw These Lines

12–29. ▶ Pattern and details necessary for making this box. (Enlarge pattern 200%.)

Cutting Line for ⅛" Plywood

Celtic Knot

2½° to 3°

¾"

¾"

3"

⅛" Plywood

Section

Scroll Saw Kerfs Cut at 2½° to 3°

Step One

Step Two

Round-Over

Step Three

Glue

Bevel Sawing and Shaping of Lid Design

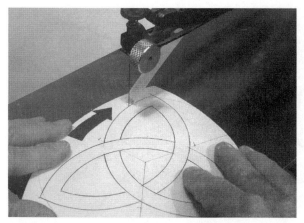

12–30. ▶ With the saw table tilted left, saw a bevel all around the outside of the "knot" design feeding the stock clockwise to make the cut.

12–31. ▶ Saw out the triangular-shaped inside pieces, bevel-cutting with the table tilted left and feeding the workpiece counterclockwise into the blade.

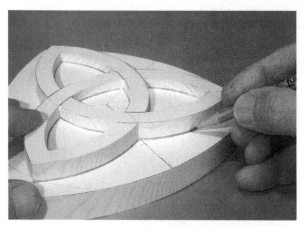

12–32. ▶ When the bevel-sawing has been completed, the knot piece raised in relief, and interior triangular pieces pressed downward, level with the background, draw light lines to indicate the portion of the beveled edges in relief that can be shaped.

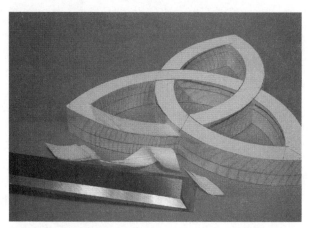

12–33. ▶ Tapering one of the six areas necessary to create the over-and-under effect.

12–34. ▶ Shaping and rounding over the bevel-sawn edges. The pencil line made freehand along the center of the design aids the shaping.

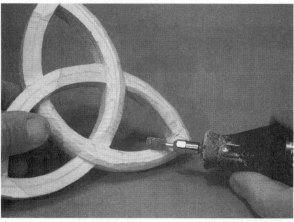

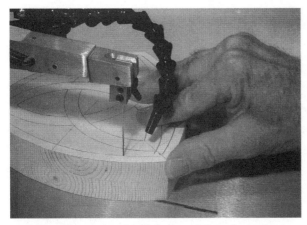

12–35. ▶ Saw two (or three) layers of ¾-inch stock to make the box walls.

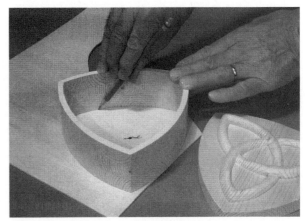

12–36. ▶ Tracing the inside shape onto plywood, which is cut and tacked under the lid to keep it aligned. (Note: Trace outside the box and cut the bottom as shown in 12–29.)

Concentric Bevel Cuts

Stackable circular rings or other design shapes cut with bevel-sawn edges are glued together to form bowls or vessels from a single flat board (**12–37 to 12–42**). This technique is used to prepare roughly shaped bowl blanks for finish-turning and -sanding with the lathe or with handheld power shaping and smoothing tools.

Bevel-cut rings are easy to make. Some experimentation will be necessary to determine the appropriate combination of bevel angle and the best width to cut the rings. This will vary with the thickness of the stock.

To give you some idea of where to start, **12–39** shows an 8-inch-square board that's ¾ inch thick. Concentric rings were marked off at ⁵⁄₁₆-inch increments along a radius. When bevel-sawn with the table set to 22 degrees, the pieces line up, one on top of the next, pretty well. If you want to form a bowl with the sides angled at 45

degrees, then rings ¾ inch wide, sawn from material ¾ inch thick, can be stacked together.

You have to find the combination of ring width and bevel angle that works best for the material and the slant angle wanted. Once this is determined, lay out and drill the blade-threading holes (**12–40**). A scrap of wood cut to the bevel angle helps to guide the angle direction of the drill. Remember, every ring should be cut with the work held in the same relative location to the blade for each successive cut. Usually it is easiest to keep the workpiece to the left of the blade, as shown in **12–41 and 12–42**.

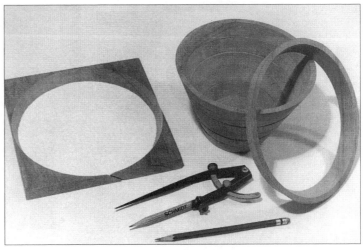

12–37. ▶ Individual, concentric bevel-sawn rings cut from a single flat board are stacked to make hollow vessels, bowls, dishes, etc.

12–38. ▶ Inverted hollow forms can be used for various bases and pedestals for artwork, lamps, etc.

12–39. ▶ An 8-inch-square board that's ¾ inch thick produces stackable rings ⁵⁄₁₆ inch wide with 22-degree edge bevels. Here all of the rings have been sawn.

12–40. ▶ Drilling blade-threading holes at the bevel-sawing angle.

12–41. ▶ Close-up look at concentric bevel-sawing. The table is tilted left and the cut is made on the line and sawing at an angle.

12–42. ▶ Cut each ring in the same manner, keeping the stock to the left of the blade. Use a counterclockwise feed, pivoting the work from the disc's center while keeping it perpendicular to and directly to the left of the blade.

Bowl Variations

The late Carl Roehl, a Wisconsin woodworking artist, was a master at making bowls and various-shaped vessels based upon the concentric-ring process that he employed to transform single flat boards into unusual three-dimensional forms. Some of his basic concepts and patterns are included here. Round bowl "rough-outs" were made of glue-stacked rings intended to be finish-turned and sanded on the lathe. The plans (patterns) for the rings were developed on an edge view of the board (blanks) (**12–43 to 12–45**).

12–43. ▶ Side view of Carl Roehl's small practice bowl featuring a "full-flair" top ring.

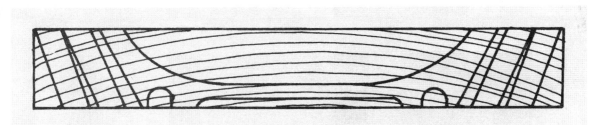

12–44. ▶ The edge-view cutting plan for the bowl shown in 12–43.

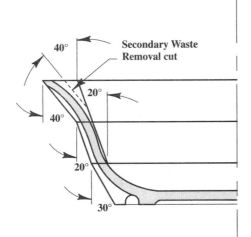

12–45. ▶ This cross-section drawing provides a bevel-sawing plan with the cutting angles to make a rough shape for finish-turning. Enlarge it 200 percent.

In addition to round bowls, other Roehl designs were made with additional scroll-sawn decoration and unusual shapes, as shown in **12–46 to 12–50**. Bowls with scroll-sawn pierced top edges are truly unusual, as were his bulbous bowls that turned inward at the top. Roehl also made bowls of non-round shapes, including rectangular ovals (**12–51**), fluted heart-shaped bowls, and various wooden flower vases, all using bevel-sawn rings cut from a single, flat board. Mr. Roehl also did extensive trendsetting work with unusual inlays using exotic woods and brass.

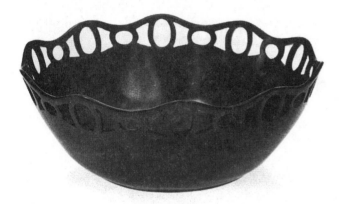

12–46. ▶ A basic round bowl with a scroll-sawn edge.

12–47. ▶ Carl Roehl five-layer bulbous bowl made from 1-inch-thick stock.

35°
20°
15°
20°
30°

Enlarge 200% for Full-Size Pattern

12–48. ▶ A cross-sectional plan for making a five-layer bulbous bowl from 1-inch-thick stock. Enlarge it 200 percent.

12–49.▶ The two top layers are decoratively pierce-sawn before being glued to the other, lower layers of the bowl.

12–50.▶ When the two pierced-sawn upper layers are completed, they will be glued to the lower rings as shown.

12–51.▶ A rectangular-shaped bowl made from concentric bevel-sawn rings.

CHAPTER THIRTEEN

INLAY WORK

I nlaying is the process of inserting a contrasting material into a surface, usually for the purpose of visual decoration (*13–1 and 13–2*). There are many different ways woodworkers prepare inlays and fit the pieces together. In scroll-sawing, there are two primary techniques: vertically stack-cutting the inlays and bevel-sawing them. Each method has certain advantages and limitations. This chapter briefly examines both techniques.

Many exciting projects exhibiting beautiful and artistic workmanship can be made employing scroll-sawn inlay techniques. The potential for incorporating inlays into your work is almost limitless. Even ¾-inch solid wood can be prepared with inlays for turning.

Prior to the refinement of the modern scroll saw, inlay work was pretty well limited to thin pieces of wood. In fact, the term "inlay" became synonymous with veneer work and marquetry. Essentially, for marquetry work, the same concepts do apply, and are discussed in Chapter 14.

VERTICAL STACK-CUT INLAYS

This technique involves simply stacking two or more pieces of wood of unlike color or species and then cutting various inlay pieces, or components, apart from the entire workpiece (*13–3*). Then you interchange the pieces as you glue them to complete the entire workpiece again. Sand and finish as necessary. The keys to this inlaying technique are to use as fine a blade as possible and to be sure that your saw table is adjusted perfectly square to the blade.

13–1. ▶ Typical solid-wood scroll-cut inlay for a box top. The background completely surrounds the inlay.

Inlay

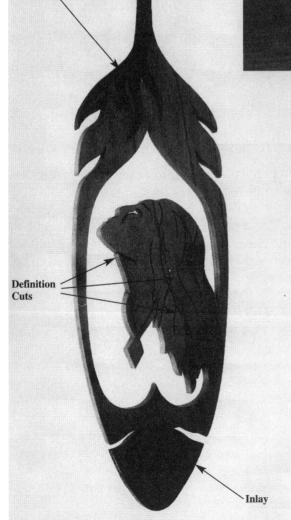

Definition
Cuts

Inlay

13–2. ▶ Another kind of scroll-sawn inlay is only partially surrounded by the background.

13–3. ▶ Stack-sawing ¼-inch mahogany and poplar. The inlay pieces on the right were vertically sawn and cut free from the workpiece.

One problem associated with the vertical stack- (or pad-) cutting method of inlaying is that, upon close examination, the saw kerf may be visible in certain areas of the completed piece (**13–4**). This problem can be alleviated by using the bevel-sawing inlaying technique discussed later, but this method also has its disadvantages.

13–4. ▶ A glue-filled kerf may be visible along some of the inlay's edges when employing the vertical stack-cutting inlaying technique.

The primary advantage of vertically stack-cutting inlay work is that it is fast and easy and you end up with two finished products or as many as the number of layers of different woods you stack together. There is no serious amount of waste associated with this method. This same technique may also be called "stacked segmentation" or "intarsia" work. (Refer to Chapter 22 for more information about this scroll-sawing technique.)

BEVEL-SAWN INLAYS

Cutting thick solid-wood and thin veneer inlays and basic veneer-marquetry techniques all involve bevel-cutting two layers of stock at once. This technique may yield considerable waste since essentially material equaling one entire layer is thrown away or at least it is not usable in the current project. This is certainly a waste; however, there are ways to conserve stock, depending upon the size and shape of the inlay.

The primary benefit of bevel-sawn inlays is that the inlay fits perfectly into the background panel—so perfectly, in fact, that no opening or saw kerf is evident along the joint line (**13–5**). Inlaying thick wood, however, requires a good scroll saw capable of making true, unwavering edge cuts in heavy stock. If there are any belly-like bulges on the cut edges or the blade drifts and wanders during cutting, all of your efforts and material will be wasted.

13–5. ▶ A perfect-fitting bevel-sawn inlay makes a focal point for this turned vase without any evidence of a saw kerf.

Review Chapter 12 to learn the essentials of bevel-sawing before undertaking the bevel inlay work presented in this chapter. Use the finest blade possible that will still handle the thickness of cut and kind of materials to be sawn. The smallest possible blade-threading hole is desired if one is necessary.

SOLID-WOOD INLAYS

Illus. **13–6** shows the relationship of the factors involved in bevel-sawing an inlay. Notice that this drawing shows the inlay inserted into the background panel from the bottom up. Changing the feed direction from counterclockwise to clockwise will create an inlay that is inserted from the top down.

Because the background stock and the inlay material are cut simultaneously, as in stack-cutting (refer to Chapter 9), the two pieces must be temporarily fastened together. This can be accomplished by using a little rubber cement, masking tape, a drop of hot-melt glue, or small pieces of double-faced tape.

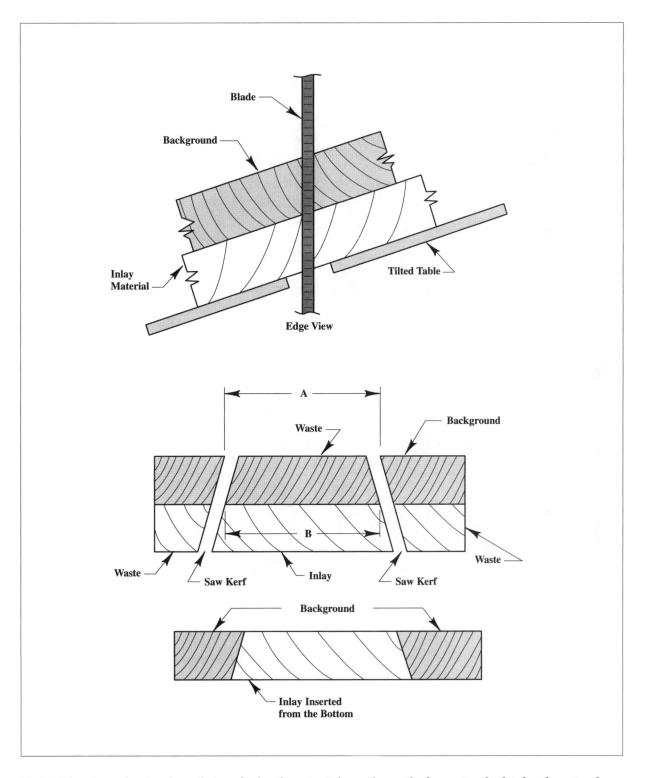

13–6. ▶ Edge views showing the technique for bevel-sawing inlays. Above: The factors involved in bevel-sawing the inlay. Center: With the correct table tilt, distance "A" will equal distance "B." Below: The inserted inlay fits perfectly, with no kerf space visible.

Trial-and-error practice cuts are the easiest way to determine the optimum amount of table tilt that is suitable for the blade width and stock thickness being used. If you change blade widths or material thicknesses between jobs, the saw table will have to be readjusted. For a flush inlay, the opening of the bevel-cut background has to be equal to that of the bevel-cut inlay (**13–6**, center).

Illus. **13–7 to 13–12** show the step-by-step procedures for making a simple flush heart inlay. The stack-

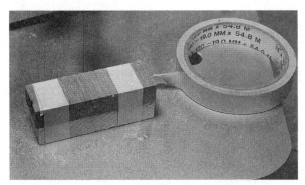

13–7. ▶ **Making a flush heart inlay. Here two scrap pieces of stock that are equal to the thickness of the eventual workpieces are being prepared for a test cut.**

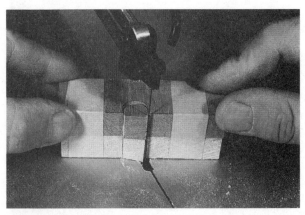

13–8. ▶ **Making the test cut.**

13–9. ▶ **With the correct table tilt, the upper piece slips snugly into the lower cutout.**

13–10. ▶ **Use the edge of the scrap test piece to establish the correct drill angle for blade-threading. The hole location is selected at the least-conspicuous corner. The workpieces are arranged for a light-colored wood inlay to be inserted into the bottom of the darker wood. The cut will be made with the workpiece rotated clockwise into the blade. If the cut were made in a counterclockwise feed direction, the slant would bevel outward, and the dark piece would be inlayed into the top of the light wood.**

ing arrangement of the two pieces and the direction that you feed the workpiece into the blade have to be thought out before you drill the blade hole, as shown in **13–10**. The directions you drill the hole and feed the material into the blade (clockwise or counterclockwise) will determine if the inlay will fit into the background piece the way it has been planned (**13–11 and 13–12**).

The inlay can be planned and cut out so it will be inserted into the background piece from either the bottom or the top. Either way is perfectly acceptable

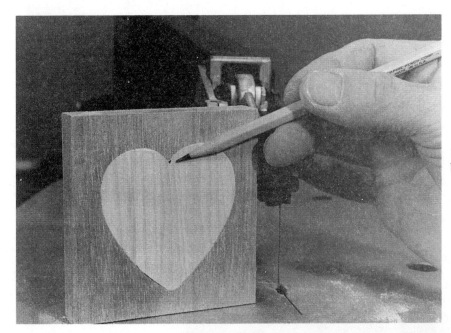

13–11. ▶ **The inlay in place. The blade-entry hole will be filled.**

13–12. ▶ **The completed inlay is on the left. The waste pieces on the right will be discarded.**

as long as you plan it that way. The top insertion is usually preferred if you're gluing the inlay into the background and applying the glue to the bevel-cut edges. With a bottom insertion, there is a tendency for the glue to be pushed up and out onto the top face of the project. This is generally undesirable.

INLAYS FOR WOOD TURNING

The procedures used to produce inlays for wood turning (**13–13 to 13–18**) are essentially the same as those just described. Inlays are simply set into boards that are laminated or glued together to make the blank for turning. The usual procedure—but one especially important for wood-turning inlays—is to prepare the components so the grain runs in the same direction. The inlaid pieces are turned as usual along with the other parts that comprise the turning. The key is careful planning with a preestablished shape and contour that best take advantage of the inlay design.

Although the inlays shown are used for spindle-turning projects, the same idea can be applied to many types and kinds of turning. Bowls, lidded containers, plates, etc., all can be glued together with stock having preinserted flush inlays.

13–14. ▶ A test cut checks that the table-tilt angle is correct.

13–13. ▶ Pieces with layouts completed for making inlays on a laminated turning blank.

13–15. ▶ Bevel-sawing the inlay. The background is on top. The workpiece is fed counterclockwise into the blade, and the table is tilted left.

13–16. ▶ The inlays cut and glued in place.

13–17. ▶ The turning blank glued up.

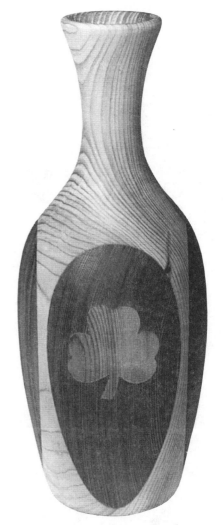

13–18. ▶ The completed turning.

SCULPTURED INLAYS

Sculptured inlays can be made by working the surfaces with contoured carving, texturing, etc. Some of the edges can even be worked or rounded over, as shown in **13–19 to 13–21**. However, inlays with rounded-over edges tend to have deep shadows, and the tight fit produced by bevel-sawing cannot always be fully appreciated visually.

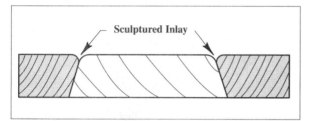

13–19. ▶ A sculptured inlay.

13–20. ▶ A look at the rounded edges on the background and the inlay.

13–21. ▶ The inlay in place. No kerf spacing is visible, just a shadow.

BEVEL-SAWN JOINERY

Gluing together irregular scroll-sawn edges and/or edge-joining interconnected cuts of wood of different species or colors without gaps or evidence of the kerf is another bevel-sawing operation similar to inlaying. Illus. **13–22** shows a project that has a narrow, dark wood strip with irregular sawn edges glued between two light-colored pieces so it appears as an inlay. This work is easily accomplished by bevel-sawing. Cutting with the inlay on top of the background as shown in **13–23 to 13–26** saves material and is very accurate.

To make the inlay and the space for it at the proper location, the background pattern is applied first. Next, a registration or reference line must be established so the inlay and its opening will be cut in the correct place. In this case, the horizontal line under the Kokopelli's feet was used for the reference.* Then apply the pattern to the inlay piece using the top edge as a reference for the correct positioning. Now, glue or tape the inlay piece (with the pattern) to the background as shown in **13–23**, again using the same reference line.

Make trial bevel cuts on scraps of the same thickness to establish the table-tilt angle and blade combination that will produce the flush inlay (refer to **13–14**). With the saw table tilted to the right, saw the bottom edge as shown in **13–24**. Cut the top edge of the inlay as shown in **13–25** to complete the inlay shape.

The concept of making bevel-cut, irregularly curved glue joints that are gap-free can also be employed to make wooden bowl and face-plate turnings and incorporated into spindle-turned designs and any number of projects with flat surfaces such as cutting boards, box tops, cabinet fronts, small tabletops, etc. One application to make almost interconnected irregular joinery cuts is shown in **13–27**. The preparation steps of wood selection and pattern placement are shown in **13–28**.

Stacked bevel-sawing ensures perfectly matched joints (**13–29 to 13–31**). Since both pieces of the joint are cut simultaneously, the margin for error has been eliminated.

Incidentally, patterns for silhouettes can be enlarged from side-view photos taken with instant or digital cameras, from conventional photography, or using other methods.

---

*The Kokopelli is a figure commonly found in petroglyphs and pottery throughout the American Southwest. It is regarded as a fertility symbol.

13–22. ▶ The irregular dark strip inlay fits perfectly because the abutting edges were bevel-cut simultaneously.

13–23. ▶ The inlay piece with its cutting pattern is double-face-taped (in the proper position) to the background piece with its pattern already applied to the work source.

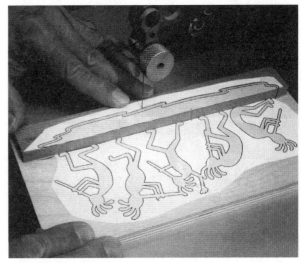

13–24. ▶ Here the table is tilted right and the bottom line of the inlay piece is being cut.

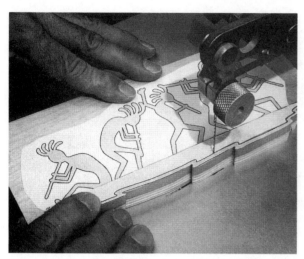

13–25. ▶ With the workpiece rotated end-for-end, the second bevel on the inlay and the background edges are cut simultaneously.

13–26. ▶ The inlay ready to be glued in place and the discarded waste pieces.

13–27. ▶ Interconnecting child-silhouette profiles are bevel-cut at the joint lines to make a perfect fit with no visible saw-kerf gaps.

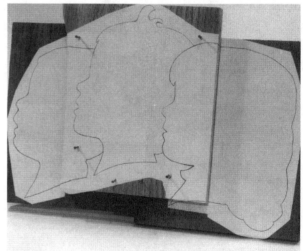

13–28. ▶ The first step in bevel-sawing the child-silhouette profiles shown in 13–27. Paper patterns and woods of contrasting colors are selected and arranged for overlapping and stacked bevel-cutting.

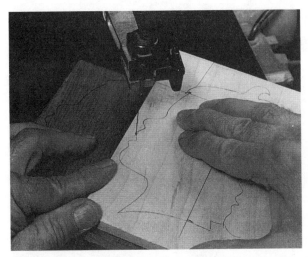

13–29. ▶ Bevel-sawing two pieces at once will make the perfectly matched joint. Here the pieces are held together with double-faced tape during the bevel-sawing.

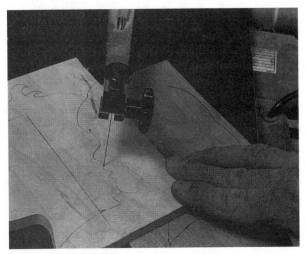

13–30. ▶ Cutting the second joint in the same manner.

13–31. ▶ An option is to glue the assembled and glued pieces to a plywood backer that is cut smaller all around.

CHAPTER FOURTEEN

MARQUETRY BASICS

arquetry is the ancient art of selecting, cutting, and fitting different-colored veneers together to create a picture or design that is glued to a flat background surface (**14–1 and 14–2**). This art form dates back to the early Egyptians and Romans. Marquetry has grown in sophistication over the centuries.

The true inlay of wood upon wood originated in Italy in the 13th century and was used predominately in church decoration. In the 17th century, the Italians began to make more general use of marquetry in the decoration of household furniture. Since then, many masterpieces have been created around the world (**14–3 and 14–4**).

Marquetry is a vast and fairly complex subject to master. This chapter is only an introduction intended to give you basic techniques to get started. The marquetrarian possesses patience and skill, plus the love and knowledge of fine woods. Only the fundamentals can be covered here. There are, however, a number of good books devoted to the subject. There is also a national association dedicated to the advancement of marquetry that has many local chapters located around the country. It is the American Marquetrarian, Inc., a nonprofit society with membership open to everyone. Initial membership dues are $25 and $20 per year thereafter. Membership includes a quarterly magazine providing news, patterns, instructional articles, and supply sources. Contact: David Peck, Editor, 726 Road N, Redwood Valley, California 95470.

14–1. ▶ The effective use of just six or seven veneers creates this entire project.

14–2. ▶ A nice look with just two different veneers inlaid into a third veneer background.

14–3. ▶ Marquetry tabletop entitled "Primal Woodworking" by Silas Kopf, one of today's premier marquetry artists.

14–4. ▶ Another whimsical marquetry creation by Silas Kopf entitled "Linda." The upper door is actually flat with concealed hinges, but the artist has effectively presented a different impression.

There is another association that will provide information on marquetry or any other aspect of scroll-sawing. The Scroll Saw Association of the World was formed in 1997 to "bring scrollers from around the world to learn from each other and provide a scroll saw information network." With S.A.W. as the acronym, this volunteer-driven association does the following: it establishes and supports local clubs; it publishes a quarterly newsletter and an annual membership directory that includes a current resources list of videos, material supplies, vendor ads, etc.; it organizes scroll-sawing competitions and contests; and it has on going programs that promote public awareness of scroll-sawing as an art form and help its members grow professionally while enjoying social fellowship. S.A.W can be contacted at 610 Daisy Lane, Round Lake Beach, Illinois, 60073.

This chapter discusses two fundamental scroll-sawing marquetry techniques: stack- and bevel-sawing. Most scroll-saw marquetry work requires very slow blade speeds. The more detailed the design, the slower the blade speed and feed must be to control the cut. Begin with moderately fine blades such as a 2/0. (Review Chapters 10 and 13.)

STACK-SAWING TECHNIQUE

The stack-sawing method of sawing veneers is referred to by those who do marquetry as the "pad method." This is the easiest way to make veneer inlays. The pad method allows you to produce multiple projects all at one time and is fast, easy, and beneficial to production-type marquetry operations. The major disadvantage is that the cut pieces have saw-kerf gaps that are visible in the finished product.

In pad- or stack-sawing, many layers of veneer are cut at one time. The layers are planned to include any number of different species or colors of wood that can be effectively cut in one operation. The saw-table setting should be square, at 90 degrees to the blade. An auxiliary table with a small blade-hole opening should be attached with double-faced tape (**14–5**).

Illus. **14–6 to 14–14** show the basic steps involved in pad- or stack-sawing marquetry. Illus. **14–15** shows the saw kerf spacing problem that is typical with this method of veneer marquetry. The filled-in saw-kerf space is always more evident when two

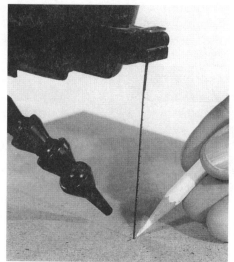

14–5. ▶ An auxiliary table with a small blade hole is essential for support when sawing marquetry veneers.

14–6. ▶ Three layers of different-colored veneers will be used to make three identical initial panels, each with a different combination of veneers.

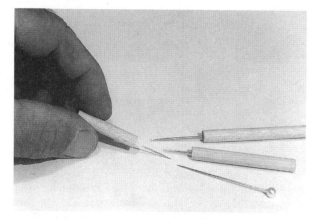

14–7. ▶ Tools for making blade-threading holes in veneers. Needles driven into dowels work well.

14–8. ▶ Three layers stacked and taped to a cardboard waste backer.

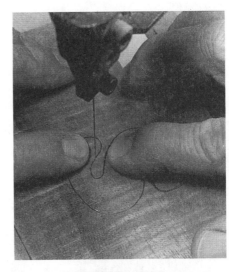

14–9. ▶ Keeping pressure close to the blade to prevent chattering. A foot switch is recommended.

14–10. ▶ When pieces are cut out, interchange them with others for desired color combinations. Insert each inlay faceup into the background piece and apply gummed veneer tape over the face, covering all saw cuts.

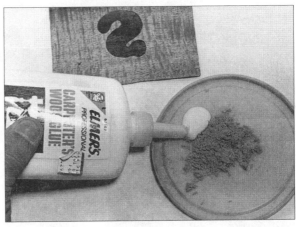

14–11. ▶ Glue mixed with sanding dust can be used as a filler. Work it into the saw-kerf gaps from the back (untaped side). Remove all excess.

14–12. ▶ Gluing the veneer assemblies to the backers, each separated by waxpaper or plastic film.

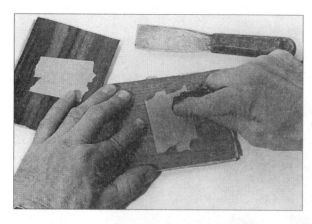

14–13. ▶ Remove veneer tape from each face. A slightly dampened rag will soften the tape. Scrape the face clean with a putty knife.

14–14. ▶ Resulting identical inlays ready to be sanded and finished.

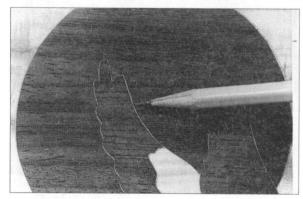

14–15. ▶ Typical saw-kerf visibility that results from the stack-sawn or pad method. Notice how more evident the kerf is where dark wood meets dark wood than where light wood joins dark wood.

darker pieces meet each other. The saw kerf is not as noticeable when a light wood butts next to a dark wood, which is also shown in **14–15**.

BEVEL-SAWING TECHNIQUE

This marquetry sawing method is based upon exactly the same procedures discussed in Chapters 12 and 13. This is the technique preferred by most mar-

quetry veterans because the results are much more professional. The table must be tilted to an appropriate angle so the kerf will be closed when the inlay is inserted into the background.

Although this method has the advantage of no visible kerf in the assembly, there are two disadvantages. First, you can only create or saw out one marquetry picture (or inlay) at a time. Second, there is more wasted veneer with this method. However, there are "tricks of the trade" professionals use to minimize waste of quality, expensive veneers.

Illus. **14–16 to 14–24** show how to bevel-cut a veneer inlay for an initial and insert it into a background. The same technique is used to make more complicated pictures because each design element is cut out individually, one part at a time. Each successive cutout part becomes another inlay inserted into the background. Work continues until all pieces or parts have been cut out and inlaid according to the pattern. All pieces are taped to the background using gummed veneer tape.

When done, the entire assembly of taped-together veneer pieces is bonded to a plywood or hardwood panel. This panel then becomes a part for a piece of

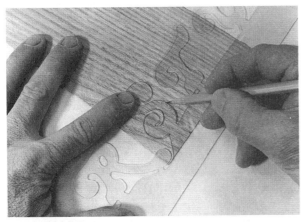

14–16. ▶ The inlay design is laid out on the selected veneer.

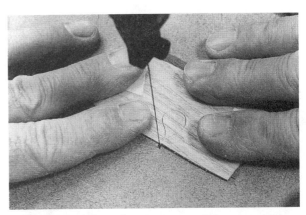

14–17. ▶ Two pieces of scrap veneer of the same thickness are bevel-cut for a test inlay to check the correct table tilt for the blade size used.

14–18. ▶ The test inlay must be fit flush without any visible kerf space.

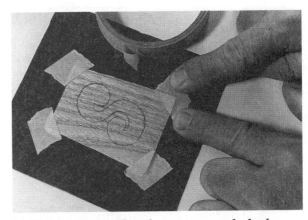

14–19. ▶ Positioning the inlay veneer over the background veneer.

14–20. ▶ Making the blade-threading hole. (See 14–7.)

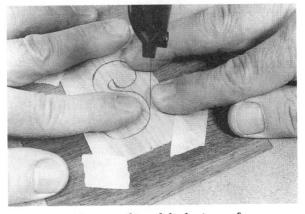

14–21. ▶ Bevel-sawing through both pieces of veneer. Here the table is tilted left and the workpiece is fed counterclockwise into the blade.

14–22. ▶ The inlay is set into the background and secured with veneer tape applied to the front surfaces.

14–23. ▶ The back surface exhibits a perfect fit without any visible saw-kerf spaces.

14–24. ▶ The completed inlay shown enlarged. Notice there is also no trace of the saw kerf or the original blade-threading hole.

furniture, a tray, a box lid, a framed wall hanging, or other project.

Bevel-sawn marquetry is a very challenging art form with many levels of difficulty and proficiency. Producing highly detailed pieces requires careful selection of veneers for color, grain, and figure, and each part must be cut and fitted perfectly.

SCROLL SAWS SPECIALLY DESIGNED FOR MARQUETRY

Expert artisans such as Willard Bondhus have taken this art form beyond what typical scroll saws can do. The need for a machine that cuts at the slowest possible speed with the finest of blades is a basic requirement for those practicing at the top of this art form.

The extremely fine blades advanced marquetrarians and experts need to use as a rule do not work in most scroll saws. The slowest speeds of most scroll saws are much too fast. Only the Diamond and Excalibur saws have speed controls that run at just a few strokes per minute. Very fine blades must be carefully tensioned, and any machine vibration is unacceptable.

Willard Bondhus prefers his own shop-made scroll saws over commercially manufactured machines to give him the performance features required. One of the earlier saws made by Bondhus incorporates some parts from the Tool Company's kit saw. This saw is driven by a 1/15-horsepower motor from a discarded Xerox machine and has a number of innovative features such as a handwheel option that provides ultra-slow cutting control when needed.

Illus. **14–25 and 14–26** show another Bondhus shop-made scroll saw designed exclusively for marquetry. Making this saw involved a combination of basic woodworking and metal-fabricating skills. Essentially, it is a motor-powered hand-frame saw that works on the C-arm principle. It has a stroke length of approximately one inch, and a foot-operated speed control. A used motor is belted down to convert speed into power to control sawing. Saws operating at high speeds are difficult to use and control when cutting thin veneers. Employing a system of pulleys reduces the blade speed and increases the power ratio.

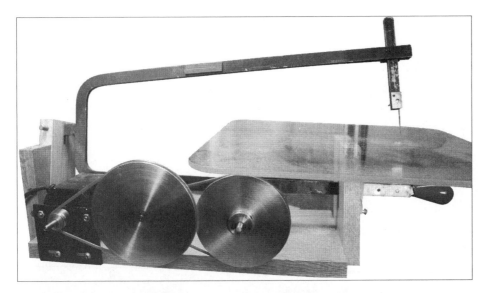

14–25. ▶ **The current shop-made Bondhus marquetry saw has a clear-plastic horizontal table and a metal C-arm fixed at an 11-degree angle (to the table). The saw carries extremely fine, user-annealed, metal-piercing blades in the 4/0 to 6/0 range.**

14–26. ▶ **Marquetrarian Willard Bondhus at work on his current shop-made scroll saw designed exclusively for marquetry.**

The horizontal table is ¼-inch clear plastic that provides visibility when installing blades in the lower clamp. The saw frame was made from ¼ × ¾-inch steel that was heated and bent. It is permanently fixed at 11 degrees to the saw table, the required angle.

The aluminum pulleys, ¼ inch thick × ¾, 1, 4, and 4½ inches in diameter, were turned in a drill press using files to finish the shape and to form the round grooves for the belts. The shafts are ³⁄₁₆-inch drill rod with brass sleeve bushings. The drive belts are ⅛-inch round rubber bands that are available at stationary stores for office machines. The frame rides up and down on a ³⁄₁₆-inch-diameter brass rod crank.

The blades used in the Bondhus marquetry saw are Nos. 4/0 to 6/0 metal-piercing blades of the hardened, brittle type recommended only for hand frames. Bondhus anneals or softens them to a point where they may not cut metal but will still cut veneers perfectly. The blades are annealed by placing them in a frying pan with sand on the kitchen stove. When the sand gets hot enough to burn the edge of a piece of veneer, they are heated for a few more minutes and then left to cool in the sand.

MARQUETRY WITH SCULPTURED OVERLAYS

Marquetry with sculptured overlays (**14–27 and 14–28**) is a new artistic concept developed and perfected by Robert Johnson of New Jersey. Johnson has given flat marquetry a spectacular three-dimensional effect that embellishes the background marquetry itself. The works are absolutely marvelous.

Johnson calls his work "relief inlay." It is actually a combination of several techniques, including basic inlay marquetry, lamination, and sculptural overlays that may be further accentuated with wire-brushing, burning, bleaching, and staining. Illus. **14–29 to 14–31** are close-ups that depict Johnson's workmanship and unusual techniques.

14–27. ▶ **These sculptured sailboat pieces overlaid onto a flat marquetry background were created with a combination of techniques by Robert Johnson.**

14–28. ▶ **Colorful laminations cut and sculptured into hot-air balloons and overlaid onto a veneer background.**

14–29. ▶ Wire-brushed mountains and sculptured trees. There is no evidence of a saw kerf.

14–30. ▶ Close-up look at the overlaid sculptured sails.

14–31. ▶ Hot-air balloons are inlays into themselves that are sculptured and then overlaid onto a one-piece background.

CHAPTER FIFTEEN

INCISE-CARVING

ncise-carving is the cutting of deeply engraved and sharply notched designs into a flat background. This work is typically more quickly and efficiently accomplished with an expensive template-guided router system. Experienced carvers deftly make incised slicing cuts using a variety of hand chisels. Serious scroll-sawers can also simulate incise-carving, but on a limited basis. Incise-carving with the scroll saw is still another bevel-sawing technique that allows you to showcase your scroll-sawing skills.

There are essentially two different methods involved in incise-carving. One, called the "two-cut" method, involves sawing two angular (bevel) slicing cuts, each from drilled starting holes at each end of the pointed design elements *(15–1)*. The "on-the-spot bevel-cornering" method is more complicated because it involves making very sharp inside and outside turns *(15–2)*. Each design element (or letter character) is cut all around almost nonstop with just one starting hole. In both methods, triangular, cross-sectional waste pieces are removed.

TWO-CUT METHOD

Incise-carving techniques with a scroll saw can be used to create calligraphy with moderately curved characters or Old English signs and a variety of deeply carved designs to decorate furniture, small doors, boxes, etc. The results look very impressive despite the fact that certain cutting procedures must be followed and the scroll saw is not perfectly suited for incise-carving. The following factors may at times make using the scroll saw for incise-carving problematic, depending upon the job at hand and the disposition of the scroll-sawer:

15–1. ▶ Incise carvings made by the "two-cut" method compared to pierced work shown at the upper right. Notice that the elements of most bevel-cut pierced designs have two pointed ends.

15–2. ▶ A more challenging style of incise-carving is best done using softwood such as this butternut. This technique involves making a number of on-the-spot turns to complete one letter.

1. It is best if the design begins and ends at a point (**15–3**).

2. The blade-entry holes must be drilled at the correct angle (**15–4 and 15–5**).

3. Two blade threadings and two cuts are required to complete each design element.

4. Threading and clamping the blade in the saw is more difficult when the table is tilted.

5. This work is easier to perform with softwoods such as pine, butternut, basswood, and redwood.

6. You will have a see-through saw kerf when viewed at the sawing angle, but only a shadow line when viewed straight on.

7. Gradual curves cut easiest. Cutting a teardrop design (**15–1**, lower right) is possible, but difficult.

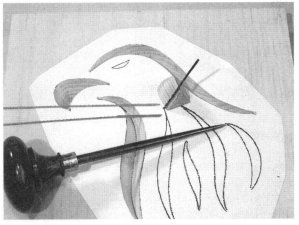

15–4. ▶ Use a bevel-cut waste piece to help guide the drilling angle.

15–3. ▶ Notice how all elements of the design begin and end at a point.

15–5. ▶ A modified blade with a narrowed end on the right allows smaller starting holes.

Determining Table Tilt

The more vertical the cut, or the less amount of bevel to it, the better. The narrower the width of the design element, the better. Review **15–6**, which shows the relationship of the overall width and depth of the cut to the amount of saw-table tilt. Increasing the depth of cut when possible will help to reduce the amount of table tilt required and make the sawing process easier.

When working with ¾-inch-thick material, it is generally best not to exceed a 25-to-30 degree table tilt or have a design element wider than ¾ inch. Depending upon the design, you can cut so the bottom of the "V" is almost through the workpiece.

Some experimentation and practice cuts in scrap will give you an idea of what to expect before tackling a major project. It doesn't matter if you tilt the table left or right as long as you are comfortable with it and you saw in the correct direction.

Draw your own cutting scheme, similar to **15–6**, on the edge of a scrap piece. Use the inclined line(s) to help you set the table tilt to the blade (**15–7**). It's okay to be off a degree or two. No one will ever know. Make a saw cut into the scrap piece to a point of about ¾ inch from the edge, and then make an on-the-spot, 360-degree turn (**15–8**). This will give you an inverted cone-shaped waste piece from the underside that can be used as a guide to drill the blade-entry holes.

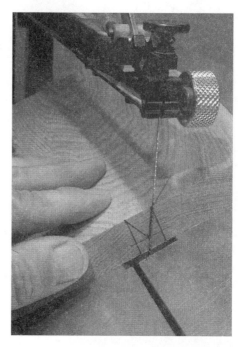

15–7. ▶ Set the table tilt equal to the cross-sectional cutting plan.

15–8. ▶ On a test piece of equal thickness, cut inward and make a 360-degree on-the-spot turn to create this inverted cone.

15–6. ▶ Develop a cross-sectional plan on the edge of the wood to establish the table-tilt angle based on the widest area of the pattern and the desired depth of cut.

Drilling Blade-Entry Holes

Mount the pattern as usual with spray adhesive. At each starting point, indent the surface slightly with a scratch awl to help start the drill. Determine the direction that the bevel of the cut is to slant and drill the blade-threading holes accordingly. It may be a lot easier, in the long run, to drill starting holes somewhat larger in size than normally required for vertical cutting. A No. 5 PGT blade, with the top end ground narrower as shown in **15–5**, and a ¾₄-inch drill bit are recommended. Remember, you need to drill two holes, one at each end of each design element (**15–9**). Also, be sure the holes slant in the correct directions to permit making the cuts that will remove triangular-shaped sections from the workpiece (**15–10**).

Blade-Threading

This is the most frustrating aspect of this work, but it gets easier with practice. Different scroll saws will present different problems. Because the table is tilted, the work tends to slide off the table. You also have to guard against kinking the blade. This work will quickly give you a good clue as to how "user friendly" your scroll saw really is. It may be helpful to remove the hold-down guard and blower hose if they interfere.

Sawing Technique

Making a cut is easy once you get the blade threaded and tensioned. You may find that the blade pinches or catches in the starting hole if it's not drilled perfectly. This may cause the workpiece to move up and down when you turn on the power. Check this first before turning the power on. Move the saw arm by hand to run the blade through a stroke or two before turning on the power. Another method, with the power off, is to lift or move the workpiece up and down on the blade a couple of times to free the teeth and start the cut. Make the cuts following the pattern lines.

After sawing is complete, fill the blade-entry holes (**15–10**). Some patterns suitable for the "two-cut" incise-carving technique are given in **15–11**. Enlarge them as needed up to 200 percent for ¾-inch-thick material.

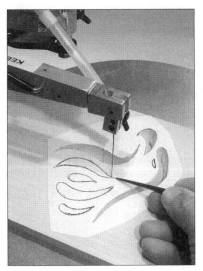

15–9. ▶ The table is tilted left and the first cut is completed. The next steps are to remove the blade, rotate the work end-for-end, rethread the blade, and make the second cut.

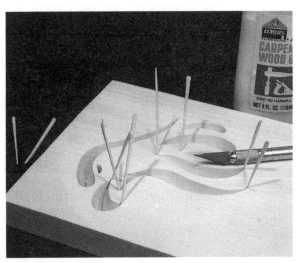

15–10. ▶ Toothpicks can be used to fill blade-entry holes if the project is to be painted.

15–11. ▶ **Examples of patterns for "two-cut" incise-carving. These patterns can be enlarged as desired up to 200 percent.**

ON-THE-SPOT BEVEL-CORNERING

On-the-spot bevel-cornering techniques require a good scroll saw that will sustain greater-than-usual tension and which has clamps that do not permit the blade to slip. There are two important factors involved with this method of incise-carving to be aware of before starting:

1. This work is best done in softwood because you must use moderately wide blades and make almost 360-degree on-the-spot turns. This results in blade friction, which causes burning and blade breakage when worked in hardwood.

2. The results are not perfect. Each corner will have a small notch or "spin gap" (hole) that looks like an overcut. These minor defects will

require filling if you want to mask their appearance. The results, however, are visually electrifying when viewed beyond an arm's length (**15–2 and 15–12**). Illus. **15–14 to 15–16** will lead you through practice sawing of the Old English letter "S."

The density of the wood species selected will influence the level of cutting difficulty for this type of bevel-sawing. Butternut ¾ inch thick was used for the sign shown in **15–2 and 15–12**.

Select a fine blade and drill the smallest possible hole at an outside corner of each letter for blade-threading (**15–13**). The narrower the blade, the better it is for on-the-spot turns. The blade should, however, be suitable for cutting thick stock and withstand

15–12. ▶ An incised bevel-cut sign. Notice the waste pieces shown in the foreground.

15–13. ▶ Blade-threading holes should slant toward the inside and be drilled at outside corners rather than inside corners.

the stress and tension. Try Nos. 3 and 4 blades if you have difficulty with No. 5s.

The angles of the drilling and sawing must be fairly close to equal. The angle for the sawing of stock ¾ inch thick can vary from 14 to 18 degrees. This will give approximately a ½- to ⅝-inch width at the face of the letter when the "V" cut is made almost all the way through the thickness of the board.

To determine the maximum width for the letters, make several trial on-the-spot turns at different table angles in a scrap piece of the same thickness. Measure the diameter at the base of the cone-shaped piece. Lay out the patterns on the workpiece with the widest part not exceeding the diameter of the cone produced by the trial-and-error bevel cut with an on-the-spot turn.

The scrap test piece used for the on-the-spot turn can be used as a drilling guide (refer to **15–13**). This will ensure that the holes are drilled at the same angle the table is tilted to. It's best to drill the blade-threading holes at outside corners rather than inside corners.

When all the holes are drilled, thread the blade through the workpiece and begin sawing. *Caution:* Make sure you feed the stock so that the slant of the letter face is toward the center. With the table tilted left, the letter is cut out by feeding the stock counterclockwise into the blade (**15–14**). Make the cut on very sharp turns by spinning the workpiece in a clockwise direction, as shown in **15–15**. Always make every sharp turn (both inside and outside ones) with the stock pivoted around the blade in a clockwise direction (**15–17**). This means that on some turns you will have to rotate the work almost 360 degrees to stay on the line.

The techniques will obviously require some study and practice, but the results are impressive and unusual. Illus. **15–18** shows a back view of the completed sign.

15–14. ▶ **A practice bevel cut, in which the work is fed counterclockwise into the blade.**

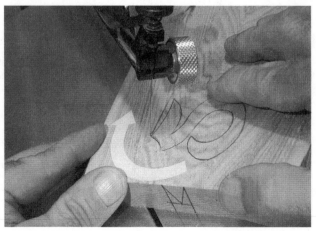

15–15. ▶ **Here the table is tilted left and the workpiece is being rotated clockwise around the blade, making a complete 360-degree on-the-spot turn at this point before the cut is continued.**

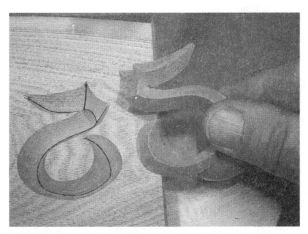

15–16. ▶ A close-up look at the completed cut, all started from a single blade-entry hole, and the waste piece removed.

15–17. ▶ Another example showing the counterclockwise feed for cutting a letter "r." At this outside corner, a near full 360-degree on-the-spot, clockwise turn will be made before continuing.

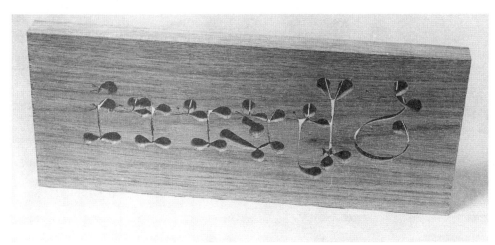

15–18. ▶ Rear view of the "Sherri" sign. Notice that all cone-shaped voids are located where on-the-spot turns were made to facilitate sharp bevel-cut cornering.

CHAPTER SIXTEEN

FINE FRETWORK

Fretwork is the sawing of ornate and sometimes extremely delicate decorative designs, usually with numerous inside openings *(16–1 to 16–3)*. This chapter examines some typical examples of small, basic fretwork projects and techniques and also reviews work by some of the world's masters that involves very delicate and/or large pieces with thousands of inside cuts.

Mastering fretwork is sometimes more of an issue of dedicated repetition and patience than it is of pure sawing skills. The nature of fretwork requires a high number of blade-threading holes, and each time an opening is cut, the blade needs to be clamped and unclamped often just to cut many tiny openings *(16–4)*. This type of work can be frustrating and become more of an exercise in personal fortitude than one of sawing expertise.

Some fretwork, however, requires very exact cuts. Two such examples are the lines of the ovals surrounding the dragon in *16–4* and the parallel state-border lines of the United States map that is shown in *16–5 and 16–6*.

Fretwork can be incorporated into all kinds of woodworking projects and today a pattern for any subject you may want is probably available. Fretwork is found in decorative and functional home accessories—furniture, signs, architectural embellishments, toys, clock mechanisms *(16–7 and 16–8)*, wildlife art, models, ornaments, religious symbols, business logos, silhouettes of every imaginable subject, and even prayers and passages from the Bible. There are two important keys to fun and successful fretwork scroll-sawing: having a scroll saw with a fast and easy blade-threading system and selecting the right material.

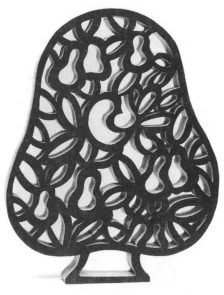

16–1. ▶ Fretwork wall hangings or trivets can be sawn from stock of any thickness.

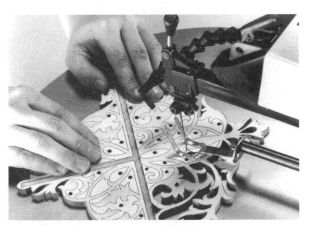

16–2. ▶ Cutting the back piece for a fretwork wall shelf.

16–3. ▶ A completed shelf.

16–4. ▶ Sawing this classic dragon design by John Polhemus with many very small openings requires both skill and patience.

16–5. ▶ This United States map, sawn by John Polhemus from a piece of 1 x 9¼ × 14¼-inch solid mahogany, is so fragile it is protected on both sides with clear acrylic plastic.

16–6. ▶ A closer look at the ¹⁄₁₆-inch-wide ribbon-like state boundaries. This work requires exceptional concentration and very skilled cutting.

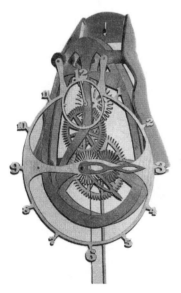

16–7. ▶ One of many working clock designs by Rick Hutcheson features gears sawn from Baltic-birch plywood and gravity power obtained from a weight hanging on a cord.

16–8. ▶ Pages from Wildwood Designs' fretwork pattern catalog.

Scroll saws for fretwork should have the following features in declining order of importance:

1. Fast and easy blade-threading.
2. A slow speed option or variable-speed control.
3. Minimal vibration.
4. A large worktable to support the work.
5. A minimal-size table opening for the blade.
6. A workable hold-down that is easily moved out of the way.

By and large, you will only get these features from a mid-priced saw. (Turn to pages 82 and 83 for a description of a new concept in scroll-saw design intended especially for cutting fretwork from thin materials.) An inexpensive machine or one that accepts just pin-end blades will quickly lead to frustration when attempting the more detailed and challenging fretwork pieces.

Should you have a saw that has a large opening in the table, you will want to cover it with an auxiliary table that will provide support for the work close to the blade. This is very important when sawing fragile work.

Fretwork involves spending long periods of time at the saw, so you want to be as comfortable as possible. Use a stool or chair and a foot switch. Provide yourself with good lighting and do whatever you can to safely handle the dust and work without any kind of strain.

WOOD MATERIALS FOR FRETWORK

Since fretwork is so labor-intensive, it is impractical to use nothing but the best possible choice of material. The prudent woodworker will not invest excessive time and effort making fancy fretwork from low-grade or inappropriate material. Nor does he or she use high-priced, rare, or the highest-quality wood when cutting crude, marginal designs or utility objects.

Wood, as we know, ranges from poor quality and cheap to material that is of a high grade and expensive. In the final analysis, you will always appreciate using the better material.

Solid Woods

All early fretwork was cut from thin solid wood because it was easier to dry than thick wood and plywood wasn't available. Serious fretworkers and the masters of fretwork art today still prefer solid wood because the edges look better and projects that are viewed from both sides appear more uniform overall.

Traditionally, fretwork is associated with thinner material, and early scroll saws cut thinner woods much easier than thick stock. Many of the patterns for today's fretwork are either simply redrawn designs from the past or new patterns developed for thin material because that is what has normally been used. Gradually, however, we are seeing new fretwork patterns and projects intended for ¾-inch and thicker material. Today, beautiful solid woods are available in almost any thickness or species desired.

Thin-Wood Warpage

Thin wood has a tendency to cup, that is, to curve across the width of a board. This is especially true with plain- (or flat-) sawn boards (**16–9 and 16–10**). Quarter-sawn wood will not cup or move nearly as much. A curved bending that occurs lengthwise is referred to as "bowing."

Cupping and bowing can be corrected fairly easily and quickly if the stock is ¼ inch or less in thickness. Slightly dampen the concave side of the board with a moist rag or a vaporizer spray like those used in liquid glass-cleaner bottles. Then carefully apply heat to the convex (opposite) side of the board. Use a flameless heat source such as a hair dryer or an electric hot plate.

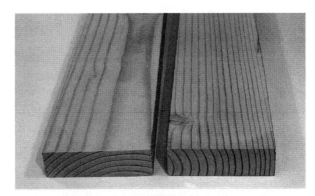

16–9. ▶ Plain-sawn wood (left), and quarter-sawn at the right. Plain-sawn boards have been cut so that the annual rings make an angle of less than 45 degrees with the surface of the board. Quarter-sawn boards have been cut so that the annual rings form an angle of 45 to 90 degrees with the surface.

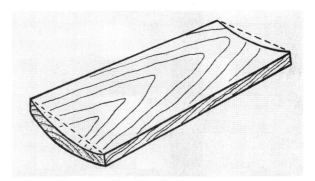

16–10. ▶ Plain-sawn boards have greater tendencies to cup, have wilder, more distracting grain patterns, and expand or shrink more with changes in environmental humidity.

Once you have fret-sawn the wood, warpage is not usually a serious problem because the openings made in the stock relieve or cut through those stresses that induced the wood to warp in the first place. Good finishing practices also help to minimize subsequent warpage.

Plywood in one form or another is widely used for fretwork projects. In spite of the fact that plywood has unsightly edges, and some kinds tend to have poorly bonded outer plies that splinter easily, flake and chip off at corners, or separate from narrowly sawn shapes, quality plywood offers may advantages. It is uniform in thickness, has minimal warpage tendencies, and is usually stronger than solid wood, which makes it a good choice for very fragile designs. Plywood's major advantage, however, is that it is ideal for projects that are of large size. Wide, thin, one-piece boards are not commonly available, and if they were, would probably be unacceptable for a variety of reasons.

Cheap building or construction plywoods including fir, Southern pine, and lauan should absolutely be avoided. Hardwood architectural plywoods and "door skins" may be usable, but it's difficult to predetermine if their face veneers have been well-glued in manufacturing (**16–11**). Most thin hardwood plywoods sold in the United States have only one good face. If plywood is available with two good sides, it is extremely expensive.

In recent years, imported Baltic- and Finnish-birch plywoods have become popular with woodcrafters. These materials are stronger, have more plies per given thickness, and have void- or gap-free interiors and edges (**16–12**). Other imported species are Italian poplar and jelutong, both of which are good, economical choices for projects requiring opaque, painted finishes. Remember, however, it is nonsensical to invest a lot of time and effort into a project using poor-quality material (**16–13**).

Fretwork-sawing skills can be quickly developed. Review the basic scroll-sawing techniques discussed in Chapters 5 to 10. Concentrating on preparing the blade-entry holes and cutting one opening at a time produce good results.

Because fretwork is so fragile and delicate, it is always best to finish-sand the surfaces before applying the pattern. Incidentally, fretwork can also be cut from plastic, metal, and materials other than wood. Fretted designs can also be cut in paper, so be sure to explore all possibilities.

16–11. ▶ Hardwood veneer plywoods are available in many species, but should be selected and used with caution.

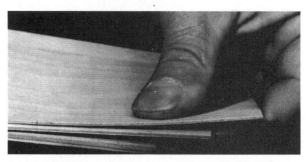

16–12. ▶ Light-colored ⅓₂-, ¹⁄₁₆-, and ⅛-inch Finnish plywood with void-free edges. Baltic birch with similar characteristics is available.

16–13. ▶ Examples of fretwork cutting problems primarily related to poor material choice. Weak fibers and poorly glued face veneer cause splintering and separation. Using a blade that is too coarse and an excessive feed can cause similar results.

BLADE-ENTRY HOLES

Use ⅛- to 3/16-inch-diameter drill bits for larger openings and 1/16-inch-diameter drill bits or smaller for tighter work. The key is to minimize grain tear-out or splintering. The bit may grab and tear the wood fibers outside the holes and extend the tear-out beyond the waste area if casually drilled too close to the line.

Use a high bit-rotation speed and a slow feed to get the cleanest holes. A support waste backer held tightly against the bottom surface of the workpiece is also essential.

Sometimes it is necessary to drill on the line such as when making "veining" or "definition cuts," as shown in **16–14**. This technique was first called veining because early fretwork patterns had many leaf designs with single-line cuts that represented the veins of leaves and foliage. Sometimes it is necessary to make very fine veining cuts that require very small blades and matching entry holes. If the material is very thin, such as veneer, a sharp-pointed knife or needle can be used to make a narrow slit or open a blade hole.

In addition to drill bits in the usual fractional sizes, small-numbered drill bits are available to drill holes even smaller than 1/64 inch. **Table 16–1** gives the decimal equivalent of the smallest-wire-gauge-numbered drill bits available, beginning with No. 80, the smallest size.

Table 16–1

Drill No.	Size
80	.0135"
79	.0145"
1/64"	.0156"
78	.016"
77	.018"
75	.02"
74	.0225"
73	.024"
72	.025"
71	.026"
70	.028"
69	.0292"
68	.031"
1/32"	.0313"

16–14. ▶ **Silhouette by John Polhemus is accentuated with "definition" or "veining" lines. Some cuts originate inside, and some are cut inward from an outside edge.**

Once all blade-entry holes have been drilled, turn the workpiece over and sand away any feathering or splintering that occurred around the holes. If you don't do this, extending fibers may catch at the scroll-saw table edge or opening and obstruct feeding.

CUTTING ORDER

Always leave the most delicate sawing for last; this will lessen the chances of accidental breakage. If there is an excessive amount of waste wood surrounding the pattern, trim it with a roughing-out cut for easier handling.

Usually the interior is cut first, especially if the pattern is small or the outline is elaborate and fragile. If the pattern is large with delicate or fragile interior cutouts, then cut the outside first. Each design must be judged individually.

Also take into consideration the order in which you will saw interior parts. If the cutting of a certain opening will leave a delicate part unprotected, then cut that opening last (**16–15**). If the table hole surrounding the blade is too large, a scrap plywood backer or an auxiliary zero-clearance table on which to support the work is recommended.

Using the right blade, the best available material, and careful sawing techniques will allow you to handle the most delicate of fretted sawing jobs confident that the chances of breaking fragile parts are reduced to the very minimum.

SAWING ACCURATELY

Sawing accurately can be accomplished by practicing the basics of scroll-sawing. You do need well-drawn patterns. Be sure the table is square to the blade and practice controlled feeding to saw straight lines and true circles and ovals. A slip or miscut will be more noticeable on these cuts than if sawing a free-form design. Do not get into the habit of relying on sanding or filing to correct a miscut. Plan to saw either on the inside or the outside of the line and then try to stick to that practice.

If your blade seems to wander or "float" away from your intended cutting path, stop and locate the cause. Is it the grain of the wood, not enough tension, the type of blade, the feed or blade speed? Whatever the problem, correct it before continuing, because

16–15. ▶ The "short" grain and pointed claws of the dragon cutout are very fragile. This would be one of the last openings to be cut. Notice the narrow parallel cut, which also requires care and concentration.

fretwork requires a major investment in scroll-sawing time not to be wasted with excruciating miscuts. Practice and experience ensure confident and pleasurable fret-sawing.

FRETWORK ASSEMBLIES

As discussed previously, fretwork is often made of very thin stock, so there generally is not sufficient material for assembly with screws or nails (**16–16**). Fast-setting super or instant glues are especially useful where nails or small screws may split the wood. Many butt and miter joints are, therefore, simply

glued together, which may require some innovative clamping techniques when conventional woodworking glues are used. Illus. **16–17 to 16–21** depict typical steps involved in making and assembling a fretwork project that has mitered butt joints.

Tab-and-slot joints (**16–22 and 16–23**) were used for at least a century before good, easy-to-use adhesives arrived. This is still an excellent joinery technique for thin material that otherwise provides minimal gluing surface areas. Other wood joinery techniques are discussed in Chapter 18. Not all projects require joints (**16–24**).

16–16. ▶ Using a high-speed rotary tool to drill pilot holes in hardwood for a butt-joint assembly nailed together with brads.

16–17. ▶ This fretwork basket, designed by Julia Meader of the Timber Lace Company and sawn by Julie Kiehnau, is a typical fretwork project requiring glued miter joints.

16–18. ▶ A disc sander makes the 15-degree beveled edges.

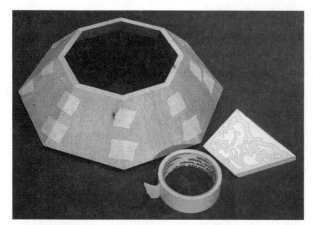

16–19. ▶ A dry assembly with tape checks the fit of the compound miters before sawing.

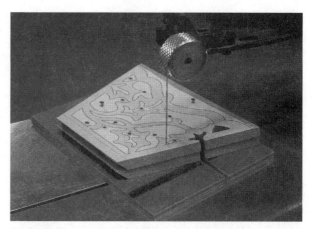

16–20. ▶ Fret-sawing by stack-cutting two sides at once supported on a waste piece of scrap plywood paneling.

16–21. ▶ All pieces sawn, ready for the final glued assembly with tape used as a hinge and clamp.

16–22. ▶ Tab-and-slot joints will secure the assembly of this fret-work wheelbarrow made from 1/8-inch stock.

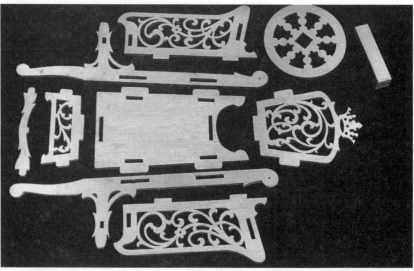

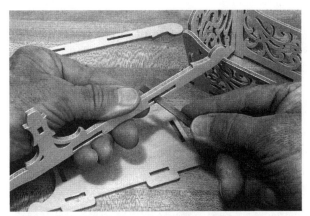

16–23. ▶ A small file is used to adjust the size of a slot.

16–24. ▶ Router and fretsaw techniques were employed to make these boxes without requiring usual joinery.

16–25. ▶ Ground blades can be used to produce clean, smooth cuts even in tight turns with ¾-inch oak right off the saw.

technique works with remarkable success. (See page 189 for illustrated sample cuts.)

CARVED FRETWORK PROJECTS

Hand-carving on fretwork surfaces sawn from thicker, solid woods gives a special added dimension and visual appeal to certain projects. One class of work that does not require advanced carving skills is "arabesque" ornamentation. This work is distinguished by creating an image of interlacing patterns. Two intriguing examples of century-old designs are shown in **16–26 and 16–27**.

THICK-WOOD FRETWORK PROJECTS

Basically, the same techniques employed to saw fretted openings in thick wood are used for thin material. The primary difference will be the size and type of blade selected. The objective is to get clean, smooth cuts without any burn marks (**16–25**). There is no easy way to remove burn marks from tight inside turns. Make test cuts in the waste area of a project before starting any finished cuts. If you get any burning, change to a new, sharp blade immediately.

Tip: Cherry, maple, and some other hard dense woods have burning tendencies that can be minimized with packaging tape. Simply cover the line of cut with clear tape. It seems to have some magical ingredient that lubricates or cools the blade. This

16–26. ▶ This flat, carved fretwork, which appears as an interlaced or woven design, is known as arabesque ornamentation.

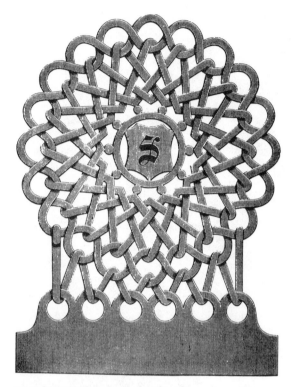

16–27. ▶ Another example of arabesque carving.

16–28. ▶ This small table of an old Swedish design has simple carved Arabesque ornamentation.

Arabesque work can include floral or foliage patterns as well as the more-complex geometric designs. Many of the old Swedish fretwork patterns included simple versions of arabesque designs. Illus. **16–28 to 16–33** show a small hexagonal table project that is a fairly elementary example of arabesque ornamentation.

Simple, basic carving skills go a long way to create interesting scrollwork. Much of this is flat surface work that can be done with just a sharp chisel. A curved gouge or V-tool is helpful for making curved stop cuts and shoulders.

If you're not a carver, simply wood-burning shallow crossing lines is a good alternative approach (**16–31**). A little practice with a test piece is recommended before applying any new technique to a project in which you have already invested sawing time.

Serious scroll-sawing wood carvers can shape leaves, round over vines, and make other design elements fully three-dimensional (**16–34**).

16–29. ▶ First, make vertical stopped cuts to sever the grain fibers.

16–30. ▶ Make slicing cuts to taper the thickness of the wood until a depth of ⅛ inch or more is reached at the deepest point.

16–31. ▶ Woodburning of the crossing and/or veining lines is an alternative for noncarvers.

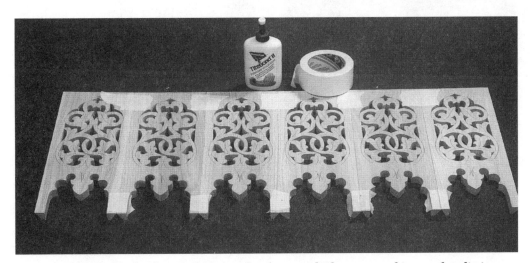

16–32. ▶ The completed sides. Masking tape has been applied to act as a hinge and preliminary clamp for the glued assembly.

16–33. ▶ **Loops of twisted rope provide extra clamping pressure.**

16–34. ▶ **Carved fretwork by Joan West.**

LARGE AND DELICATE FRETWORK

Some of the large (or actually huge) fretwork projects being created today are absolutely awe-inspiring (**16–35 to 16–38**). In addition to being large in size, some of this work is also incredibly delicate and fragile. This work is not for the timid and should only be approached with the realization that you must be fully committed to a long-term and perhaps stressful effort. As you may know, the two largest scroll saws available today are the RBI 26-inch and the Excalibur 30-inch scroll saws. Some of the largest pieces being made far exceed these throat limitations. Pieces up to six feet tall have been made using 18- and 20-inch scroll saws.

One technique is to make the project in stackable tiers. Robin Wirtz, one of the world's most ingenious and skilled fretwork artists, has developed some clever and inventive techniques to make large fretwork panels that seem to exceed the limits of normal possibilities (**16–38 to 16–43**).

16–35. ▶ **This Eiffel Tower made of 3/16- and 1/4-inch solid walnut by James Reidle stands 36 inches high. This project consists of several independently made stacked sections.**

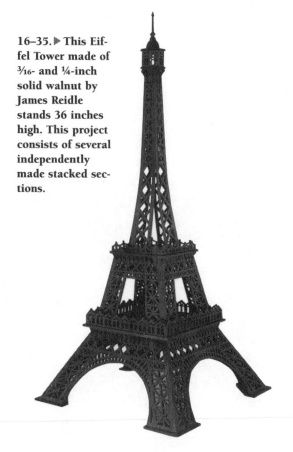

16–36. ▶ A close-up look shows highly skilled sawing and demonstrates excellent continuity of the straight and curved-line cuts.

16–38. ▶ "Flight of Fancy" by Robin Wirtz is made of ½-inch solid ash and measures 16 × 32 inches. Notice the astonishingly thin and delicate curly Q's that seem to just dangle.

16–37. ▶ The Dome Clock stands 50 inches high. It is a resurrected design from the 1800's. This one was made of 5/16-inch butternut by the late James Reidle Sr. in the 1940's using a foot-powered scroll saw.

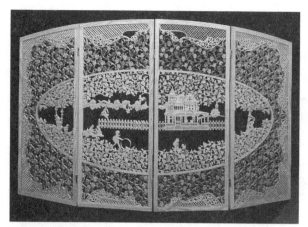

16–39. ▶ A typical Robin Wirtz project, this fireplace screen—entitled "Summer Dreams"—measures 45 inches high and 6 feet wide with 5,654 inside cuts.

16–41. ▶ This folding screen by Robin Wirtz is 6 feet, 11 inches high x 6 foot wide. It is cut from ½-inch ash set in 1-inch frames.

16–40. ▶ Close-up of Robin's ½-inch-thick solid-ash screen. Notice the horizontal grain direction of the fretwork panels.

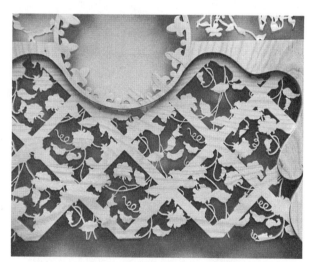

16–42. ▶ A close look at the delicate cutting of curly Q's in solid ash with horizontal grain.

16–43. ▶ This design—entitled "Hummer"—is another delicate piece of fretwork by Robin Wirtz. It measures 32 inches high × 8½ inches wide and has 868 inside cuts. The grain runs horizontally and the project is made in either two or three sections, depending upon the throat capacity of your saw.

16–44. ▶ One of Robin's earlier scroll saw set-ups shown during construction. The entire tabletop will be covered with plastic laminate.

While many people are naturally curious as to what brand of saw Wirtz uses (a DeWalt 20-inch saw), that is not as important as how she "outfits" her scroll-sawing center. To totally eliminate scroll-saw-induced vibration, Wirtz has a large, custom-built auxiliary table (**16–44**). The scroll saw, with its stand, is placed in the corner of the shop and bolted to the floor. The saw table is attached to the two walls in the corner and does not touch any part of the saw. Thus, if there is any saw vibration, it is not transmitted to the workpiece. The table is covered with plastic laminate and waxed so the workpiece moves easily (**16–45 to 16–47**). The front edge of the saw table is well-rounded, so the work doesn't get caught on it.

Each of Wirtz's project panels is made in sections of a size that permits being sawn and rotated within the throat-capacity limits of her scroll saw (**16–47**). White ash is Wirtz's choice of wood because it is strong, hard, not brittle, and has good resistance to shock or impact while still having a beautiful pattern and color.

The grain of each panel section must run horizontally to permit being glued to other sections and to systematically increase the vertical dimension of each panel. The pattern is applied to the workpiece with 1-inch-wide, double-faced tape (refer to **16–46**). The entire back of each pattern is covered with the

tape. Spray adhesive does not hold to the very narrow cuts or endure the excessive handling involved.

Wirtz uses No. 2 and 2/0 blades for fine detail and No. 5 reverse-tooth blades for general sawing. When sawing curly Q's and delicate designs, cut the insides first and avoid any sideways pressure when making sharp turns.

Each section is cut complete, one at a time, except for about 1/8 inch all along the top and bottom edges that abut to the next adjoining section. The sawing that is left undone in these areas generally consists of simple straight or easy cuts that can be made through the glue line after the glued has cured.

16–45. ▶ Robin's original patterns are developed with a CAD program. Here's her color computer printout ready for sawing. Notice the plastic laminate that covers the table.

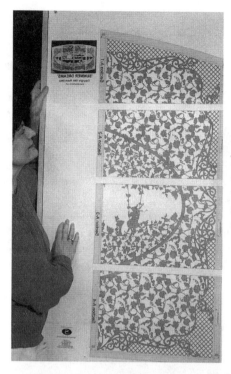

16–46. ▶ The patterns for just one of the four panels for the fireplace screen shown in 16–39.

When the sections are glued, the fret-sawing along the joints is completed and the clamping tabs are sawn off. Each completed panel is stored, temporarily fastened to a sheet of plywood (16–51). The project is painted on one side with an airbrush. The back side is not painted but clear-finished so the project can be reversed for those who prefer a natural look. Finally, each panel is inserted into a grooved frame and connected with hinges.

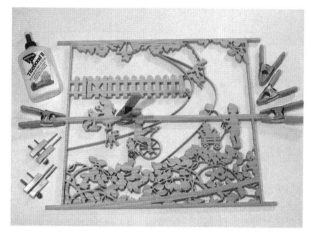

16–48. ▶ Building a large vertical panel from smaller sections. Notice the two outside gluing tabs and the small amount of sawing still to be completed. The remaining inside cuts are mostly straight through the glue line and will be completed after the glue cures.

16–47. ▶ Robin at work on a panel section.

Wirtz also cuts "clamping tabs" into the outside waste, near the glue line, for clamps to grip on to (16–48 to 16–50). Specially made clamps designed to provide pinpoint pressure along the glue line are also used. The sections are glued together lying flat on a piece of plywood prepared with a crosswise-cut opening. The glue-joint work is performed over the plywood opening so the work can be inspected and clamps can be applied from either side as necessary.

16–49. ▶ Clamping is done on a piece of plywood over an opening to provide access for the clamps and allow inspection from both sides. Specially made clamps are used to produce pinpoint pressure where needed.

16–50. ▶ Sawing is almost completed in each section except for approximately ⅛ inch along each joint, which will be cut after gluing.

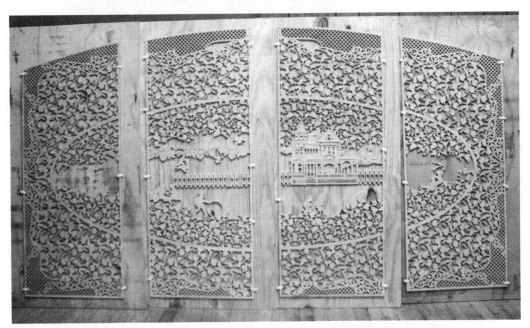

16–51. ▶ The completed sawn sections have been glued into individual panels, which are then safely stored against a piece of plywood for protection while they are finished with air-brushing and the outside frame work is being prepared.

CHAPTER SEVENTEEN

APPLIQUÉS & OVERLAYS

ny figure or design glued or fastened onto a flat background is called an overlay or
appliqué. Generally, this work serves a decorative or ornamental purpose; however, practical work such as overlaying the hour numbers of a clock or applying letters to a sign also
fits into this category of work (17–1 to 17–3).

Scroll-sawn signs are discussed in Chapter 23, and some examples of sculptured overlays applied to marquetry backgrounds are illustrated in Chapter 14. Almost any project can incorporate overlays or appliqués
to give its surfaces more visual impact. A very basic example is shown in 17–3 in which a sculptural effect
is obtained by gluing several layers of wood with rounded edges to a flat surface.

Overlays can be used to conceal material imperfections or structural joints, as shown in 17–4. Overlays
can also be combined with other scroll-sawing techniques such as with pierce-sawing and inlay work
(17–5). The size and character of the design should determine the best thickness for the overlay. Most scroll-
sawers tend to use wood that is too thick, creating a heavy look. As a general rule, the smaller and the more
delicate the design (17–6), the thinner the overlay should be.

17–1. ▶ This clock face sawn by Carl Weckhorst features overlaid numbers and decoration.

17–2. ▶ Here a decorative overlay becomes the focal point of this fretwork project.

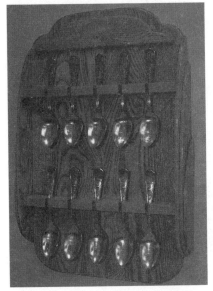

17–3. ▶ The layering of solid-wood pieces with rounded edges to the sides of this spoon rack by Don Zinngrabe creates a sculptural effect.

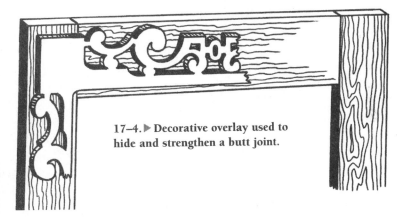

17–4. ▶ Decorative overlay used to hide and strengthen a butt joint.

17–5. ▶ Another clock face made by Carl Weckhorst combines pierce-sawn numbers and decorative overlays.

17–6. ▶ These small pins of maple and mahogany crafted by John Polhemus were sawn with a 2/0 blade. Tiny droplets of instant glue bond the overlays to the background.

Plywood ⅟₃₂ or ⅟₁₆ inch thick is often a good choice for overlay and appliqué material. Finnish- and Baltic-birch plywood make very suitable overlays. They are durable, yet have "soft" grain figures and colors that suggest an appropriate delicateness.

Thin solid woods and veneers can be used as overlays (**17–7 and 17–8**), but they require careful sawing and handling. The wild or coarse-grain figures on some woods prove to be unattractive when used for overlays and plain fretwork as well. Another general guideline to keep in mind is that overlays are often made from a material that contrasts in color with the background. Light-colored overlays, however, look good on almost all backgrounds. Be careful when using dark overlays on light backgrounds—this could make the overlay appear heavy, which may be contrary to the look you are trying to achieve.

Overlays should be cut carefully because the material usually contrasts with the background and miscuts will be obvious. When the overlay is delicate and the material is thin, a suitable fine blade will be necessary. It may be necessary to sandwich thin material between two waste boards while sawing. If you are cutting several overlays together in a stack, use a backer board to support the bottom layer.

Another factor to consider when using solid woods is to maintain consistency of the grain direc-

17–8. ▶ **Solid-wood initial overlay on a solid-wood box. The grain direction of the overlay is the same as that for the solid-wood top.**

tion. Since woods swell and shrink with changes in humidity, the grain of the overlay and the grain of the backer should run in the same direction (**17–8 and 17–9**).

Use an auxiliary table with a zero-clearance opening around the blade when sawing thin and delicate work. Saw out the inside opening of the larger intricate overlays first. Be careful when sawing thin and narrow parts. (Review Chapter 10.) Saw carefully with a firm and easy feeding motion. Apply some pressure to the delicate areas near the blade with your fingers or use the eraser end of a pencil.

17–7. ▶ **Carved butternut overlay on the back of a walnut hand-mirror project created by Joan West.**

17–9. ▶ **Locate the desired position of the overlay with two dots or small pencil marks so it can be placed quickly when gluing.**

GLUING

Several kinds of glue can be used: instant or super cyanoacrylate glue, yellow carpenter's glue, or a permanent-bond spray adhesive. Apply glue carefully if the overlay is very delicate. Usually there are some larger areas where glue can be used a little more liberally, and small areas that should only be "spotted."

Thin overlays are difficult to clamp because the material is usually flexible so it is a problem to obtain uniform pressure. You may need a caul or pressure pad (flat board) under the clamps. If the object is difficult to clamp, use a sandbag, bricks, or a stack of books for weight.

One effective method for applying glue to the overlay is to first apply a thin coat of glue onto a piece of glass (or any smooth, flat material), drop the overlay on it, and then press gently to coat all areas. If careful when applying the glue, you will not have to clean up excess glue that has oozed out around the edges.

Illus. **17–9 to 17–14** show the steps involved in gluing an overlay with regular woodworking glue. It can be difficult to position overlays, so make sure that you have prepositioned your piece before applying glue. Before gluing, lay the overlay on the background and mark its location lightly with a pencil (refer to **17–9**), pinprick two positioning points, or set in three stick pins for guides when you lay the glue-applied overlay in place.

Another technique is to save the waste cut from sawing around the overlay and temporarily tape it in place to the background. This serves as a placement guide for the overlay and contains it so it doesn't slip while clamping.

After the overlay is glued in place, put something flat on it to distribute pressure and weigh it down. Use a heavy piece of plastic or plate glass (with smooth edges for safe handling). This way, you can see when the overlay moves if excess glue accumulates (refer to **17–12 and 17–13**).

The best kind of glue to use depends upon the circumstances associated with the inlay itself. Large-size overlays will require slower-setting glues or a quick method of applying the glue and a suitable clamping technique.

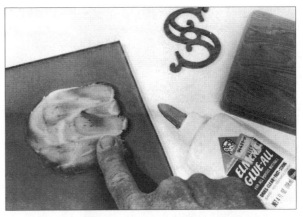

17–10. ▶ **Spreading an even coat of glue onto a piece of flat glass or plastic.**

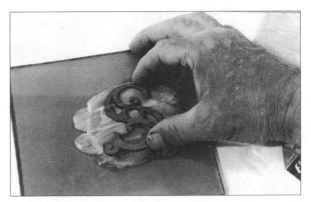

17–11. ▶ **Carefully drop the overlay onto the glue spread on the glass to transfer an even coat to the gluing surface of the overlay.**

17–12. ▶ **A piece of glass or clear plastic is used to distribute clamping pressure, and it allows you to inspect the work.**

17–13. ▶ Carefully remove any glue "squeeze-out" after it sets, but before it cures hard.

17–15. ▶ Fretted ¹⁄₁₆-inch birch plywood overlays create a nice look on these purchased basswood tissue boxes.

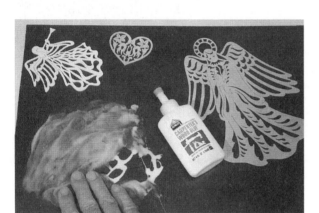

17–14. ▶ Thin ¹⁄₃₂-inch plywood overlays ready for gluing. Glue is being spread on a flat laminate countertop in preparation for transferring it to the backs of the overlays.

Spray Adhesive

Using spray adhesive has several advantages. It is easy and quick to use. Some permanent-bond spray adhesives will also bond unlike materials. Use spray adhesive to bond wood, metal, or plastics to each other. It is excellent for gluing woodcut silhouette designs to translucent plastic for making lamps. Spray adhesives also bond wood letters to Corian to make attractive desk name signs. (Refer to Chapter 19 for information on cutting Corian.) If you cut the letters from thin veneer, it looks almost like an inlay, which is also attractive.

Use a spray adhesive that requires just hand or roller pressure and no clamping. This is ideal when applying large-size overlays that are difficult to reach with clamps (**17–15**). Spray adhesives also work well for applying thin overlays to curved backgrounds.

When using aerosol adhesives, it is important to direct the spray so it is at a right angle straight toward the back surface of the overlay (**17–16**). If done carefully, very little of the adhesive overspray will collect on the edges of the overlay.

A good spray adhesive for overlay work has a low "soak-in" quality and a fast, aggressive tack. (Adhesives that soak into the wood require more adhesive.) Usually, just hand pressure or a roller to press the overlay tightly to the background is all that is required. *Caution:* Always use adhesives and finishes in a well-ventilated area.

Warning: Certain finishes such as Danish oil and lacquer-based finishes may actually dissolve some kinds of spray adhesive. A water-based polyurethane topcoat may be a better choice of finish when a spray adhesive is used. Always make a compatibility test of

17–16. ▶ Direct the spray of the aerosol adhesive at a right angle to the surface of an overlay to minimize any glue buildup of adhesive at the edges.

17–17. ▶ Before finishing, an optional step is to use a flutter-wheel abrasive (shown in a hand drill) to smooth and soften the sharp sawn edges of the overlay.

17–18. ▶ This dramatic-looking project features a wood fretwork background with fretted brass overlay wording and symbols. (Photo courtesy of Robert Becker, *Creative Woodworks & Crafts* magazine.)

the adhesive and finish beforehand.

Depending upon the look you want and the thickness of the background, decorative nails or screws can also be used to attach overlays. Brass escutcheon pins or small brads with painted heads can also be used. Plastic and metal overlays need to be predrilled, and fragile solid woods should also be drilled when using metal fasteners (**17–18**).

OVERLAYS OVER INLAYS

Combining overlays over overlays can sometimes create a very special project (**17–19**). Regular square-edge, carved arabesque, or simple overlays with slightly rounded edges applied onto a background with a flush inlay(s) are all interesting and reasonable possibilities.

Applying overlays over inlays allows you to incorporate a wider variety of colors or more kinds of wood or other materials into your artistic efforts. The neat thing about this technique is that there is no need to waste time trying to make a perfect fit around the inlay because the work can be designed so the overlay covers or hides all the edges of the inlay. The inlay(s) will only show through one or more of the openings cut out of the overlay.

The key to inlay work, of course, is to make it fit flush to the background so that the overlay that is eventually applied will have a level surface for gluing. The recessed surfaces for the inlay can be made with careful bevel-cutting techniques using the scroll saw. (See Chapter 13.) It would be advantageous to use a router or a hand chisel to cut inlay recesses partway into background surfaces should you have work that you do not want to cut through.

Illus. **14–27 to 14–31** on pages 242 and 243 show some beautiful examples of sculptured overlays applied to marquetry backgrounds.

17–19. ▶ An example of the possibilities involving overlays placed over inlays. This can provide an endless variety of colors and interesting decorative effects.

JOINERY

*T*he capabilities of a good scroll saw can be employed to make a number of useful woodworking joints (**18–1 and 18–2**). As in most areas of scroll-sawing, well-executed joinery cuts
depend upon accurate layout and the scroll-sawer's proficiency for following lines precisely.
The ability to cut next to a very sharp, fine line or to actually split the layout line is sometimes an essential
skill for joining two parts perfectly together. (Refer to Chapter 8 for information about scroll-sawing basics.)

This chapter discusses a few historically popular joints that have been made with the scroll saw and were
used to assemble scrollwork long before modern adhesives and special metal fasteners became available.
(Illus. **16–22** on page 260 shows the tab-and-slot joint used centuries ago for assembly of thin fretwork.
Techniques for using the scroll saw to prepare wood for making interlocking or contoured edge-to-edge
joints are discussed in Chapter 13.) Some of the more typical woodworking joints including lap joints, flat
miters, cope joints, and even through dovetails can be sawn with the scroll saw.

Some of the joints illustrated here obviously could be made easier and faster using other woodworking
tools such as table saws and routers. On a nonproduction basis, however, you will find the scroll saw to be
an effective joint-making tool, particularly if your shop is not equipped with other such equipment. On pages
289 to 293, you will learn how to make a novel hinged joint and an elegant pin-and-cove joint using the
scroll saw with assistance from a router.

18–1.▶ **Halved joints may be cut entirely with the scroll saw. The two "halves" of the joint slide into each other. An assembled project shown at the right requires no glue and is easily disassembled if desired.**

18–2.▶ **The classic 19th-century pin-and-cove joints found in fine antique furniture and incorporated into this CD organizer were made with the scroll saw and the router.**

JOINT-MAKING TIPS

The following tips will prove helpful when you use the scroll saw to cut joints:

1. Use the widest blade possible, and be sure your table is set perfectly square to the blade.

2. Select easy-to-cut woods with uniform density. Use plywood where strength is a priority. When using solid wood, be sure it is free from warp and well-dried.

3. Always sand surfaces before sawing any profiles.

4. Check patterns for fine, thin lines; these are essential for sawing accurate joint components.

5. Avoid excessive use of glue.

6. Be cautious when using nails or screws to assemble thin wood; in fact, avoid their use whenever possible. They do not look good and tend to split thin wood.

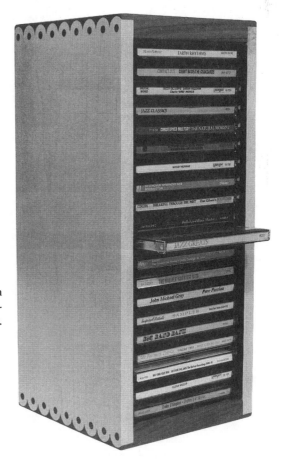

TAB-AND-SLOT JOINT

Tab-and-slot joints are cut entirely with the scroll saw itself. They are a type of mortise-and-tenon joint. In fact, these terms are often used interchangeably.

One variety of this joint, when assembled, is not easily visible (**18–3**). Other types, often called "through" or "open" mortise-and-tenon joints, are not hidden (**18–4 and 18–5**).

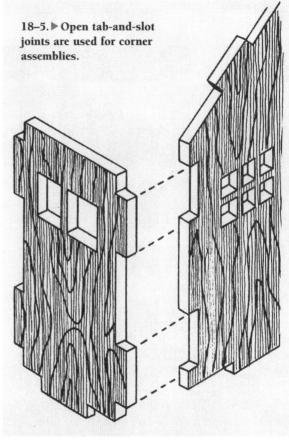

18–5. ▶ **Open tab-and-slot joints are used for corner assemblies.**

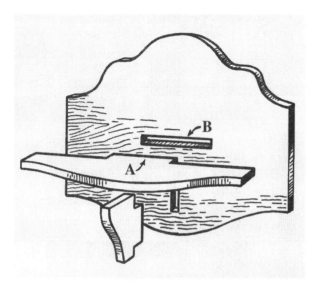

18–3. ▶ **The simplest form of tab-(A)-and-slot-(B) joint. When properly made, the joint is strong and not easily detected.**

18–4. ▶ **Visible tab-and-slot joints were widely used to assemble early fretwork projects.**

Locked Tab-and-Slot Joint

The locked tab-and-slot joint (**18–6 to 18–8**) is another joint sawn entirely with the scroll saw. It is somewhat difficult to lay out because the slots have to be offset slightly from the tabs, as can be seen in **18–8**. Locked tab-and-slot joints are good to use in various utility-type projects and in toy-making when building and dismantling play barns, fences, models, bridges, boxes, etc. It also should be mentioned that plywood is an especially good material to use when you are incorporating this joint into projects that will be roughly used, like toys.

18–7. ▶ A close look shows the "hooks" or "stops" of the tabs and the longer slots that allow the parts to slide and interlock.

18–6. ▶ A locking tab-and-slot joint was used to assemble this entire project.

18–8. ▶ A close look at the shelf tabs extending through the slots and then pulled forward to lock in place. The result is a strong joint, but it leaves an undesirable opening behind each tab as shown.

HALVED JOINT

Halved joints consist of slots that match in their widths and are cut into the workpieces, permitting the two parts to slide together to make an assembly without requiring glue. They are machined entirely with the scroll saw, but must be laid out and sawn very accurately (**18–9 to 18–14**). In fact, when using patterns with halved joints, be sure to check the material thickness with the slot sizes of the pattern. Usually a slight modification to the pattern is required. Make sure that you have sawn the parts just slightly oversize so that they can slide into each other without being forced—especially when you are using solid wood (**18–11 and 18–12**). In some cases, the slightest pressure may split the wood.

On the other hand, take into account the fact that if you are going to sand the faces, you will reduce the thickness and the needed widths of the openings. Sometimes, depending upon the character of the design, it may be more advantageous to saw the halved slots before sawing any of the remaining profiles. Often, a long halved slot temporarily weakens the work, in which case the slot should not be cut until last. Remember that the quickest and easiest way to attain a perfect fit with all such joints is to carefully lay out the joints and then saw them very accurately (**18–14**).

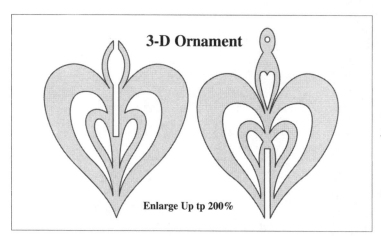

3-D Ornament

Enlarge Up tp 200%

18–9. ▶ A small three-dimensional heart ornament pattern incorporates a halved joint.

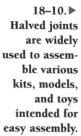

18–10. ▶ Halved joints are widely used to assemble various kits, models, and toys intended for easy assembly.

18–11. ▶ This elegant lamp project made of exotic solid hardwoods requires careful sawing and fitting of the halved joints used in its construction. (Photo courtesy of Robert Becker, *Creative Woodworks and Crafts* magazine.)

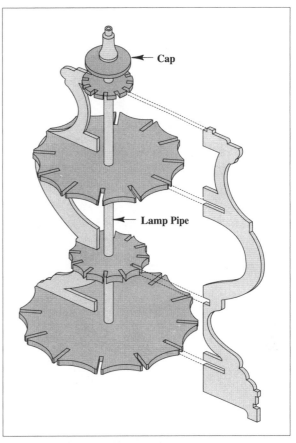

18–12. ▶ The lamp assembly details. (This drawing is adapted from a copyrighted pattern and instructions featured in *Creative Woodworks and Crafts* magazine.)

18–13. ▶ Three-dimensional birds assembled with the halved joint.

18–14. ▶ Almost every project requires some final adjustments of the slot widths so the components slide freely together. Here a scroll sander is used to trim the opening.

LAP JOINT

The lap joint (**18–15 to 18–18**) is a useful structural-frame corner joint for thicker stock. The width of the framing stock cannot exceed the thickness-cutting capacity of your scroll saw. The thicker the material the better, because both parts of the joint need to be sawn while it is supported on its edge, as shown in **18–17**.

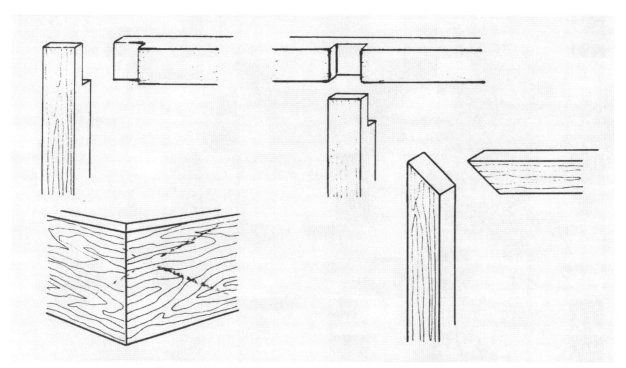

18–15. ▶ Some corner joints that can be cut easily on the scroll saw include, from left to right, corner lap, middle lap, and flat miter joints.

18–16. ▶ A corner lap joint made with the scroll saw.

18–17. ▶ Joint work such as this requires a wide blade, good tension, and accurate layout.

18–18. ▶ The basic cope joint. A cut piece is shown above; the assembled nonmitered inside corner joint is shown below.

COPE JOINT

The cope joint is commonly used for fitting moldings into an inside corner without using a conventional miter joint. Illus. **18–18** shows the cope-sawn and the assembled joint. To make this joint, only one piece is cut to the profile shape of the molding. The cut in this one piece is made simply by starting with a 45-degree miter cut on the end, as shown in **18–19**. The profile cut is then eas-ily made by sawing precisely along the miter line, which gives the exact curve required. This cut is made with the blade and table adjusted square to each other at 90 degrees.

No table tilting is required to make the cope cut. Illus. **18–20** shows the cope cut in progress. The resulting surface will be the coped end that matches the profile of the molding. This second piece should now butt perfectly against the first piece.

18–19. ▶ One piece (at left) is square-cut to length. The end of the second piece is miter-cut at 45 degrees before it is cut to the matching profile as shown in 18–20.

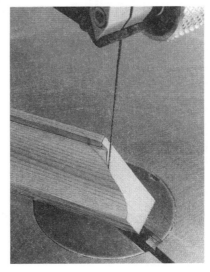

18–20. ▶ The miter-cut end is sawn precisely on the miter line to make the profile of the "coped" cut.

COPE DOWEL JOINT

Model-makers often use this joint to join dowels to each other to make various structures. Cabinetmakers can use this joint for making door and drawer pulls or handles. To get good intersections (**18–21**) , saw the ends of the dowels to a profile that equals the diameter of the mating dowel.

When a simple work-holding fixture is used, this type of cut can be easily made on the scroll saw. Simply bore a hole through a piece of scrap wood, as shown in **18–22**. If you are making a cope cut in the end of a ¾-inch diameter-dowel, then bore a ¾-inch hole. It may be difficult to insert and remove the dowel for cutting unless a slot is cut lengthwise or horizontally into the jig. Transfer layout lines to the top surface of the fixture to indicate the diameter for the end cope desired. The same idea works for making a coped cut into the side of a dowel. The fixture shown in the photos can be used for sawing both end and side coping cuts.

The cuts on the dowels are made by sawing precisely along hole surfaces bored into the fixture. Be careful not to cut into the fixture material or cut too far away from it (**18–22**).

Illus. **18–23 and 18–24** show some very easy-to-make drawers for workshop storage of small parts. The pulls are simply side-cope cuts on one-inch dowels that provide a finger grip. The dowels are glued into holes bored completely through the drawer front and secured with a finish nail driven vertically into the dowel.

18–21. ▶ **Coped joints are perfect for connecting dowels. The simple jig at the right is helpful for making coped dowel joints.**

18–22. ▶ **Cope-cutting the end of a dowel in the fixture.**

18–23. ▶ **The dowel finger-pull on this small-parts drawer was made by cope-cutting.**

18–24. ▶ **The pulls on these workshop storage drawers are simply side cope cuts on one-inch dowels that provide a finger grip.**

FLAT MITER JOINT

With the assistance of a very basic and simple fixture, you can make perfect-fitting flat miter joints. The key is to carefully make the jig or fixture, which is not difficult. Use a piece of ¼-inch plywood about 6 inches × 12 inches. Lay out two lines 90 degrees to each other for fastening two ¾-inch × 1¼-inch guide strips. Glue and nail them in place so they make a perfect 90-degree inside corner. Don't worry about the quality or fit of the mitered corner on the fixture. It is of no importance, because you will be running the saw through it anyway. Any miscut .miter

(**18–25**) is corrected by making successive passes and shifting the pieces together after each pass, until there are no longer any gaps remaining (**18–26 and 18–27**).

Sometimes the two pieces of flat miter (**18–28**) can simply be held against a square or plastic draftsman's triangle (**18–29**). Repetitive cuts are made through the joint as necessary until a perfect, gap-free fit is achieved. *Tip:* To reinforce miters cut in thin stock and miters that are visible only from one side, simply glue lengths of finish nails across the joint as shown in **18–30**.

18–25. ▶ **Poorly fitting flat miter cuts can be easily corrected with the scroll saw.**

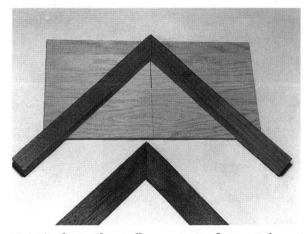

18–26. ▶ **Above: The scroll saw mitering fixture. Below: A poor-fitting flat miter joint ready to be corrected with the help of the fixture.**

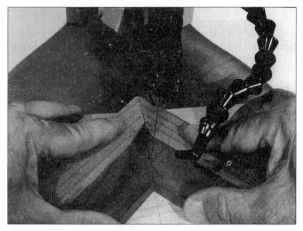

18–27. ▶ **Workpieces are handheld tightly against the guides of the jig with the joint as tight as possible. Successive saw cuts are made through the gap of the joint until the joint closes perfectly without any gaps.**

18–28. ▶ **Flat miters cut for a thin fretwork picture frame.**

18–29. ▶ **If any gap exists at the miter joint, hold the pieces tightly against a square or draftsman's triangle as shown and make a cut through the joint. Repeat as necessary until the joint fits tightly.**

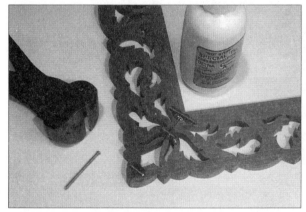

18–30. ▶ **Epoxy or glued nails applied to the back surface of this fretwork mitered frame strengthen the joint without worry of splitting the thin, delicate joint with conventional nailing practices.**

THROUGH DOVETAIL JOINT

Through dovetails (**18–31**) are beautiful corner joints and a symbol of high-level craftsmanship. Dovetails can be made with the scroll saw remarkably easily. One advantage of dovetailing with a scroll saw is that no special jig or fixture is needed; in fact, all that is needed is a good scroll saw with a table-tilt capability and a sharp, narrow blade with good tension.

Make a practice joint before attempting this work on a major project. Make sure that your stock is of uniform width and the ends are cut square. Set the pieces on edge, with the choice surfaces (faces) to the outside. Determine which piece is to be the pin piece and which is to be the one with the tails. In **18–31**, the tail piece is on the left and the pin piece is on the right. Start with the pin piece first. It is the more complex of the two parts to

18–31. ▶ **This through dovetail joint was cut with the scroll saw without the aid of any jigs or fixtures. At left is the "tail" piece; the other part is called the "pin" piece.**

make. It is far easier to make the tails fit previously cut pins.

Lay out the spacing and angular marks for the pins on the end of the board. Usually angles of 14 to 15 degrees are standard, with 15 degrees recommended here simply because it's easy to find on the saw tilt scale. On the inside face, draw a line square across the board to represent the thickness of the tail or other member of the joint. Then "square-in" lines extending from the end of the board to the line on the inside face. This will now give you the left and right angles of the pins and their length. Illus. **18–32** clearly shows the pin layout and how to make one of the bevel or

18–32. ▶ **The pins have been laid out, and one side of a pin is being bevel-sawn. Make all cuts saving the layout lines.**

angular cuts that forms one side of the pin.

To make the pin "bevel-ripping" cuts, tilt the table correspondingly to 15 degrees. You can only cut one side of each pin at this first table setting. Cut the full length of every pin.

Next, to make the second cut on each pin do one of two things: either reverse the blade so it cuts rearward and leave the table at the same adjustment, or tilt the table to the identical degree setting but in the other direction. Illus. **18–33** shows the first approach used on saws that have tables that tilt in one direction only. Install the blade so the teeth face away from the operator and make the cut by pulling the work toward you.

18–33. ▶ **Bevel-ripping the second side of the pins. Here, the blade is installed rearward so the teeth point away from the operator. The cut is made by pulling the workpiece toward the operator. Use this technique on scroll saws with tables that tilt just one way. Otherwise, the operator has the option to tilt the table to a new setting to make the second bevel cut on each pin.**

Once all of the bevel-ripping cuts have been completed, adjust the table to a perfect 90-degree setting. Now, cut out the majority of the waste between the pins, as shown in **18–34**. Carefully follow the layout line so that the pins are all of uniform length. You will have to leave little wedge-shaped waste pieces next to each pin.

Remove the wedge-shaped waste pieces that remain on each side of the pins with a sharp knife (**18–35**). Practically any knife will handle this job—the only requirement is that the knife is sharp enough to slice off the end-grain fibers. The completed pin member is shown is **18–36**.

18–35. ▶ The remaining triangular waste pieces next to the pins can be cut away with a sharp knife, chisel, or hand coping saw.

18–34. ▶ Once each pin has been bevel-sawn on both sides with the table tilted, cut out the spaces between the pins with the saw table set at 90 degrees. Notice that all material except the little wedges next to each pin is carefully sawn away.

18–36. ▶ A completed pin piece. Notice that the sharp pencil lines have (for the most part) not been cut away.

Making the tail member is easy, although accuracy in the layout and cutting is essential. Use the finished pin member as a pattern for laying out the tail member. Carefully trace around it as shown in **18–37**. Use a square and mark the depth of the tails so they equal the thickness of the mating pin board.

Sawing the tails is easy. However, it is imperative that you do not cut beyond your layout lines. Use a fine blade such as a No. 2 or 4. Try to save the layout lines. Utilize the "on-the-spot" turning capability of the saw to make the sharp inside corner cuts required for this job (**18–38**).

The joint should fit together without much problem provided you saved the line when cutting the tail member. This should create a tight joint that may

require some tapping with a hammer and a scrap block to bring the joint together—exactly the type of fit you want.

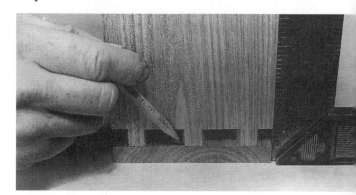

18–37. ▶ Transferring the outline of the pins to the tail piece.

18–38. ▶ With the saw table at 90 degrees, cut the tails as shown. Utilize on-the-spot cornering techniques and save the layout lines to complete the tail pieces.

HINGED CORNER JOINT

This hinged joint (**18–39**) is more decorative than functional. As with dovetailing, however, people will be amazed that this unusual joint was made primarily with the scroll saw. The design of the hinge limits its range of movement, but for picture frames, toys, and similar projects, it has some useful applications.

There are two keys to making the hinged joint:

1. The dowel pin of the hinge appears to run all the way from top to bottom, but it does not. Two short lengths of dowel, one inserted from the top and the other from the bottom, provide the pivoting mechanism (**18–40**).

2. The two halves of the hinge are created by sawing one piece of stock in two, by cutting along the interlocking square-shaped fingers as shown in **18–41**. Use a No. 5 or 7 blade.

Basic specifications for making this joint with ¾-inch-thick stock as shown in the photos are as follows: The square "fingers" of the hinge are ¾ × ¾ inch; the roundovers (**18–42**) have a ⅜-inch radius; the dowels are ¼ inch in diameter x 2½ inches in length; the inside vertical holes are ⁹⁄₃₂ inch in diameter; and the top and bottom pin holes are ¼ inch in diameter.

18–39. ▶ The decorative hinged corner joint on this project has a limited swing range, but it's perfect for connecting these standing picture frames.

18–40. ▶ Drilling for the dowel hinge pin is done before sawing the square hinge fingers to separate the two halves. A shop-made V-block guides the bit.

18–41. ▶ Sawing the square hinge fingers as shown creates the two "leaves" of the hinge. Careful, consistent sawing directly on the line and sharp-turn cornering are important.

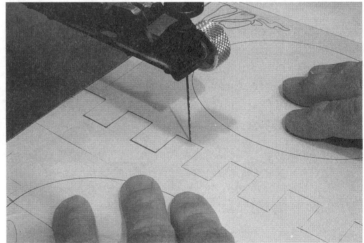

18–42. ▶ A router table is used to round over the hinge edges.

PIN-AND-COVE JOINT

The pin-and-cove joint (**18–43 and 18–44**) is believed to have evolved from a joint that originated in Europe over a century ago. Occasionally, it appears as a drawer joint found in quality antique furniture. The original joints were made with very complex machines that produced integral dowel pins cut on the end grain along with the scalloped female cuts. Today, with a router and scroll saw you can imitate joints that look exactly the same as those made long ago. The only tools or accessories required are a template, a router and bit, a scroll saw, and a drill.

You can either make the template yourself (**18–45**) or purchase a ready-made one of tough plastic. The template serves three functions:

18–43. ▶ These elegant 19th-century pin-and-cove joints are made using a router and a scroll saw. A template is required. You can either make one from Baltic-birch plywood, as shown at the left, or use a commercially produced one made from polycarbonate plastic, as shown at the right.

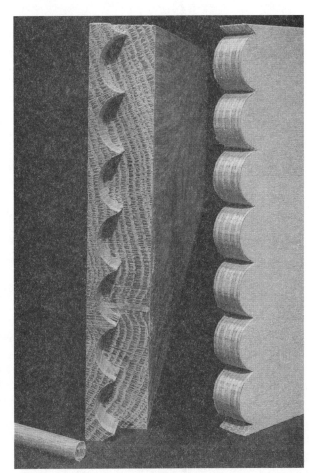

18–44. ▶ Components of the pin-and-cove joint. The routed female scallops are shown at the left, and the matching male scallops cut with the scroll saw are at the right.

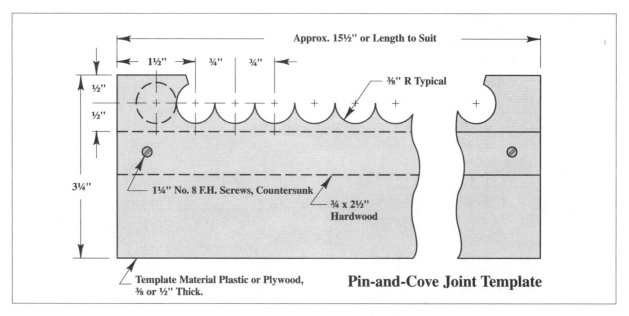

Approx. 15½" or Length to Suit

1½" ¾" ¾"

½"

½"

3¼"

⅜" R Typical

1¼" No. 8 F.H. Screws, Countersunk

¾ x 2½"
Hardwood

Template Material Plastic or Plywood,
⅜ or ½" Thick.

Pin-and-Cove Joint Template

18–45. ▶ Construction details for making your own pin-and-cove template.

1. It is used with the router and a ⅝-inch-diameter pattern bit (with a ½-inch cutter length) to cut the scalloped recesses (**18–46 and 18–47**).
2. The template is also used to lay out the wood for scroll-sawing the matching scallops (**18–48**).
3. The template is used as a positioning device for drilling the dowel pinholes.

The basic procedure is as follows:

1. Purchase or make a template using a ¾-inch-diameter bit, boring a row of holes ¾ inch center to center (refer to **18–45**).
2. Rout the female scallops with the workpiece clamped vertically as shown in **18–46 and 18–47**.
3. Lay out male scallops as shown in **18–48**.
4. Cut the male scallops with the scroll saw as shown in **18–49**. *Tip:* Cut straight into the apex between the curves. Then back the blade in to start the cut from the point of the apex.
5. Make a trial fit.
6. Glue and clamp the joint together, checking for squareness.
7. After glue has cured, drill the pinholes as shown in **18–50**.
8. Insert dowels with glue (**18–51 and 18–52**).
9. Cut and sand the dowels flush.

18–46. ▶ View showing how the template is used with a pattern-type router bit to machine the female scallop cuts of the joint. (A pattern-type router bit has a ball-bearing guide the same diameter as the bit that follows the profile of the template.)

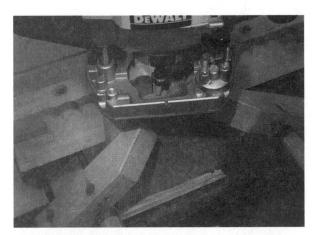

18–47. ▶ The routing operation.

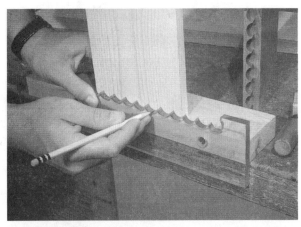

18–48. ▶ Laying out the male scallops for scroll-sawing.

18–49. ▶ Scroll-sawing the male scallops. Notice the relief cuts made inward to the apex of each scallop.

18–50. ▶ Setup for drilling the pin holes. A center-drilled ¾-inch-diameter dowel held cradled against the template locates each hole, and the tape on the bit gauges the hole depth.

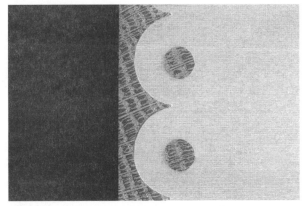

18–51. ▶ A close look shows how the grain direction of these oak dowel pins matches the end grain of the oak stock.

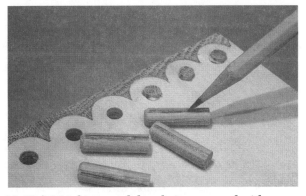

18–52. ▶ Matching wood dowel pins prepared with a marked line to reference the grain direction.

CHAPTER NINETEEN

SAWING PLASTICS

he techniques for scroll-sawing various types of plastic have advanced tremendously in recent years (19–1 and 19–2). Previously, you were doing pretty well if you could saw acrylic plastic, for example, without frictional heat fusing the kerf back together behind the blade. Illus. 19–3 to 19–6 clearly show this problem and the importance of having some sort of mask or tape preapplied to the surface to help dissipate frictional heat.

Contemporary blade designs and sawing procedures commonly produce scroll-sawn surfaces that almost look polished. In many cases, sanding and polishing the scroll-sawn edges of the plastics can be virtually eliminated. Recently discovered sawing techniques and the easy accessibility of special plastics afford the average scroll-sawer more freedom and satisfaction when working with plastic. Project designs and patterns developed especially for plastic are steadily emerging, and most popular plastics can now be sawn almost as easily as wood.

There are a number of keys to successful plastic-sawing that must be observed. One major factor is the selection of the best sawable material. Some plastics look alike, but have distinctly different characteristics (19–7). All plastics, by and large, saw cooler and smoother if the surface is covered with duct tape or packaging tape in addition to the factory-applied protective mask (19–8 and 19–9). Other keys to successful plastic-sawing include the appropriate blade, the optimum blade speed and feed, and blade modification if necessary to provide clearance in the kerf to reduce side friction.

19–1. ▶ Cuts in acrylic plastic. Shown are a ⅜-inch-thick eagle sawn by Bill Pickens, test cuts on a single ½-inch-thick piece, and two ⅜-inch stack-cut pieces. Notice that all sawn edges have near-polished surfaces.

19–2. ▶ Highly detailed fretwork in ⅛-inch acrylic mirror stock sawn by Don Frechette.

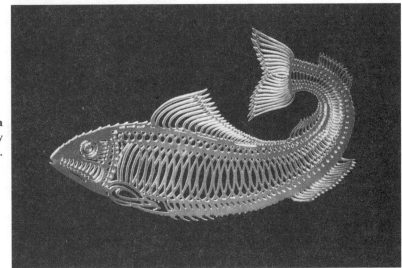

19–3. ▶ Sawing ¼-inch acrylic with a No. 7 skip-tooth blade. This shows a typical problem when sawing unmasked plastic. Notice the molten plastic gumming the blade and fusing the kerf together.

19–4. ▶ The cut edges with "globs" of melted plastic clinging to them clearly demonstrate the problem of frictional heat.

19–5. ▶ Masking tape applied to plastic and then sawn under same conditions as the cut shown in 19–4. Notice the sawdust-like waste.

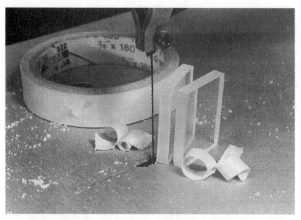

19–6. ▶ A close-up look at the pieces sawn in 19–5. Notice that they have cleaner cut surfaces than the plastic cut in 19–3 and 19–4. They are, however, not as smooth and as polished-looking as they can be (refer to 19–1).

19–7. ▶ Left: Clear acrylic. Right: Tinted polycarbonate. Under the same conditions, the acrylics cut smoother and are less expensive, but are more brittle.

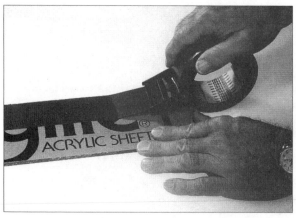

19–8. ▶ Duct tape applied to the top surface either lubricates the blade or keeps the cut particles from reentering the kerf. This prevents the cut from fusing.

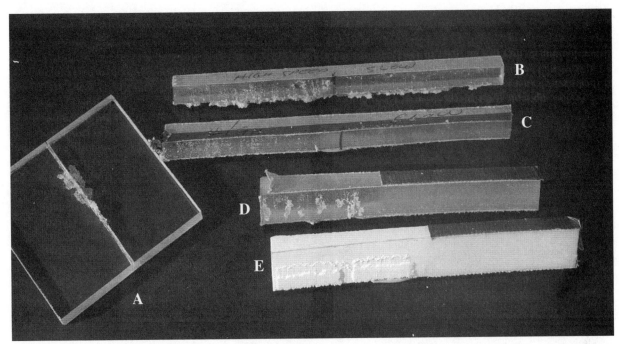

19–9. ▶ **Various plastics cut with a No. 7 double-tooth blade. (A) Unmasked acrylic with a fused kerf. (B) One-quarter-inch masked acrylic. The left side was cut at 1,725 strokes per minute, and the right at 850 strokes per minute. (C) One-quarter-inch acrylic with mask and duct tape. The left side was cut at a high speed, the right at a slow speed. (D) Three-eighth-inch polycarbonate cut at a slow speed. The left side was cut with only a mask, and the right was cut with a mask and duct tape. (E) One-half-inch Corian cut at a slow speed. The left side was cut with no mask or duct tape, and the cut shows fusing; the right was cut with duct tape, and has a clean cut.**

TYPES OF PLASTIC

There are perhaps a thousand or more different types of plastic material in use today. The average scroll-sawer, however, probably has access to just a dozen or two. Acrylic sheet plastics are very popular and easily accessible, but there are three different formulations of acrylics that look similar, yet cut very differently. In addition to the various kinds of acrylic plastic, scroll-sawers can also cut ABS (acrylonitrile butadiene styrene), epoxies, melamines, nylon, phenolics, polycarbonates, polyesters (including reinforced polyesters [fiberglass]), polypropylenes, polystyrenes, PVC (polyvinyl chloride), vinyl, Teflon, and other plastics. Of all the sheet plastics, the acrylics are the most widely used.

Acrylic Plastics

Acrylic plastics with brand names such as Plexiglas, Lucite, Acrylite, and others are generally made in three different ways. In descending order of scroll-saw cutting quality, these are: 1) cast, 2) continuous cast, and 3) extruded. *Cast-manufactured acrylics* are made by pouring molten liquid plastic resin into a mold, and then curing it between sheets of plate glass. *Continuous-cast acrylics* are made by producing sheet plastic on reels in very long lengths. The thickness of these acrylics is not as consistent as that of cast-manufactured acrylics. *Extruded acrylics* are made when a screw feed system forces melted resin through openings that give it its form, similar to the way toothpaste is forced from a tube.

You can, for example, purchase Acrylite FF, which is continuously extruded, or Acrylite GP, which is cast. They look similar, but have very different scroll-sawing qualities. Usually acrylics over 1/10 inch in thickness are cast or continuous cast.

Extruded plastics are the least expensive, but the most difficult to cut. Slight changes, however, in blade size, speed, or side-clearance modification and feed rates can make a dramatic difference in cutting. If you have problems, try a slower blade speed, a slower feed rate, and a larger blade. Observe the chips (sawdust) coming to the top of the kerf. If there are not individual sawdust-like particles, slow down the feed rate.

It is also interesting to note that certain colors of acrylic tend to cut better than others.

Polycarbonate Sheet Plastics

Polycarbonate sheet plastics such as Tuffak look much like the acrylics, but are generally tougher. They are also more expensive and cut easier, but the scroll-sawn surfaces do not finish as polished as acrylic surfaces.

Polystyrenes

Polystyrenes and other soft, thermoforming plastics will cut much like the extruded acrylics (**19–10**). Slow blade speeds and feed rates are required for the cutting of most plastics. Additionally, the surfaces need to be covered with tape and the blade may need to be modified to provide side clearance in the kerf. Each type and thickness of plastic reacts differently to various sizes and types of blade, feed rates, and blade speeds. Consequently, it is always necessary to test the variables in scrap stock before making finished project cuts. Sometimes slowing the blade speed just 50 to 100 strokes per minute can make a big difference.

Solid Surface Materials

Solid surface materials such as Corian (**19–11**), Avonite, and Surell are readily cut with a scroll saw. Again, however, the surface or cutting lines need to be covered with either duct tape or clear packaging tape. Slower feed rates are also required. Blade modification to provide side clearance may be necessary (**19–12 and 19–13**). Other trade names of hard surface material include Fountainhead and Gibraltar.

Of all brands, Corian, made by DuPont, is the most popular for scroll-sawing. That is because there are now several mail-order companies that sell small quantities of Corian to scroll-saw hobbyists. Most other brands of hard surface material are sold exclusively to trained dealers that currently do not make their material available to the general public.

Corian consists of 30-percent acrylic polymer and 70-percent natural materials. It is available in 80 different colors and granite-like patterns. The most popular thickness is ½ inch, and the colors and patterns run all the way through the material so it never wears away and does not delaminate.

Decorative Plastic Laminate

Decorative plastic laminate (also know as HPL [high pressure laminate]) is the most common type of countertop surface covering. It is available in hundreds of colors and pattern variations including wood grains, marble, slate, and others. It is a standard ¹⁄₁₆ inch thick and very hard and brittle. The

19–10. ▶ Left: Undesirable cut on ¼-inch-thick extruded acrylic plastic made with a No. 5 crown-tooth blade at 400 strokes per minute and with a slow feed. Center: Same extruded acrylic plastic, but cut with a No. 9 crown-tooth blade, at the same speed and approximately the same rate of feed. Right: Piece of ⅛-inch extruded acrylic (covered with transparent film) with a fused cut that is shown alongside a clean kerf made when masking tape was applied to the surface. A No. 5 crown-tooth blade was used for both cuts at approximately 550 strokes per minute and a slow rate of feed.

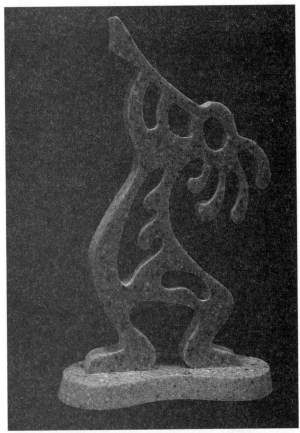

19–11. ▶ **This figure is made of Corian; notice the smoothly cut edges, shown just as they came from the scroll saw without any subsequent sanding or polishing.**

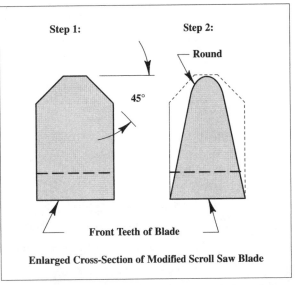

19–13. ▶ **Technique for shaping the cross-section of the blade to obtain clearance.**

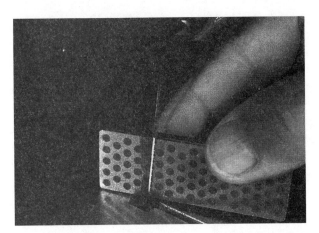

19–12. ▶ **Modifying the blade with an abrasive "stone" (in this case, a diamond hone) to remove material from the sides of the blade and behind the teeth, to provide clearance and less friction in the kerf.**

most well-known brand is Formica. This material is best cut at slow speeds with a fine-tooth, metal-cutting blade.

Scroll-sawn decorative laminates make good overlays and attractive signs and ornaments. They can be glued back to back for projects such as ornaments that are visible on both sides. New laminates have the color running through the material; this ensures that the laminate will be visible on both sides of the project.

BLADE SELECTION AND MODIFICATION

Generally, the two best types of blade to use for cutting sheet acrylics and solid surface material such as Corian are the ground-tooth and the crown-tooth blades manufactured by Olson Saw Company. To make an occasional cut, a skip- or double-tooth blade might work, but for continuous sawing and the best possible results, the ground or crown-tooth blades are recommended. The crown-tooth blade cuts cool, probably because the teeth carry the chips so they exit from both the bottom and the top of the workpiece.

In most cases, the action of the blade burnishing against the sides of the kerf, which gives wood such a very smooth cut surface, is actually the major cause of friction and heat when cutting plastic. This, and the fact that most saw blades smaller than the No. 12's do not have any set, makes it understandable why cutting plastics requires some modification to the material, cutting speeds, and to the blade itself.

Remember the general rule of using the largest blade possible that still allows you to cut the detail needed, provides the quality of cut desired, and keeps enough teeth in contact with the work relative to the material's thickness.

To provide clearance, reduce side friction, and allow making sharper turns than usual with a wider blade, modify the blade's cross-sectional shape as shown in **19–12 and 19–13**. Illus. **19–14 and 19–15** show some cuts made with modified ground and crown-tooth blades, respectively. Illus. **19–16** shows the types of jewelry item that can be made with a scroll-saw blade that has been modified.

19–14. ▶ **Stack-cutting two layers of ⅜-inch acrylic. Notice the bright area of the blade that has been removed with an abrasive stone to provide clearance.**

19–16. ▶ **Small jewelry items cut from Corian, brass, and silver.**

19–15. ▶ **One-eighth-inch acrylic cut with a No. 2 crown-tooth blade.**

OTHER TIPS AND SUGGESTIONS

The type and brand of plastic, its thickness, the amount of detail required, the speed range and stroke length of your saw, and of course the blade used all have an impact on plastic-sawing success. There is, for example, a notable difference between scroll-sawing Corian hard surface material and Surell. The latter dulls blades more quickly, so more frequent blade changes are necessary. Generally, it has been the author's experience that the patterned Corian cuts cleaner than the single, solid-color types (**19–17**).

If using blades with reverse teeth, pay attention to what they are doing. You may be better off lowering the blade position in the blade clamps so the reverse teeth do not carry the plastic sawdust upward, back into the kerf. When sawing thin material, you may find that you are cutting the majority of the stock's thickness on the upstroke.

19–17. ▶ This handsome dolphin, designed by Barry Gross, is made of sculptured ½-inch Corian with inlays.

At the first indication of any problem, slow the feed rate. If that doesn't help, slow the blade speed. A blade speed between 500 and 700 strokes per minute is a recommended starting point. Expert scroll-sawer Bill Pickens uses modified ground blades and suggests starting at 650 strokes per minute for sawing most acrylics. He has also stated that the ½-inch bronze-colored acrylic made by Rohm and Haas cuts great at 675 strokes per minute. Another of his favorite acrylic plastics is ⅜-inch-thick amber.

Bill will also snip off ¼ inch from the bottom of his modified blade, thus lowering it in the saw. This places the transition area where the blade was honed well below the table and reduces the number of reverse teeth that cut. (Refer to the test cuts shown in **19–18 and 19–19**.)

An old trick when sawing plastic is to lubricate the cutting line by rubbing it with the corner of a block of paraffin, a candle, or a crayon. Another approach is to apply a saw-blade lubricant directly to the blade to prevent chips from clogging it. Lubricants are available as a solid wax stick or as a liquid in a spray dispenser.

Plastics-sawer Don Frechette developed a unique lubricating system for stack-cutting extremely fine detail with 2/0 blades to cut the fish project shown in **19–2** on page 295. He sandwiched 30-weight, oil-saturated thin cardboard between the two or three layers of stacked ⅛-inch-thick acrylic plastic mirror. After sawing at a slow speed, the oil was removed with soap and water.

When scroll-sawing plastic mirror, do not apply any kind of tape to its back side. It may pull off the

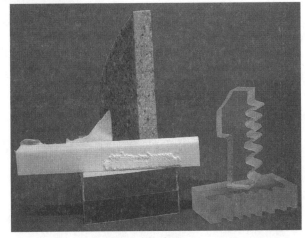

19–18. ▶ Cuts in Corian and thick cast acrylic all made using Olson's No. 9 PGT blade. The vertical piece of Corian has a scroll-sawn edge almost as smooth as its flat surface. The white Corian on the left-center of the photo shows a smooth cut on its left half, with masking tape on its top surface; the right half shows how the chips have fused together on the wall of the kerf when cut without the tape. In the foreground on the left are two pieces of ½-inch-thick cast acrylic, each with factory masking tape, stack-cut at 700 strokes per minute and a slow feed rate of approximately two linear inches per minute. In the foreground on the right are tight radius cuts in ½-inch-thick acrylic plastic (made with factory masking on).

reflective backing when removed. It is best to fasten it to a waste plywood backer held together with brads driven through predrilled holes on the waste sides of the cut. This way, sawdust, chips, and/or any roughness on the saw table will not scratch the reflective backing of the plastic mirror.

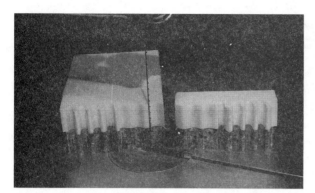

19–19. ▶ **Stacked and tight-turn practice cuts made with a No. 9 ground blade through two layers of ½-inch-thick Corian, each surface covered with masking tape and held together with double-faced tape.**

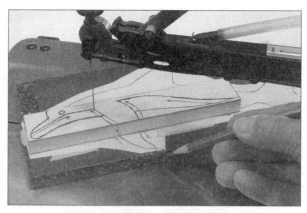

19–21. ▶ **Small piece of white Corian held in place over the bottom layer ready for stack-sawing.**

Plastic inlays can be made following the same procedures used for wood. Illus. **19–20 to 19–23** show how the edge inlays of the dolphin project in **19–17** were made by stack-sawing. Illus. **19–24** shows a product that can be used to polish projects such as the dolphin project.

Liquid plastics of various colors and some with contrasting granules can be used as pour-in inlays for small scroll-sawn designs such as lettering and decorative accents in Corian and other solid surface materials. Simply cut the design with the scroll saw, tape off the bottom so the liquid doesn't run out, mix and pour in the product, and sand it flush after it cures. One such product available to scroll-sawers by mail order is sold under the trade name Inlace.

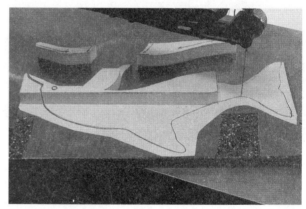

19–22. ▶ **The double-thickness inlay areas are cut before the outside profile.**

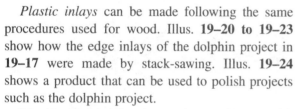

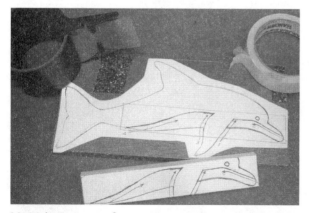

19–20. ▶ **Corian surface preparation for sawing the dolphin shown in 19–17. Two separate workpieces are covered with duct tape, and the pattern is applied as usual over the tape.**

19–23. ▶ **With the inlays glued in place with epoxy or instant glues, the edges are rounded over and the entire project is sanded and polished.**

19–24. ▶ **The Wonder Wheel (nylon impregnated with abrasive) is available from Judy Gale Roberts's studio. It is ideal for polishing metal and shaping Corian, as well as for detailing intarsia pieces.**

PHOTO CUTOUTS

Photo cutouts, also referred to as "photo sculptures" (**19–25 and 19–26**), are simply photographs glued to plastic or wood that are then profile-cut with the scroll saw and mounted to a wood base. There really isn't any kind of sculpture work involved. Original "photo sculptures" are made with photos permanently glued to a white, opaque plastic. Solid white is preferred because it not only blends with the white photo paper, the white does not show the scratches on the sawn edges that can result from poor scroll-sawing techniques.

A permanent spray bond adhesive is recommended to get the best bond. It is usually best to roughen the surface of the plastic slightly with 100-grit abrasive. Apply the glue according to the manufacturer's instructions, which usually suggest using a roller to apply pressure.

19–25. ▶ **Photo "sculpture." A photo permanently glued to white opaque plastic (or to plywood) is profiled with the scroll saw.**

19–26. ▶ **Spray adhesive bonds the photo. The photo outline is cut with a tab added to the bottom that matches a slot cut into a ¼-inch-thick solid-wood base.**

CHAPTER TWENTY

SAWING METAL & OTHER HARD MATERIALS

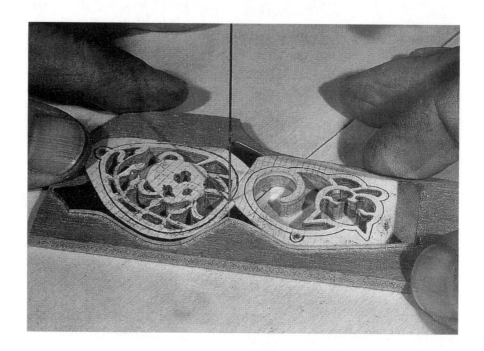

P rojects involving sawing metal to create jewelry (20–1), models, novelty items, and decorative hardware, and a variety of ornamental (20–2) and utility metal-cutting jobs (20–3 to 20–5) are all within the normal capabilities of most scroll saws. A good scroll saw should cut hard materials up to ½ inch thick and some easier-cutting metals up to ¾ inch thick. A number of metals do cut remarkably easily.

Copper (20–3), brass (20–6 and 20–7), aluminum, silver, bone, ivory, and even steel plate (20–8) can be sawn to extraordinarily fine detail with the sawn edges relatively free of conspicuous saw marks. Notably hard materials such as glass, ceramics, and stone can also be sawn; however, cutting such materials may be pushing the limits of scroll-sawing practicality. Nonetheless, lubricants, coolant-delivering accessories, and special diamond blades are available for those insistent on using the scroll saw to cut darn near everything.

20–1. ▶ Examples of extraordinary metal-sawing detail by Monty Gould.

20–2. ▶ Painted sheet aluminum ornament made by Karl Gutbrod.

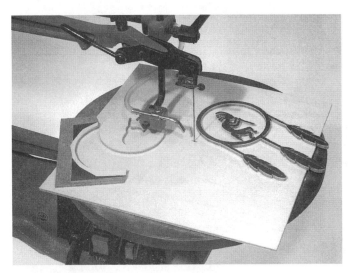

20–3. ▶ Sixteen-gauge copper sawn while bonded to a ⅛-inch hardboard waste backer with pattern adhesive. Double-faced tape holds a piece of ⅛-inch plywood in place as a protective auxiliary table.

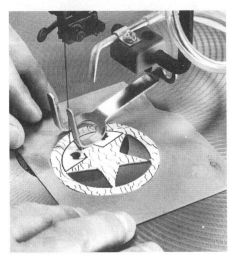

20–4. ▶ Sawing sheet metal. Notice that the blade teeth are so fine they are barely visible.

20–5. ▶ Sawing square tubing. Notice the coarser blade.

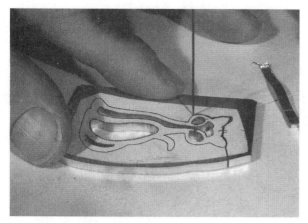

20–6. ▶ Sawing ⅛-inch brass.

The ability to saw any hard material hinges upon selecting the most sawable kind of material, selecting the best type and size of blade, and employing the best blade speed and feed rates. It is also essential to have a good saw with a true vertical blade travel and to possess good feeding skills to keep the blade from rubbing against the sides of the kerf. It is especially helpful to have some supporting tricks to cool or lubricate the cutting action to minimize friction. Many materials, however, can be cut dry, clean, and relatively quickly without lubricants or special cooling techniques (refer to **20–7**).

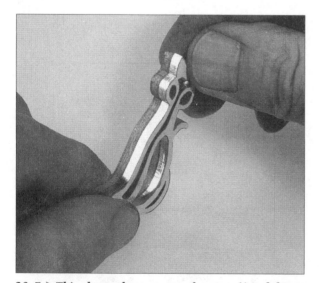

20–7. ▶ This shows the very smooth cut on ⅛-inch brass sawn while temporarily bonded to a plywood waste backer.

20–8. ▶ Detail cut into ¼-inch steel plate with a Hegner saw.

MATERIAL SAWABILITY

Any problems encountered when sawing metal and metal-like materials can often be attributed to *not* selecting the most sawable kind of material. Like the variable cutting qualities of different acrylic plastics, the sawability of a particular metal cannot be determined by its classification or looks. Basic metals are composed of various mixtures and ratios of other metals (alloys), which give the metals different characteristics and, consequently, a wide range of sawing qualities. Brass, for example, consists of copper and zinc in various combinations. It may also contain quantities of aluminum, lead, or tin. To maximize scroll-sawing efficiency, purchase brass labeled as "dead soft" or "half hard." It consists of 85-percent copper and 15-percent zinc.

Like brass, other metals vary in their composition and hardness. There are hundreds of aluminum alloys available that have a very wide range of scroll-sawing qualities. Hardness or softness is not necessarily related to a material's sawability. Some soft metals, such as certain aluminums, tend to load or "gum" the teeth of fine-tooth blades. Some aluminums and brass may, on the other hand, be so hard that if they are at all cutable, the sawing process is very slow and the blades wear down much too quickly.

Metals are sold by the square foot or square inch and by weight. Metal thicknesses are expressed by gauge numbers as well as fractional and decimal equivalents as identified in **Table 20–1**. Always ask your supplier about the machining characteristics of the material before buying. If cutting scrap or recycling some unknown material, you will find out very quickly how cutable the material actually is once you attempt a test cut.

Table 20–1

Gauge Chart

Thickness	Gauge	Decimal Equivalent
▬	14	.064
▬	16	.50
▬	18	.40
▬	20	.032
▬	22	.025
▬	24	.020
▬	26	.016
▬	28	.013
▬	30	.010

Table 20–1. ▶ Gauge chart with popular metal thicknesses.

METAL SOURCES

Metals for scroll-sawing can be obtained from many sources. A manufacturer's scrap piles are a good source. Used or new aluminum house siding is very cutable. Many old signs are painted on usable sheet aluminum. An old silver spoon, for example, can be flattened and provide the perfect material for special pieces or jewelry (**20–9 to 20–11**).

20–9. ▶ A silver spoon is a good material source when making jewelry pieces.

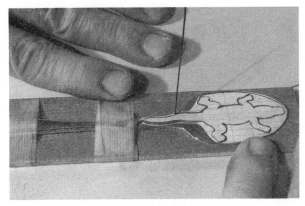

20–10. ▶ A flattened silver spoon being cut into a pin.

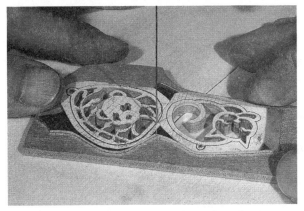

20–11. ▶ Jewelry-making with sterling-silver sheet, a very expensive material.

BUYING METALS

Mail-order companies specializing in hobby, craft, and jewelry-making materials provide small quantities of various metal materials. Check your local Yellow Pages under "Metal Fabricators" and "Salvage" for companies that may sell off-cuts and scraps at good prices.

BLADES

Blades for metal-cutting have as many as three times the number of teeth per inch, and they are harder and more brittle than woodcutting blades of comparable sizes. Fine teeth are necessary for sawing hard and thin material.

Caution: Some metal-piercing blades are very brittle and are recommended only for use in handheld saw frames. They may dangerously shatter when broken if used in scroll saws. Some Swiss and German manufacturers, however, produce 5¼-inch fine metal-piercing blades that are sufficiently flexible and suitable for use in scroll saws. Still, however, the finest blades (5/0 to the 8/0 sizes) are not recommended because they are so fine and delicate. A 4/0 blade, for example, has 72 tpi (teeth per inch) and, obviously, it is intended to use for cutting extremely fine detail. Almost the same detail, however, can be cut using 2/0 or 0 blades with 62 and 56 tpi, respectively.

Jeweler's metal-cutting blades with 42 tpi are recommended for material up to ⅛ inch thick. Use blades with 50 tpi for material up to ¹⁄₁₆ inch thick. Metal-cutting blades with 30 tpi and less can be used for material ³⁄₁₆ inch and thicker. As a point of reference, a No. 5 jeweler's blade with 36 tpi will cut ⅛-inch-thick brass running at 1,350 strokes per minute with a cutting rate of about one linear inch of feed per 15 to 17 seconds.

Diamond Blades

Diamond blades (**20–12**) are available to cut or actually grind away mother-of-pearl, ceramics, glass, and stone. These blades are made of round piano wires onto which industrial diamond abrasive particles have been electroplated.

Diamond blades are available in a coarse 60-grit size to a finer 180-grit. They range in length from 5⅛ to 5⅜ inches, and can be trimmed to length with side-

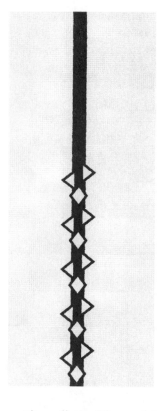

20–12. ▶ Diamond blades are piano wires electroplated with industrial diamond abrasives.

cutting pliers. Diamond blades have diameters of .027 or .032 inch.

Diamond blades can be used dry, but they work best with liquid coolants such as water or cutting oils, which can be messy around the scroll saw. Soft lubricant sticks and mist-spray lubricants are worth a try. Glass and other very hard material can be lubricated with water.

Even though diamond blades actually cut (or abrade) on both the upstroke and downstroke, because they do not have conventional teeth they cut very slowly. Diamond blades should not be used for cutting softer materials because loading will likely occur.

COOLANT SYSTEMS

Coolant systems (**20–13**) are available from distributors of RBI and Hegner scroll saws. The RBI unit consists of a drip-tank system with a feed line that delivers the desired amount of liquid to the blade. An adjustable needle valve sets the drip rate. Hegner's system operates from a foot pump that delivers fluid as needed through a nozzle mounted to the hold-

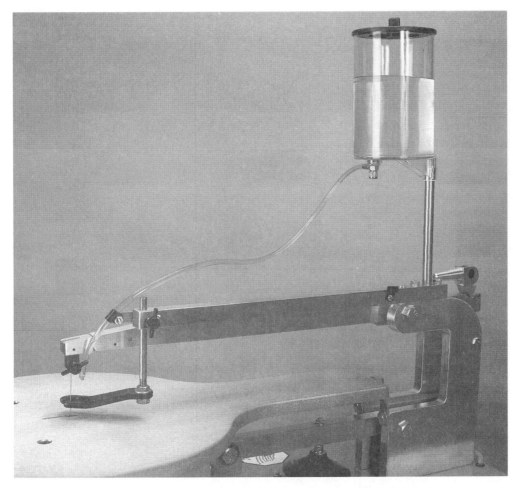

20–13. ▶ R.B.I.'s drip-tank accessory has a valve to control the coolant drip rate.

down arm. The RBI and the Hegner coolant accessories are easily adaptable to other brands of scroll saw.

It's been said that some scroll-sawers have tried the intravenous liquid-feeding apparatus used in hospitals with good success for dispensing lubricants and coolants to the cutting area of the scroll saw. If you ever have a hospital stay, be sure to request that your used implement leaves with you!

TIPS FOR CUTTING METALS AND OTHER HARD MATERIALS

Always employ prudent safety practices, especially the wearing of eye protection. Here are some additional tips that you may find helpful to use either alone or in combination with other techniques. Always test in a trial-and-error mode:

1. Clean and polish the surfaces before applying the pattern. Use liquid polish if the material is free of scratches, etc. Rough, scratched surfaces will need to be worked with silicon-carbide or aluminum-oxide abrasives and power-buffed with a cotton buffing wheel and tripoli polishing compound (**20–14**).

2. Copper, brass, and other materials may come with protective varnished surfaces that need to be removed before applying subsequent finishes and special coatings such as patina solutions (**20–15**).

3. Protect the surface of your saw table with an auxiliary table made of thin plywood or hardboard (refer to **20–3**).

4. Protect the bottom surfaces of your workpiece from scratches by mounting your work to a

20–14. ▶ **An old electric motor converted to a buffer consists of a cotton buffing wheel on a threaded motor-arbor adapter that fits onto the motor shaft.**

20–15. ▶ **Sheet copper "critters" scroll-sawn, bent to shape, and treated with a patina finishing solution.**

waste plywood or stiff cardboard backer. Thin metals can be temporarily bonded to backers with spray pattern adhesive (refer to **20–3**).

Although thicker material can be cut without a backer, at least a single piece of bottom waste backer has advantages. It allows the pattern to be applied directly to the material rather than to the top layer of a "sandwich." With a bottom backer, the bottom work surface is not exposed to the cutting chips, which otherwise will scratch surfaces. A backer also gives more thickness to the work, making it easier to grip and control with your fingers when feeding.

5. Thin metals in the 30- to 18-gauge-thickness range are best sawn sandwiched between two pieces of waste plywood.

6. Apply a generous coat of paste wax to the bottoms of backers. This will help to lubricate the blade and improve feeding.

7. Use the hold-down whenever possible.

8. Always feed the workpiece in a direction that is directly into the front of the blade. Often there is a tendency to apply some of the feeding pressure to one side of the blade when sawing curves. This forces the blade to rub against the sides of the kerf, which increases blade friction, heat, and premature blade failure. When cutting small pieces, check for the correct feeding direction by occasionally relieving the feed pressure entirely to see if the blade shifts or pushes the workpiece sideways on the table.

9. Thin metals can be stack-cut. Layers of soft copper and aluminum, for example, can be stack-cut simply by nailing, taping, or gluing them to a waste plywood backer.

10. Try ground wood-cutting blades to make an occasional cut in nonferrous metal if you don't have metal-cutting blades on hand.

11. Stick, mist, and liquid lubricants really do help. Use bar soap, paraffin, a candle, or a crayon if you don't have commercial lubricants. Soft metals, including some aluminum, may be best cut using liquid lubricants.

12. Try covering the lines of cut with duct or packaging tape when sawing hard-to-cut materials.

13. Some metals may require annealing (softening) before they can be cut. This requires heating the metal to a specific temperature and then cooling it in the appropriate manner—with water, oil, sand, or a special solution, or by just allowing it to cool slowly in the air.

14. *Caution:* The cut edges of metal are sharp. Soften them with a buffing wheel charged with an abrasive compound (**20–16**).

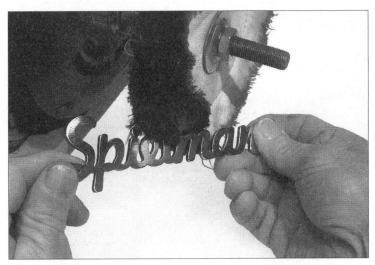

20–16. ▶ **Buffing polishes surfaces and softens sharp edges.**

CHAPTER TWENTY-ONE

SAWING PAPER

Scroll-sawing paper is easy and fun. It is surprising that more scroll-sawers do not take advantage of the practical and novel things that can be done with paper and the scroll saw *(21–1 and 21–2)*. Cutting up a stack or two of 3 × 5 note cards, for example, will quickly produce enough ornaments to decorate an entire Christmas tree or produce a supply of unusual greeting cards. You can easily create filigree name tags and placecards for an entire banquet or produce any number of unusual holiday and party decorations.

The single major key to sawing paper and paper-like sheet products is to clamp the individual sheets (several or hundreds) tightly together into a stack-sawing "sandwich." This can be accomplished with tape or nails *(21–3 and 21–4)* as done with the hidden book compartment and the stationery projects shown. When professional scroll-sawer John Polhemus cuts stationary, he shrink-wraps his stack with the pattern on top.

Illus. *21–5 and 21–6* show how easy it is to cut and complete the secret-compartment book project. Illus. *21–7 and 21–8* show different sizes of inside cut. A discarded magazine is useful for making a practice or test cut. Simply hold or pinch one corner of the pages tightly and tape them down.

21–1. ▶ An old book with a secret compartment created with the scroll saw.

21–2. ▶ Stack-cut paper stationery can be personalized and decorated with an endless variety of pierce-cut designs.

21–3. ▶ A tight "sandwich" of paper taped between corrugated cardboard.

21–4. ▶ Two pieces of thin waste plywood are nailed together (over a metal plate) with the book pages sandwiched in between.

21–5. ▶ A No. 9 double-tooth blade makes the cut from a blade-entry hole. A freeform-cutting pattern was selected to eliminate the difficulty of sawing parallel to the lines of print or to the edge margins.

21–6. ▶ The completed sawn opening and the stack of waste.

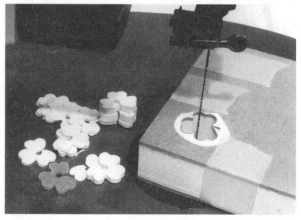

21–7. ▶ Pierced design completed with a No. 4 skip-tooth blade. Notice the smooth walls of the cut.

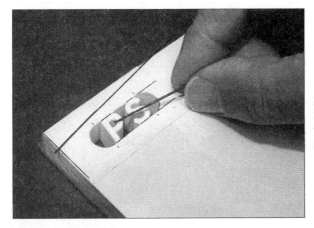

21–8. ▶ The tiny cutout for the letter "P" was sawn with a 2/0 skip-tooth blade, and the blade-entry hole was made with a No. 63 drill, a wire-gauge drill that is between $\frac{1}{32}$ and $\frac{3}{64}$ inch.

DRILLING TIPS

When drilling blade-entry holes, maintain downward pressure close to the hole during drilling. Drill the smallest-size hole possible. Drill at a high speed and drill the holes well away from the cutting line when possible. Often the paper will "hump up" around the hole when drilling, particularly if you feed the bit too fast.

BLADES

Almost any blade cuts paper, but to be sure you get the cut you want, make a test cut on the corner of an old magazine first as described above. Regular skip, double-, and crown-tooth blades all work well. Paper-sawing tends to dull most blades more quickly than cutting wood of the same thickness, so be prepared.

STACK-SAWING FABRIC

Stack-sawing felt and other fabric can be done just like sawing stacks of paper. The key is to be sure that the layers in the stack are tight and that you have stiff cardboard or waste plywood on both the top and bottom.

SAWING DELICATE DESIGNS

Surprising detail can be scroll-sawn into paper, but it is not as defined as when cutting wood and other materials. Use an auxiliary table with zero clearance around the blade opening to provide maximum support of the work. Or, use waste plywood for the top and bottom of the sandwich to provide additional support near the blade. Waste plywood on top minimizes the tendency of the paper to hump up around the bit when drilling holes that, because of the nature of the design, must be located close to the cutting line. Ensure that your table is square to the blade and sufficient tension is maintained. Use fairly high blade speeds and a feed rate that allows for complete control. Experiment with blade types and speeds until you get the results desired.

CHAPTER TWENTY-TWO

SEGMENTATION & INTARSIA

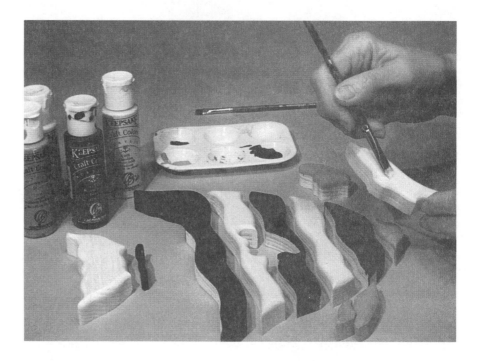

*S*egmentation and intarsia projects *(22–1 and 22–2) involve simple scroll-saw work in combination with elementary wood-shaping techniques. The results are beautiful pieces of art that look like low-relief carvings. Essentially, the processes involve scroll-sawing individual parts or primary elements of a design, shaping the edges, and then gluing the parts together to create the whole. There are several alternatives to the shaping and finishing processes to give this work variety. By and large, however, this work can be categorized as either "segmentation" or "intarsia."*

The major difference between segmentation and intarsia is that intarsia is made from many different colors and/or species of wood individually cut and fitted to each other (22–1), while segmented projects are most often cut from just one single piece of wood (22–2). The processes involved to shape or form the individual pieces are essentially the same. Finishing techniques, however, vary. Most intarsia is finished with clear topcoats to expose the natural color of the wood and its grain or figure. Segmented projects can also be finished naturally to take advantage of grain, etc.; however, various pieces can be stained and/or painted to conceal the less-desirable woods and to provide interest and color (22–1, 22–3, and 22–4).

22–1. ▶ Intarsia consists of all-natural wood colors as exemplified in this work by noted intarsia artist and author Lucille Crabtree.

22–2. ▶ Segmented sun face in butternut with painted eyes.

22–3. ▶ Segmentation in pine. Left: Some segments stained. Right: All-natural finish.

22–4. ▶ A combination of segmentation finishing options: natural, stain, and acrylic paint. Natural and stain finishes have been used on one project, and a natural finish and acrylic paint on the other.

Segmentation is easier and faster because less time is involved in selecting and fitting the various kinds of wood together. Segmented projects are usually made from inexpensive materials, and generally just one piece is required. Initial costs are less because an inventory of various-colored or exotic woods is not required. In a typical intarsia project, maple and walnut may provide the light and dark colors and padauk a brilliant red (**22–5**).

22–5. ▶ Garnet Hall's 49-piece intarsia cardinal. Notice the wood-burned veining detail on the leaves and acorns.

CUTTING THE INDIVIDUAL SEGMENTS OR COMPONENTS

The individual segments or components of a particular design can be cut with a scroll saw (**22–6**). As many as six pattern copies may be required for each intarsia project, whereas just two are required for segmentation work. Keep one as a master and to use

later to assist with assembly. With scissors, cut up the intarsia patterns so you have one full pattern profile for every part. Secure all patterns to the chosen workpieces with spray adhesive and then cut the parts.

Depending upon the complexity of the design, use blades from Nos. 2 to 5 for segmentation-cutting, and from Nos. 3 to 9 for intarsia. Make all segmentation cuts directly on the line in one continuous pass. Intarsia parts can be sawn just on the outside of the line and sanded or shaped slightly with the scroll saw, if necessary, to achieve tight fits. *Tip:* Leave the patterns attached or mark an "X" on the back surfaces of each part to keep the front surfaces oriented.

22–6. ▶ Sawing segments from a single piece of stock. Make a continuous, single kerf cut directly on the line.

SHAPING AND FORMING

Lay all the sawn pieces faceup on your master pattern and determine which parts need to be reduced in thickness or raised with shims for visual interest (**22–7 and 22–8**). Cut the shims from plywood and reduce the thickness of those pieces noted on the pattern (**22–9**). *Important:* When reducing thickness, always remove stock from the front, not the back surfaces. Mark adjoining thicker pieces so the completed contouring will appear to flow together as if carved from a single piece. Do not round over below your pencil marks (**22–10**). Smooth the surfaces of each piece as necessary.

22–7.▶ Rounding and shaping the edges of the individual pieces with a drum sander.

22–8.▶ High-speed rotary tools with various accessories are available to round over and shape individual pieces.

22–9.▶ Shape (round over) the edges of the lower pieces first. Then mark higher adjoining pieces to facilitate contouring. Notice that not all edges are rounded over.

22–10.▶ This close-up of the butternut sun face shown in 22–2 clearly shows how shims elevate the chin, nose, cheeks, and eyebrows.

FINISHING AND ASSEMBLY

Individual pieces that are to be stained or painted are done so before assembly (**22–11**). Edge-to-edge gluing is best done on top of the extra pattern copy (**22–12**).

MAKING A BACKER

Make a backer from thin plywood. Trace around the project as shown in **22–13**. Cut the backer ⅛ to ¼ inch smaller all around. Glue the project to the backer. Apply a clear, protective finish as desired (**22–14 and 22–15**).

Separated segmentation differs from regular segmentation in that the plywood backer is intentionally designed to be a visible element of the finished proj-

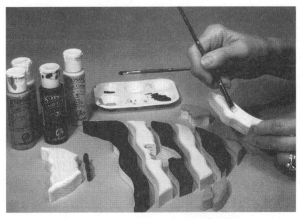

22–11.▶ Acrylic paint is applied to all visible and non-gluing surfaces of the individual pieces.

22–12. ▶ Applying glue to an unfinished edge. Glue the assembly together over a pattern copy.

22–13. ▶ Tracing the perimeter for the thin plywood backing.

22–14. ▶
Back view of typical segmentation/intarsia project.

22–15. ▶ Pattern for a practice project. Cut it from ¾-inch stock and round over all edges. Use woods or stains and paints in colors of your choice.
(Reprinted from the book *Scroll Saw Segmentation*, by the author.)

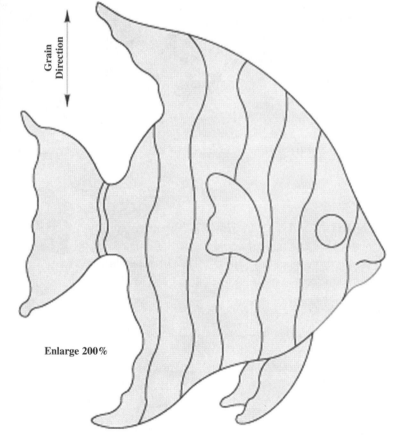

Grain Direction

Enlarge 200%

ect. The backer in **22–16** has been painted black and is exposed all around the outside edges and between the shaped and painted segments.

STACK-SAWN SEGMENTED INLAYS

Stack-sawn segmented inlays are two or more layers of different kinds of wood in contrasting colors that are stack-sawn into project segments as shown in

22–17. Thin stock (⅛ to ¼ inch) is commonly used, and the sawn edges are, as a rule, not rounded over. After sawing, the pieces are interchanged and glued together, edge to edge. Epoxy glue is recommended because it is a good gap filler and does not require usual clamping pressure. Sand the surfaces flat and add a finish (**22–18**). Illus. **22–19 and 22–20** show a pattern and projects in which this technique was used.

22–16. ▶ Separated segmentation. The backer shown here painted in black is visible with the shaped and painted segments glued on.

22–17. ▶ Left: Stack of padauk and ash ready for sawing. Right: Cut pieces are interchanged (inlaid), ready to be glued edge-to-edge over wax paper on a flat surface.

22–18. ▶ The surfaces are sanded flush and finished. The nonslip pad eliminates clamping.

22–19. ▶ Pattern for stacked segmentation ornament.

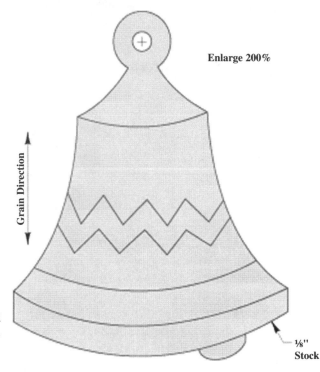

Enlarge 200%

Grain Direction

⅛"
Stock

22–20. ▶ **One-eighth-inch thick stacked segmentation projects designed and crafted by Alan Hoyt.**

PICTORIAL SEGMENTATION

Pictorial segmentation is an unusual "offshoot" segmentation technique developed by Kerry Shirts. Essentially, it can be described as stain-finished segmentation work without any rounding over or shaping of the sawn pieces. The pattern detail can be simple or complex, as shown in Illus. **22–21 and 22–22**. The more realistic works require greater detail in both pattern development and sawing. No. 5 blades are used for general cutting and No. 2 blades for the more intricate cuts necessary to define facial features and the like.

The choice wood for this work is soft maple, but other, light-colored, tight-grain woods work well.

Some pieces are left unstained, and others are colored using primarily two stain colors: light golden oak and dark walnut stains. Like basic segmentation work, the pieces are stained before assembly. The pieces are edge-glued together with some pieces set out slightly in relief from others that are either left more or less flush or set slightly back. A nose piece, for example, is typically set forward.

Refer to the books *Scroll Saw Segmentation* by Patrick Spielman, and *Scroll Saw Art: Realistic Pictures in Wood* by Patrick Spielman and Kerry Shirts, Sterling Publishing Company. Each book provides more how-to information and over 36 patterns with instructions. (See pages 344 and 345.)

22–21. ▶ A beginner's-level pictorial segmentation project by Kerry Shirts.

22–22. ▶ "Indian Elder" demonstrates the realistic facial expressions possible with the pictorial segmentation techniques perfected by Kerry Shirts.

CHAPTER TWENTY-THREE

SPECIAL PROJECT TECHNIQUES

his chapter presents brief overviews of five popular and innovative methods of making scroll-saw projects that do not require mastering new or unusual cutting techniques other than those discussed in the previous chapters. These projects are:

1. Ring vessels and simulated woven baskets 2. Toys and puzzles 3. Signs 4. Logscapes 5. Pierced portraits

VESSELS AND SIMULATED BASKETS

In Chapter 12, we introduced the basic techniques involved in making collapsible bevel-sawn baskets, a craft perfected by scroll-saw artist Rick Longabaugh. Also described in that chapter are some incredible bowls created from a single board of bevel-sawn rings, a process refined by Carl Roehl. Here we illustrate and discuss some interesting and easy-to-make vessels and simulated-basket designs developed by Joan West and John Nelson (23–1 and 23–2). These projects involve sawing simple, vertically sawn rings or layers that are glued one on top of another.

Undulating Rings

Undulating rings, when sawn from a flat board, will produce projects like the fruit bowl shown in **23–1**. Illus. **23–2** shows a typical nest of sawn rings cut from one piece of stock and a thin plywood bottom. Every other ring is rotated 15 degrees so that the convex areas of one ring will overlap the concave, curved portion of the adjoining ring. Illus. **23–3** provides a quarter pattern of a ring. Make four enlarged photocopies and tape them together to make a full pattern (**23–4**).

23–1. ▶ **This easy project designed by Joan West is made of undulating, vertically sawn rings cut from ¾-inch-thick wood.**

23–2. ▶ **A nest of rings sawn from one piece and a ⅛-inch-thick plywood bottom ready for assembly.**

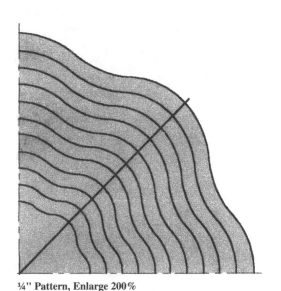

¼" Pattern, Enlarge 200%

23–3. ▶ **Pattern for rings for fruit-bowl project.**

23–4. ▶ **Nut bowl of essentially the same design concept as the bowl shown in 23–1, but made of rings with more undulations and sawn from thinner (⅜-inch) stock.** (Photo courtesy of Robert Becker, *Creative Woodworks and Crafts* magazine.)

Simulated Baskets

Simulated baskets are a design concept developed by author/scroll-sawer John Nelson in the late 1990's. The striking basket-weave look is achieved by stacking thin-walled "rings" of alternating design profiles. The basket shown in Illus. **23–5 and 23–6** is made of layers cut from ¼-inch-thick stock (**23–7 and 23–8**). This small basket measures just 3½ inches wide, 3⅛ inches high, and 5½ inches in length, and is just one of hundreds of design variations developed by Nelson. Each layer requires one full piece of wood, which leaves all of the inside as waste if making just one basket. These waste pieces, however, can be utilized to make new rings for progressively smaller-size basket designs.

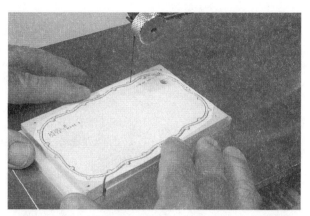

23–7. ▶ **Stack-sawing two layers of rings. The inside has been cut first, but it is left in place for support while sawing around the outside.**

23–5. **This small basket designed by John Nelson is simply scroll-sawn rings that, when stacked, give the appearance of a true basket weave.**

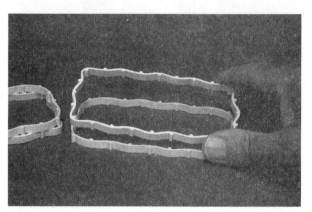

23–8. ▶ **Rings of alternating designs ready to be glued, one on top of another.**

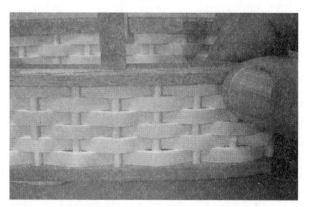

23–6. ▶ **A close look still does not convince many observers that this is not an authentic woven basket.**

TOYS AND PUZZLES

Wooden toys of all kinds for youngsters of all ages are very popular and profitable projects for scroll-saw users. There are numerous books of toy patterns and designs developed especially for scroll-sawers. Those toys shown in **23–9**, for example, feature painted wood balls that rotate when the toy is pulled. Some also incorporate the wood hinge joint discussed on pages 289 and 290 (**23–10**). Incidentally, a double V-block quickly centers and supports purchased wooden balls for drilling (**23–11**).

Various kinds of puzzle are additional projects perfect for the scroll-sawer. Illus. **23–12** shows some simple stand-up designs for very young scroll-sawers that are easy to make from solid wood. Illus. **23–13**

23–9. ▶ Pull toys made by Bob Phillips.

23–10. ▶ Before scroll-sawing to separate the hinged joint pieces, the pin holes are drilled as shown.

23–11. ▶ Drilling balls with the help of a double V-grooved block.

23–12. ▶ Stand-up puzzles made for youngsters should be cut from relatively thick stock and have fairly wide kerfs so the pieces slide together easily.

23–13. ▶ **Children's trays or inlay puzzles made of two layers of Baltic-birch plywood. Notice the one-piece border permanently glued to the back layer.**

shows typical children's tray or inlay puzzles made from Baltic-birch plywood. It is especially important to use a sufficiently wide kerf-cutting blade such as a No. 7 or 9 so the pieces fit together easily. Be sure to round all sharp edges and corners and to use nontoxic finishes. (Refer to Chapter 24 for more information about some easy finishing and decorating tips ideal for children's puzzles.)

"Jigsaw" puzzles (**23–14**) can be made by gluing posters, magazine covers, or other art onto

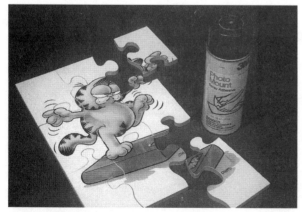

23–14. ▶ **Posters permanently glued to plywood make good jigsaw puzzles.**

Baltic-birch plywood. Use the cutting pattern given in **23–15**, enlarging it as desired. Trace over the work with graphite paper or use a temporary bond adhesive to secure the pattern itself for cutting. Adult puzzles should be made with progressively smaller pieces and narrower kerfs. A No. 2/0, narrow-kerf blade just .009 inch thick is a special blade recommended for more-difficult-to-solve puzzles. It is available from Advanced Machinery Imports.

23–15. ▶ **This pattern can be enlarged 200 percent or more to make jigsaw puzzles with pieces of different sizes for different ability levels.**

SIGNS AND PERSONALIZED ITEMS

Making wood signs (**23–16 and 23–17**) and personalized items such as hammer handles (**23–18**), plaques (**23–19**), baseball bats, and the like can be a very lucrative activity for the serious scroll-sawer. Numerous types of letter and number patterns and designs are available in books and computer programs that make generating patterns of any size or type quick and easy.

There are basically three kinds of scroll-sawn signs:

1. "Pierced" signs, where the letters are cut through (refer to **23–17**). These signs are pretty much restricted in size by the throat capacity of the scroll saw.

2. Signs with "freestanding" connected letters, such as desk name signs (**23–20**) or those with individual letters (**23–21**). (The scroll saw can

23–16. ▶ Pierced sign by John Polhemus. (Piercing is the cutting of inside openings.)

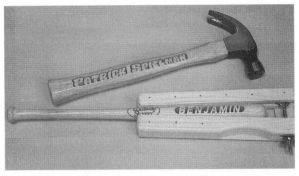

23–18. ▶ Examples of product personalization by John Polhemus.

23–17. ▶ Excellent pierced sign crafted by Harold Foos. All letters of this 20-inch-diameter sign are sawn through ¾-inch-thick oak. A black backer holds the centers of the "O's," "A's," and other letters.

23–19. ▶ Personalized wedding plaque by Cathy Peck.

23–20. ▶ Sawn desk name signs are popular.

also be used to saw letters that look engraved—as if carved into the background—or raised in relief above the background by employing the principles of bevel-sawing discussed in Chapter 12.)

3. Signs with "applied" letters or numbers, in which the letters or numbers are attached to a solid backer (**23–22 to 23–27**). As shown in **23–27**, larger signs of any size can be made with applied lettering.

The key to successful sign-making hinges on good design. Selecting the appropriate letter styles, the best material or combination of materials, and suitable finishes is very important.

23–22. ▶ **Applied letters of contrasting woods.**

23–23. ▶ **House numbers and a gargoyle overlay with a sprayed metallic finish and attached with round-head brass escutcheon pins (nails).**

23–21. ▶ **Individual letters are great decorating items. Notice the added touch of the router-rounded edges.**

Contrast is always important for visual clarity; however, effective and suitable messages can be expressed with little or no contrast between the letters and background. Two unusual examples of stunning material use are mirrored plastic letters glued to a mirrored background and Corian glued to Corian. (Mirrored plastic letters are cut from an acrylic plastic sheet that reflects images in a similar way to glass mirror.) Scroll-sawn metal and/or metal finishes also make strong visual statements. Other popular choices include bright, polished brass (refer to **23–24 and 23–25**), authentic or imitation gold leaf (refer to **23–26**), and patina finishes that make wood, brass, and copper look aged. (Refer to Chapter 24 for more information about these and other special finishes that are desirable for wood signs.)

23–24. ▶ **Sawing ⅛-inch solid brass.**

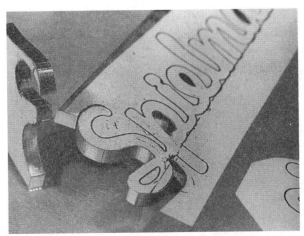

23–25. ▶ A close-up showing the smoothly sawn edge of the cut brass. (Refer to Chapter 20 for more information on cutting brass and other metals.)

23–26. ▶ The authentic gold leaf applied to just the face surfaces of this initial plaque is unequaled for durability and elegance.

23–27. ▶ The "Lord's Prayer" by Carl Weckhorst measures 30 × 35 inches, with all characters overlaid onto a contrasting background.

LOGSCAPES

Logscapes (**23–28**) were first brought to this writer's attention by Dean Larson in mid-1999. Logscapes are simply a series of silhouette-layered scenes that appear as if carved inside of a log bolt. This novel project can be made from real logs (with or without bark), shaped from a 4 × 4, or just made from glued layers of wood. The blank should have a rounded surface to simulate a half-log, as shown in the accompanying photos.

The first step is a band-saw operation in which the "window recess" is cut (**23–29**). Once this is done, the window piece is sliced off with the band saw (**23–30**). This piece should be about ⁵⁄₁₆ inch thick at the thinnest area. Sand the front surface of the window piece as necessary. Next, cut three more full lengthwise slices about ⁵⁄₁₆ inch in parallel thickness from the log. Two pieces will be used for silhouette layers and one for the back piece.

Apply the first silhouette pattern to the window piece (**23–31**) and cut away the background, leaving a parallel border edge all around. Use the window piece to lay out the perimeter cut for sawing the second silhouette (**23–32**). Cut this silhouette out with the scroll saw and use it as a pattern to draw the perimeter-cutting line for the third layer.

Next, mask off the gluing surfaces of the back piece and paint the inside surface flat-black. When dry, glue all the layers together. No finish is applied

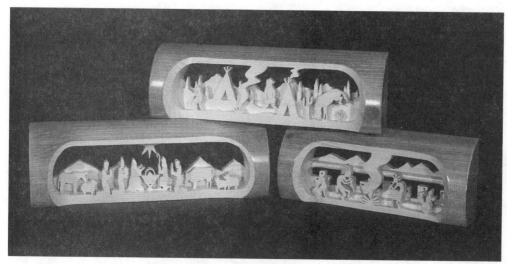

23–28. ▶ Logscapes created by Dean Larson involve band- and scroll-saw work.

23–29. ▶ Sawing the "window recess" from a prepared half-log on a band saw. This is done freehand using a 3/16- or 1/4-inch blade.

23–30. ▶ Resawing to cut the window piece from the "log."

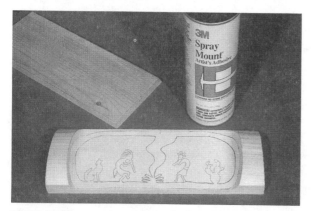

23–31. ▶ Silhouette pattern applied to the window piece.

23–32. ▶ The window silhouette is used as a pattern to make the perimeter cut of the second silhouette layer.

to the inside silhouette surfaces. The outside surfaces, however, are sanded smooth and stained medium-brown or fruitwood and finally finished with a semigloss topcoat. Some logscapes made from real logs are left with the natural bark on.

PIERCED PORTRAITS

Pierced portraits (**23–33 and 23–34**) are silhouettes or design images that represent people. They are becoming popular scroll-saw projects not only because they are unique-looking, but also because they exhibit the particular personal traits of friends and loved ones artfully cut into wood. They could also be called "reverse silhouette overlays" because of the way they are made. Obviously, the success of this work requires a good pattern, as all fine scroll-saw projects do. Patterns for this work, however, carry the added requisite that they must be true-to-life images.

Pattern development begins with a photograph that is converted to a high-contrast copy on the computer. Then the artist embellishes it freehand as necessary into a cutable design that does not compromise the subject's character or expression. Scroll-saw artist Gary Browning has produced a pierced portrait of the author from a snapshot (**23–35 and 23–36**).

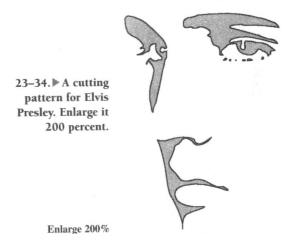

23–34. ▶ A cutting pattern for Elvis Presley. Enlarge it 200 percent.

Enlarge 200%

23–33. ▶ These pierced portraits of Elvis Presley and Marilyn Monroe, designed by Aaron Moriarity, are cut through ⅛-inch Baltic birch and then glued to a ¼-inch contrasting plywood.

23–35. ▶ Portrait of the author designed and sawn by Gary Browning. It is ¼-inch Baltic birch with felt glued to the back.

23–36. ▶ Photo from which the portrait shown in 23–35 was made.

CHAPTER TWENTY-FOUR

FINISHING BASICS

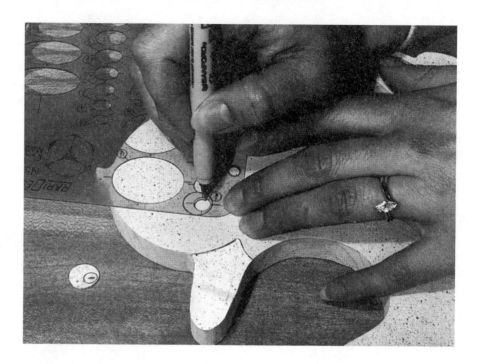

 his chapter provides a brief overview of some basic and easy-to-use finishes for various kinds of scroll-sawn project. Many of these projects—such as fine fretwork and intarsia— are highly labor-intensive, so it is very important to use the best possible choice of finish. A well-crafted project can be ruined or degraded because the most complementary finish was not selected or properly applied. Always read the manufacturer's instructions and test the finish on scrap of the same wood before applying it directly to the project.

There are hundreds of finishes in a broad range of costs and features to choose from that include new and faster finishes as well as the traditional and time-tested ones. The focus in this chapter, however, is to present a few finishes that are relatively easy to use and that provide good results. Generally, most scroll-sawing finishing needs include one of the following: *1.* Painting *2.* Staining or dye-coloring *3.* Natural finishes *4.* Special treatments, i.e., patina finish, gold leaf, etc.

The easiest approach is to apply no finish at all; for some projects such as toys, puzzles, ornaments, and small compound-sawn novelty items this might be very satisfactory. Another alternative is to overlay or laminate a decorative paper or plastic material onto your stock before sawing *(24–1)*. Also consider the effect obtained if you paint or stain the surfaces before applying the pattern and sawing. Then, just leave the sawn edges unfinished for contrast. This works especially well for silhouettes painted black.

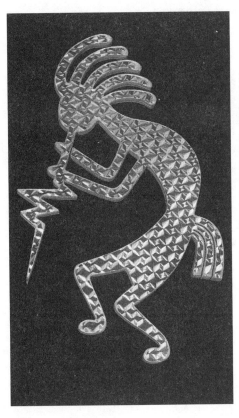

24–1. ▶ A holo-graphic sheet with a pressure-sensitive back was applied to the stock before sawing to create this piece.

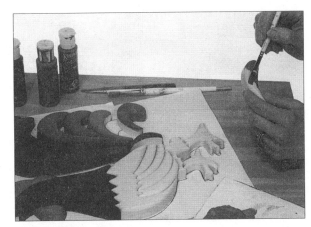

24–2. ▶ Acrylic paints are water-based and easy to use and clean up.

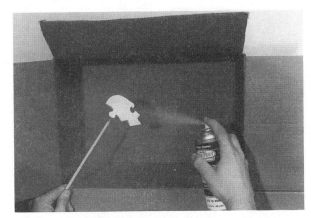

24–3. ▶ A cardboard box makes a short-term spray booth for aerosol-finishing.

PAINTING

There are many types of paint and enamel available that can be brushed or sprayed on. Country cutouts, intarsia pieces, holiday ornaments, and decorative pieces are easily brush-painted using acrylic paints. *Acrylic paints* (**24–2**) are nontoxic, water-soluble, mix easily, dry quickly, and clean up easily.

Any color and type of paint you might want is available in an aerosol (**24–3**). Be sure to check those that require primers. Certain pieces of fret-work may look good with a spray-painted finish. It must be capable of being coated uniformly, however, without runs and dust marks. High-gloss finishes magnify every dent, scratch, and dust particle, and achieving a good high-gloss finish is difficult for the average hobbyist.

Some special-effect painting techniques that work well with acrylics and are useful for decorating coun-try cutouts, puzzles, and the like are shown in **24–4 to 24–6** and discussed below. *Important:* Always test finishes, especially those involving special-effect techniques, before applying them to your project.

Spattered Finish

The spattered finish is created by simply applying the paint of one color over another by propelling droplets from a stiff bristle brush, as shown in **24–4**.

Sponge Finish

The sponge finish (**24–5 and 24–6**) is the technique of randomly dabbing one paint color over a base of another contrasting color. In addition to sponges, tex-tured cloth, crunched paper, and the like also work, with each giving a slightly different finished look.

Painted Detail Lines

Detail lines that represent facial features or other defining lines are easy to paint using paint pens (**24–7**) or felt-tip markers (**24–8**).

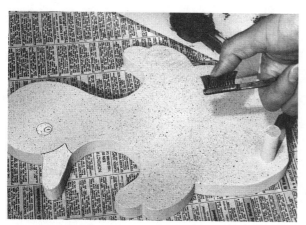

24–4. ▶ Using an old toothbrush to give a project a "spattered" finish.

24–5. ▶ Sponge-finished wooden "quilt" by Frank Droege.

24–6. ▶ Applying the second color using a sponge with a dabbing action to create a random, open pattern.

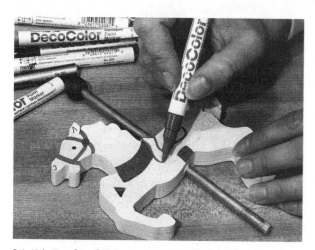

24–7. ▶ Freehand-painting lines using paint pens.

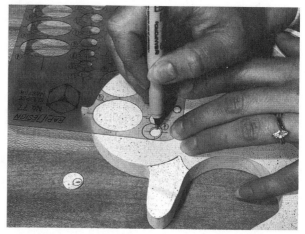

24–8. ▶ Smooth and perfectly executed lines can be made using templates, French curves, and straightedges as guides.

Decorative Dots

Decorative dots (**24–9**) can be applied one at a time using the pointed end of an artist's brush handle or another, similarly pointed object. Dots of various perfectly spaced patterns can be applied using special folk-art "dotting tools" sold in hobby and craft stores (**24–10**).

Aerosol Special-Effect Finishes

Aerosol special-effect finishes of all kinds are found in paint stores and the paint departments of various discount stores. Sprays are available that produce a variety of special finishes including crackle and simulated-marble finishes and that give a granite or stone look. They are easy to use and dry quickly (**24–11**).

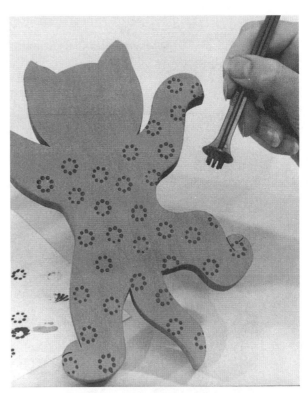

24–10. ▶ **This folk-art decorative dotting tool is one of many available featuring different patterns.**

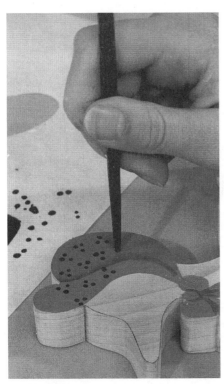

24–9. ▶ **Applying decorative painted dots with the end of an artist's brush handle.**

24–11. ▶ **Applying a textured, stone-fleck aerosol finish.**

STAINS

Stains (**24–12 and 24–13**) are used to enhance the color and natural figure (grain) of wood. However, many fine projects can be ruined quickly by unknowingly using wood materials that do not accept stains readily. For example, pine, a popular scroll-sawing wood, does not take some penetrating oil stains well. Often, blotchy and uneven coverage results. A quick test will reveal that end grain and roughly sawn edges will absorb more stain and, therefore, stain darker than side or face grain.

Gel stains seem to perform better on softwoods. Gel stains can be applied easily to smooth, uninterrupted surfaces, but attempting to use gel stains on highly detailed fretwork would obviously present many application problems.

24–13. ▶ **Dip-staining portrait segmentation pieces.**

COLOR DYES

Color dyes can be used to give woods very brilliant, transparent colors. They work best on light-colored woods such as pine, ash, maple, and oak. Dyes allow the grain to show through and are often a good departure from the common brownish wood tones.

There are two types of color dye available: concentrated powder dyes that mix with water (**24–14**), and an oil-based, ready-to-use wipe-on product called "color stain" (**24–15**). The water-based type requires raising the grain before using. The surfaces are dampened with a sponge and allowed to dry. Then the surfaces are sanded before the dye is applied. *Tip:* When using stains and color dyes, be sure to test potential topcoats for compatibility. Danish oil, for example, has the same solvents as oil-based dyes and will dissolve and dilute the color.

24–12. ▶ **A Kerry Shirts project made from one piece of soft maple. Uneven staining is more acceptable and even desirable on this piece of wildlife art because wildlife has many variations of color and tone. A piece of scroll-sawn furniture, however, is expected to have uniform intensity of color and tone.**

24–14. ▶ **Applying a water-based dye. Here a thinned-down blue is applied with a brush. This type is good for toys and water cleanup is easy.**

24–15. ▶ Direct from the bottle, "color stain" is an oil-based product applied with paper towels.

CLEAR NATURAL FINISHES

There are many types of clear natural finish, and most work great for typical wood-finishing jobs. There are two basic types: surface topcoats that simply lay on top of the surface, and penetrating topcoats that soak into the wood.

Every woodworker has his or her favorite clear finish, e.g., varnish, shellac, lacquer, vinyl, penetrating Danish oil, or the new water-based topcoats. Almost any clear topcoat finish can be used for any particular type of scroll-sawn project except when it comes to finishing highly detailed and delicate fretwork (**24–16**).

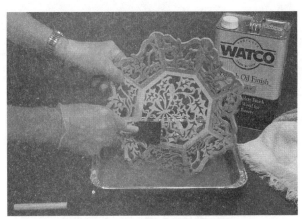

24–16. ▶ Slosh-finishing ornate fretwork with penetrating Danish oil produces an excellent rich-looking, non-glossy finish that is ideal for fine hardwoods and is extremely easy to apply. Slosh-finishing consists of splashing the finish on the wood in a combination brushing-and-dipping operation.

Because of the many tight, inside corners, narrow openings, veining or detailing kerf cuts, it's almost impossible to effectively use brush-applied or spray finishes on fine fretwork. Trying to get spray or brush-applied finish into small openings often results in an excessive buildup and runs surrounding each area. The problem magnifies if you use glossy finishes, which, this writer, as a rule, avoids like the plague.

Penetrating Danish Oils

Penetrating Danish oils are one of the easiest finishes to apply. Danish oil also works well on highly absorbent woods such as pine and butternut, but avoid using the type that has pigment added to change the wood's natural color. The surfaces must be thoroughly sanded to get the best effect, especially the end grains.

Dipping or a slosh application with a foam brush or rag is the best way to apply Danish oil (**24–16**). A flat tin contains the mess and catches the excess runoff (**24–17**). Usually, just a single application is required. Apply it liberally with a rag or foam brush, flooding all surfaces and allowing the finish to flow into all small openings and narrow veining kerfs. Keep the surfaces wet for approximately 30 minutes, so the finish can penetrate into the wood. Continue "feeding" the end grains to the point of refusal.

After about a half hour, or when the penetration rate has slowed, you have the option of a light wet-sanding with a fine wet/dry abrasive (silicon carbide)

24–17. ▶ The tin is a good way to allow excess oil finish to run off into the tray.

using the finish itself as the lubricant. This gives the product a very smooth, velvet-like feel. If the work is too delicate to sand, then omit the wet-sanding step.

Important: You must wipe off and remove any and all excess oil that remains on the surface; otherwise, it will film over and become sticky. Wipe all surfaces with an absorbent rag, removing as much excess finish as possible. Lay the project on a rag and blow the excess finish from saw kerfs and small openings not removed with the rag. Use compressed air, a tire pump, bellows, canned air, or whatever means is available.

Olive, Peanut, and Mineral Oils

Olive, peanut, and mineral oils are good to use for any projects that come into contact with food. They are applied essentially the same way as penetrating Danish oil.

PATINA-FINISHED BRASS AND COPPER

Finishing kits are available that make any material, including wood and plaster, look like aged metal. Real brass and copper are very easily and quickly given a patina-finish, which is a beautiful bluish-green aged look typically resulting from long-term exposure (**24–18**). Be sure that any protective wax or varnish has been removed so the true, raw metal is exposed. Apply a liquid patina solution with a sponge.

PATINA-FINISHED WOOD

A patina finish can also be applied to wood (**24–19 and 24–20**); however, the wood has to be first coated with a special metal-based finish. This is finely ground powder of copper or brass suspended in a water-based solution that gives the wood a real metal substrate. The patina finish reacts to this finish.

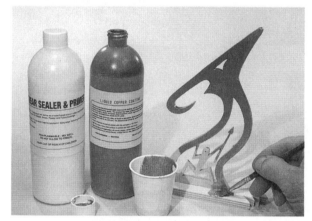

24–19. ▶ **To apply a patina finish to wood, the wood is given a special coating, which is a blend of finely ground metallic (copper) solids suspended in a water-based air-drying emulsion.**

24–18. ▶ **Scroll-sawn critters cut from sheet copper, bent, and then coated with a patina solution, which gives them a popular "aged" look.**

24–20. ▶ **When the sponge-applied patina solution oxidizes, the material coating—the wood—bears a remarkable resemblance to real metal, as shown here.**

APPLYING GOLD LEAF

Applying gold leaf (**24–21**), also known as "gilding," is an ancient art and not that difficult to do on flat surfaces such as letter faces of signs and decorative scroll-sawn overlays. There are entire books dedicated to this subject. The information here, however, is intended only to get you started and through the basics (**24–22**).

Gold and silver leafing is available as imitation or genuine, pure gold and silver products, which are obviously priced accordingly. Several mail-order companies offer supplies and starter kits in various price ranges.

The application procedures are essentially the same for all gilding work. First, prepare the surface by sanding it as smooth as possible. Apply a good, hard finish and sand it very smooth up to at least 600-grit wet/dry abrasive (**24–23**). Wipe the surface clean and dry. Next, apply the "size," which is an oil-based adhesive available as a "quick-dry" or "slow-set" type. The latter requires a 10- to 12-hour wait, versus just three hours for the former.

Apply the size smoothly and evenly (**24–24**). Ensure that it is not accidentally applied where you don't want it, so be on the lookout for runs, drips, etc.

24–21. ▶ This elegant gold-leaf-decorated scroll-sawn sign is made in two layers consisting of a fret-sawn backer with overlaid border and letters.

24–22. ▶ Supplies necessary for making the "Valitchka" sign include regular and instant glue to assemble the sign, spray-paint finish, wet/dry abrasive, a book (packet) of gold-leaf sheets (left) and "size," the gold-leaf adhesive at the right.

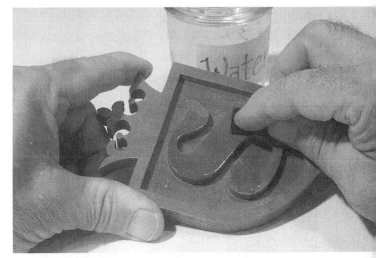

24–23. ▶ Painted surfaces must be sanded very smooth with 600-grit wet/dry abrasive.

Remove the size from such areas with mineral spirits, and use mineral spirits to clean brushes, etc.

Test the size for appropriate tack with your knuckle (**24–25**). If it sticks to your knuckle, it is much too wet. The size should be almost dry. When you drag your knuckle lightly over the surface, it should produce a squeaky sound. Best results favor a drier rather than wet size.

Transfer the leaf using the tissue paper from the "book" that carries the thin gold-leaf material (**24–26**). Try not to touch the leaf and avoid touch-ing the size directly with the tissue. Press the leaf down with the side of your hand as shown in **24–27**. Do not worry about overlaps or seams, as they will not show. After all surfaces have been covered, wipe them with a wad of cotton to remove the excess leaf and lightly burnish the gilded surfaces with moistened cotton balls.

If imitation leaf was used, varnish over the surface; otherwise, it will tarnish. If real gold leaf was used, it can be varnished for added abrasive or scratch protection, but this is not necessary.

24–24. ▶ Applying the "size" (the gold-leaf adhesive) with an artist's brush.

24–25. ▶ Testing the tack quality of the size.

24–26. ▶ One sheet of gold leaf as it comes mounted on tissue paper.

24–27. ▶ Laying down the leaf using the side of your hand. Overlap each application about ⅛ inch.

24–28. ▶ Use your fingers to transfer the leaf to small areas and fill in void spaces.

SCROLL-SAW BOOKS BY PATRICK SPIELMAN

Alphabets and Numbers (The Woodworker's Pattern Library). Over 40 styles of alphabets and dozens of number patterns for signs and home identification projects. 128 pages.

Artistic Scroll Saw Patterns & Projects. Flowers, birds, sea and water life, animals, humorous, Southwestern designs, plus patterns for metal and plastics. Developed by Dan Kihl. 144 pages (8 in color).

The Art of the Scroll Saw: Award Winning Designs. 35 award-winning designs and patterns from 27 of the world's best scroll-sawers. 160 all-color pages.

Christmas Scroll Saw Patterns. Over 200 full-size patterns, including angels, ornaments, centerpieces, etc. 164 pages (4 in color).

Classic Fretwork Scroll Saw Patterns. Over 100 easy fretwork patterns and projects. Co-designed with James Reidle. 160 pages.

Decorative & Ornamental Scroll Saw Patterns. 100 project variations and original designs by co-author Dirk Boelman. 128 all-color pages.

Fun & Easy Scroll Saw Projects. Approximately 250 easy-to-make patterns in over 100 project caragories, all in color. 160 pages.

Instant Scroll Saw Projects. 40 projects with patterns that can be color-photocopied and glued permanently to the work or used with transfer tool application. 128 all-color pages.

Scroll Saw Art: Realistic Pictures in Wood. 30 incredible projects developed by Kerry Shirts employing pictorial scroll-saw segmentation techniques. Beginner to advanced, art-quality pictures with complete how-to instructions. 128 all-color pages.

Scroll Saw Basics. Clear, step-by-step approach to the fundamental techniques of scroll-sawing. Brief, to-the-point information for beginners. 128 pages.

Scroll Saw Country Patterns. 400 popular ready-to-use designs for scroll-sawing or for use in other media such as quilts, stencils, appliquè, glass, or jewelry. 196 pages (4 in color).

Scroll Saw Fretwork Patterns. 200 full-sized patterns for stunning projects, ranging from simple to challenging. 256 pages. Co-authored with James Reidle.

Scroll Saw Pattern Book. 450 practical patterns of easy to medium difficulty. Best-selling pattern book. Co-authored with James Reidle. 256 pages.

Scroll Saw Patterns for the Country Home. 275 patterns for fast and fun, down-home projects. 200 pages.

Scroll Saw Picture Frames. Ready-to-use patterns for imaginative, better-than-store-bought frames that are works of art by themselves. 128 all-color pages.

Scroll Saw Puzzle Patterns. 100 patterns for jigsaw, stand-up, and inlay puzzles. 264 pages (8 in color).

Scroll Saw Scandinavian Patterns and Projects. Patterns for functional projects in Scandinavian simplicity. Co-authored with Gösta Dahlqvist. 200 pages (8 in color).

Scroll Saw Segmentation: Patterns, Projects & Techniques. Over 40 wonderful "segmentation" projects—easier, faster, and more economical than intarsia. Techniques fully described and illustrated. 128 all-color pages.

Scroll Saw Silhouette Patterns. Patterns for a variety of images and scenes from simple to complex. Co-authored with James Reidle. 160 pages.

Southwest Scroll Saw Patterns. Over 200 patterns designed by Dan Kihl and inspired by early cultures of the American Southwest. 168 pages.

Spielman's Original Scroll Saw Patterns. 280 original patterns featuring animals, jewelry, ornaments, and decorative accents plus much more. 228 pages (four in color).

Victorian Gingerbread: Patterns & Techniques. Plans and patterns developed with James Reidle for a full range of architectural exterior and interior detail including brackets, grilles, spandrels, corbels, running trim, etc. 200 pages (8 in color).

Victorian Scroll Saw Patterns. Very delicate and ornate patterns reproduced from early 19th century. Shelves, filigree baskets, antique frames, holders, etc. 160 pages.

METRIC EQUIVALENCY CHART

Inches to Millimeters and Centimeters

MM=Millimeters   CM=Centimeters

Inches	MM	CM	Inches	CM	Inches	CM
⅛	3	0.3	9	22.9	30	76.2
¼	6	0.6	10	25.4	31	78.7
⅜	10	1.0	11	27.9	32	81.3
½	13	1.3	12	30.5	33	83.8
⅝	16	1.6	13	33.0	34	86.4
¾	19	1.9	14	35.6	35	88.9
⅞	22	2.2	15	38.1	36	91.4
1	25	2.5	16	40.6	37	94.0
1¼	32	3.2	17	43.2	38	96.5
1½	38	3.8	18	45.7	39	99.1
1¾	44	4.4	19	48.3	48	101.6
2	51	5.1	20	50.8	41	104.1
2½	64	6.4	21	53.3	42	106.7
3	76	7.6	22	55.9	43	109.2
3½	89	8.9	23	58.4	44	111.8
4	102	10.2	24	61.0	45	114.3
4½	114	11.4	25	63.5	46	116.8
5	127	12.7	26	66.0	47	119.4
6	152	15.2	27	68.6	48	121.9

INDEX

ABOUT THE AUTHOR

atrick Spielman is the leading author on woodworking throughout the world with over 65 books published, including the best-selling Router Handbook and Scroll Saw Pattern Book, which have each sold over one million copies. The updated New Router Handbook won the National Association of Home and Workshop Writers award for the Best How-To Book in 1994. A graduate of the University of Wisconsin-Stout, he has taught high school and vocational woodworking in Wisconsin public schools for 27 years. Patrick, with the assistance of his family, owned and operated a wood product manufacturing company for 20 years. Most recently, he published and distributed Home Workshop News, a bimonthly newsletter/magazine dedicated to scroll sawing. Patrick and his wife Patricia currently own and operate Spielman's Wood Works and Spielman's Kid Works, two gift galleries located in northeastern Wisconsin that feature quality products made from wood.

Over the course of Patrick's teaching and woodworking careers, he has invented hundreds of jigs, fixtures, and woodworking aids. He has served as a technical consultant and designer for a major tool manufacturer and he continues to pioneer new and exciting techniques for woodworkers as he has done for more than 45 years